# Baltimore Iconoclast

# Baltimore Iconoclast

*William Hughes*

Writer's Showcase
San Jose New York Lincoln Shanghai

Baltimore Iconoclast

Writer's Showcase
an imprint of iUniverse, Inc.

For information address:
iUniverse, Inc.
5220 S. 16th St., Suite 200
Lincoln, NE 68512
www.iuniverse.com

A personal perspective, with satirical overtones, on the personalities, events, and movements, that make a city, like Baltimore, what it is.

ISBN: 0-595-21551-3

Printed in the United States of America

# Dedication

*Henry L. Mencken*
*Author-Journalist-Patriot*
*"Sage of Baltimore"*

# Contents

# Preface

Since the 9/11 tragedy in America, the freedoms we have long since taken for granted, like Free Speech and the Right of Association, have become seriously endangered.

The mass media, too, is fast becoming monopolized, and, unfortunately, more complicit in the errant ways of the Establishment. In the marketplace of ideas, political correctness has replaced the critical analysis of issues.

Over the years, I've written a lot of articles, many of which I've posted on my website. In order to share those opinions, with an even wider audience, and to preserve a historical record of my times, I've decided to publish this book.

Unless the present trend is radically reversed, I fear my generation may be the last one in America to engage in a robust debate of the political, cultural and social matters of the day.

In a few of my pieces, I have added an author's note, in order to bring the matter up to date, or to clarify a point or two.

My fondest hope is that some of these writings will find a place in the hearts of my fellow citizens, who are also concerned about the fragile fate of our Bill of Rights.

*Res Publica Est Res Populi*

## (The Republic is the Property of the People)

---

# Chapter One

---

## Heroes, Heroines & Mavericks

### 1. Harry Agro's Odyssey: A WWII Story
### September 21, 1984

On February 3, 1943, The *Baltimore News-Post* (the predecessor to the *News American*) ran a photograph and short paragraph on U.S. Navy seaman First Class, Harry Agro of 706 W. Barre St. The concise notice simply said that the son of John Agro was "missing in action." No other information was permitted to be given out at that time. It would take almost another three years for the full tale of the World War II odyssey of Southsider Harry Agro to become know.

The story really begins at the main Post Office on Calvert and Fayette Streets, on April 20, 1942. In the wave of patriotic fervor that followed the Japanese sneak attack on Pearl Harbor on December 7, 1941, Agro decided to do his part in his country's defense and enlisted in the U.S. Navy.

One of eight children of immigrant Sicilian parents, Agro was then a husky, hard 200 pounds, built on a solid six-foot frame. He had been working making piston rings in a plant in Southwest Baltimore. He was also very restless, ready to see some action.

"I took my basic training at Newport, Rhodes Island and had my gunnery training at New Creek, Virginia," Agro explained while sitting in his comfortable living room in his home in the Baltimore Highlands, just south of the Baltimore City line. "I was then assigned as a gunnery mate in the Merchant Marine on a cargo ship the *SS Paul Luckenbach.*"

The Liberty ship, as it was then commonly called, carried a cargo, valued at $8 million of 18 tanks, 10 B-25 planes, and other machinery and military wares bound for the Russian port of Murmansk. It sailed from Brooklyn's Navy Yard in New York harbor and met up in the North Atlantic with a convoy of close to 300 ships. Before rounding the Cape of Good Hope, off Africa's southern coast, the *Luckenbach* left the convoy and continued its journey alone into the Indian Ocean.

"It was September 22, 1942, just as night was starting to fall," Agro recalled. "I was in the galley helping one of the cooks, a black man named, 'Muscles,' with the dishes when the first torpedo struck. Muscles and I quickly ran to the back of the ship to attempt to man the aft gun. Just then two more torpedoes hit their mark, and the ship began to list badly. As we began to run forward, I got stuck in the ship's rigging used to tie down the deck's cargo, but Muscles pulled me out, and we both got over the side to one of the ship's lifeboats."

All 59 crew members of the *Luckenbach* made in safely into the lifeboats. The educated speculation was that the ship was hit by torpedoes from a German submarine, since the Indian Ocean was in the Third Reich's sphere of wartime operation.

After 26 days in a lifeboat with 14 other men, traveling 1200 miles, being stalked by sharks, living off of ship's rations and rain water, surviving a two-day storm that almost sank their craft, Agro and his mates reached the Indian port city of Malabar. He credited the instructions given by the *Luckenbach's* captain to steer northeast "no matter what," as Agro recalled, for his survival.

After a short respite in India, Agro was transferred to what was then the island of Ceylon (now Sri Lanka) to take the position of gunnery mate on yet another American cargo vessel, the *SS Sawokia*. The *Sawokia* was carrying a full cargo of jute and was headed for the US. Agro, it appeared, was finally headed home.

Only nine days out of Ceylon, the *Sawokia* was spotted by a German raider vessel, the *HK Michel*. Camouflaged as a cargo vessel, the *Michel* was actually a fierce man-of-war heavily armed with torpedoes, heavy artillery and machine guns, and even a small plane for scouting purposes.

On November 29, 1942, the *Michel* sunk the *Sawokia* in less than 15 minutes of combat. Not one trace of the *Sawokia* remained. At the time, the *Sawokia* was located about 400 miles northwest of the island of Madagascar. Only 19 of the 62 crew members survived.

All of the men, who were caught below deck when the ship was first attacked died. By a stroke of sheer luck, Agro happened to be on deck when the first bomb hit. Despite serious wounds to his head and leg, Agro managed to get off the dying ship, and after spending the night in the water, was picked up the next day by the crew of the *Michel*.

"The Germans treated us good, right as sailors. They never beat us," Agro noted, "We were on that ship for three months. They also sank a Greek and British freighter, so that there were about 85 survivors from the three vessels on the *Michel*. They ended up taking us to Singapore and turning us over to the Japanese."

It was during the two years and nine months of Japanese confinement as a prisoner of war that Agro's fortunes took a turn for the worse. "We were herded like cattle on board a Japanese ship, it must have been 400 prisoner, all nationalities. It seemed like it took forever for us to reach their northernmost island of Hokkaido, where the prison camp town of Hakodate was located," Agro said.

In the camp, Agro was forced to work 18 hours a day for 14 days straight with only one day off. He worked most of the time loading coal ships and barges, where he was personally required to load 10 tons of coal each day, carrying 90 kilos on two baskets balanced on a pole, walking up a plank and onto the vessel. He also worked in the mines, and was once forced to help build an airfield.

"They would beat you for nothing, for no reason at all. They would slap you with their fist, hit you with a stick, even with their rifle butt. Once they beat me over the head with a coal shovel," Agro recalled. "You always had to bow to them, and if you were slow getting up from your straw mat, where you slept at night in the barracks, they would hit you.

"The food was never enough. It was mainly rice, fish heads, fish bones and sometimes a soup out of seaweed. The last five months of the war things started getting better. We got some Red Cross parcels, and that really saved us," Agro said. At the war's end, Agro weighed 125 pounds.

"What was also really bad was that we never got any news from the outside world, not all the time we were there," he added. "And the biggest problem was every 14 days, they would change the guards, bring in a new set of guards, who would just start beating up on us all over again.

"They once caught an Englishman stealing some food," Agro continued, "and they stood the poor man up outside against a pole from 5 A.M. To 5 P.M. In the snow for two weeks until he died. They then put his body in a barrel and took him up the hill, where they cremated him, and brought his remains back in a jug. Of the 900 prisoners in that camp, I think only about 390 of us ever came home. The rest went up that hill in a barrel."

"The Japs always told us the war was going to last 50 or 100 years. Towards the end of the war, however, things started to change in the camp. They stopped beating us. We wondered why?"

On Agro's birthday, August 12, 1945, the U.S. had dropped an atomic bomb on the City of Hiroshima. It killed 92,000 people. On August 9, 1945, another atomic bomb was dropped on the City of Nagasaki.

Forty-thousand people were killed and equal numbers injured in both Japanese cities. The devastation wrought from both blasts was so widespread and intense that to this day, the US government has never relinquished the official films of the aftermath of the fiery holocausts.

Today, Agro lives quietly with his wife of 38 years, Madeline. He's a plumber by trade.

Asked how he was able to withstand the tortuous ordeal of the prison camp, Agro underscored his "will to live." He said, "You always had it in your mind, that you would never let those people bury you there. I never wanted to be buried on that soil. That is why I kept going. I was also young," he continued, "and that helped me. The older guys had a more difficult time. But once you get something in your head, that you want to live-no matter how bad the conditions. I wanted to get back home and that kept me going."

*        *        *

## 2. Kudos to Rep. Mario Biaggi (D-NY)
### February 12, 1981

Maryland Irish National Caucus, Inc.
110 Bosley Avenue. Cockeysville, Md. 21030

Hon. Mario Biaggi, M.C.
House of Representatives
Washington, D.C.
My dear Congressman:

For the last six years, I have been active with the Maryland Chapter of the Irish National Caucus.

I have done so in the role of member, *pro bono* counsel, and for the last year as state chairman.

During all that period of time and to the present, you have been in every respect in your position as a member of Congress and Chairman of the "Ad Hoc Committee for Irish Affairs," a true champion of the voiceless and beleaguered nationalist minority in Northern Ireland.

On behalf of all our members and supporters, I congratulate and thank you for your outstanding leadership role.

You have been an inspiration to the Irish-American community dedicated to the principle of self-determination for the Irish People.

> Sincerely,
>
> William Hughes
> Baltimore, Maryland

cc: Hon. Thomas O'Neill
Hon. Edward Kennedy
Hon. Patrick Moynihan
Hon. Hugh Carey

＊          ＊          ＊

## 3. Rep. Parren J. Mitchell & Capitol Hill Politics
### December-January, 1985

"When I look back on it, the impeachment of President Richard Nixon, Spiro T. Agnew's resignation as Vice-President, the war in Vietnam, and the aftermath of the Civil Rights movement, it was the perfect time for me to serve in the Congress," said Rep. Parren J. Mitchell.

Since 1970, Mitchell has represented in the Congress, Baltimore City's sprawling 7th district. In the November general election, the widely popular black political leader is unopposed on the ballot.

Maryland's first black congressman, Mitchell has been the driving force for championing legislation and progressive causes during his often-times controversial tenure in office. "It has been like a Shakespearian drama being here," continued Mitchell, while seated in a spacious conference room in his office at the Rayburn Building. It is only a stone's throw from the House of Representatives. "You get those hard dramatic moments and you remember them of course."

"Once, I remember being in the House getting ready to vote on a matter, and a silence fell over the whole chamber-not a whisper could be heard as it was graveled to order. It was the time," Mitchell recalled, "that Vice-President Spiro Agnew came over to plea bargain with the Speaker of the House, Carl Albert, over whether he would be tried by the House or by the courts."

Mitchell was an unrepentant foe of the Vietnam War, when it wasn't very popular to oppose the administration's policy. He fought hard in the House to end the war along with a coterie of other congressmen, that constantly grew in numbers as the conflict lingered on aimlessly.

Mitchell reminisced about another stirring time concerning that volatile issue. A congressman from Georgia, one of the House's chief hawks on the Vietnam conflict, went to the Well of the House to speak in his typical heavy Georgian accent. Mitchell recalled his words, "I cannot ask the young men, that I had killed or wounded in Vietnam to forgive me. I cannot ask the mothers and fathers of those young men to forgive me. But, I do ask God to forgive me for being part of the wrong war for so long."

"Tears came to my eyes," when I heard those words said Mitchell. Another moving incident Mitchell wanted to talk about was the Watergate crisis. He recalled receiving a telephone call late on a Sunday evening at this home in Baltimore from Speaker Albert. The Speaker said, "We are going to have to meet early tomorrow in the House. We are going to have to impeach the President. We are getting mail by the box load about Nixon. The people want him impeached, and we must follow the will of the people.

"The phone call came right after the so-called "Saturday Night Massacre." Mitchell response to Speaker Albert was, "Mr. Speaker, I asked for Mr. Nixon's impeachment a long time ago."

"Strange enough," Mitchell underscored, "a great deal was done on domestic and social programs under Nixon. He was astute enough as a politician to recognize the power of the Congress. Nixon, unquestionably set the seeds for minority businesses, although he did it for the wrong reasons. He wanted to get reelected by starting-up black capitalism."

Mitchell said blacks had access under President Nixon, Ford and Carter, but not under Ronald Reagan. "If Reagan wins," Mitchell predicted, "things will be exceedingly grim and difficult. The blessings of the system, however, are that there are checkpoints. The House will remain Democratic. I suspect we will do fairly well in the Senate. Reagan is enormously popular as a man, but his programs aren't."

America is really not a bestial nation," Mitchell said. "We don't see anyone without any help. We aren't going to see people hungry in the streets. I don't care how conservative some elements get. There is a basic decency in America, that isn't going to let those programs go by the boards."

"I am, was, and always will be a liberal," Mitchell emphasized. "When all else fails, I believe it is the duty of government to do things for people: housing, health, education and jobs. I want the Democratic Party to shift back more towards that position, rather than becoming the new 'Atari Democrats,' the middle of the road types. It is because we have a capitalistic system, that we need government to play those roles."

Although there were some rumors, that this might be Mitchell's last hurrah, he said that he is taking it one term at a time.

He also made it clear, that he had no interest in running for mayor of Baltimore City in '87. But, he said, he knew of at least 12 black men and women, in addition to State's Attorney Kurt Schmoke, who were more than capable of handling that office.

Mitchell said that he is astounded that he is now the fourth ranking member of the House's powerful Banking Committee. "I have enough support from the members and I know that if anything happens, I would be considered for the committee's chairmanship."

And then with a big belly laugh, he concluded,"Of course, the House would probably want to abolish the committee!"

# 4. Ex-M16 Agent Exposes British "Dirty Tricks"
## December, 1993

On Monday, October 18,1993, ex-British Army Captain, and M16 (Military Intelligence) operative, Fred Holroyd, stunned a C-Span audience, estimated conservatively at three million viewers, with details of the British government's sordid "dirty tricks" campaign in Northern Ireland (the occupied Six Counties), and in the Republic of Ireland (26 Counties).

The tactics revealed at the National Press Club in Washington D.C. included murders, bombings, framing of innocent victims, black propaganda, and kidnappings.

Holroyd, 52, served in the six counties from 1974-76 as a Captain with M16, the British military intelligence. He said that M16 had "no limits" when it came to any matter that the agency felt threatened the state.

He learned that intelligence in Ireland involved employing pseudo-gangs, assassinations of Republicans or Republican sympathizers; and "Ps-Ops", (persuading the nationalist population by misinformation, bribes, intimidation and smear attacks to oppose the rebel insurgents).

"Dirty tricks were and are condoned at the highest level of the British government," according to Holroyd. He said that the Special Air Service (SAS), undercover military personnel, that are "licensed to kill," are controlled directly by the office of the British Prime Minister and the Cabinet. He said the SAS, often referred to as "Margaret Thatcher's Praetorian Guard," ran "spies" in the 26 Counties.

Both the Irish and British governments "cooperated using terrorist to subdue the indigenous movement, the IRA (the Irish Republican Army),"

Holroyd said, "and the Dublin government permitted the SAS into the 26 Counties to kill and bomb."

According to this operative, the Irish police, known as the *Garda*, would "freeze areas" south of the border and allow the British to come in unhampered, to "do their thing." "British intelligence would deliberately create and provoke violence and blame it on the IRA," Holroyd said. "They (the Intelligence Service) don't question what they are doing. If they see something as being for the good of the government, then they see it as being legitimate."

Elaborating, Holroyd added, "That's fine, if the leaders of the country have some control and know exactly what the intelligence service believes in. In Ireland, the British government professed a policy that they believed in, and the intelligence service carried out another policy, which was entirely different from the government's.

In that case, 'Who is running the government?'"

When he decided to go to Northern Ireland as a soldier, Holroyd thought he would be separating the fighting parties. Unfortunately, his job turned out to be much different then he expected.

"I was allowed to prosecute a campaign against the Catholics, the Republicans, but not against the Protestants, the Loyalists. I was told, 'They are not our purview. The police, the RUC (Royal Ulster Constabulary), will do it.' The police didn't do anything…the civil power was corrupt."

Holroyd reported the atrocities to his senior officer, which turned out to be a mistake. Eventually, he was forced out of the military for taking a stand against his own government's "dirty tricks" campaign, despite 16 years of exemplary service in the British Army.

For the last 14 years, Holroyd has been trying to clear his name and set the record straight about the Irish situation, especially with the U.S. media. The British government has repeatedly tried to discredit Holroyd as a credible source, even committing him to a psychiatric hospital. The

British doctors, however, refused to certify that there was anything wrong with him.

He issued a challenge to the British government to charge him under the draconian "Official Secrets Acts." Holyroyd said nothing would give him more pleasure than to backup in court, with solid evidence, the charges that he has been publicly making. He also stated that no statements he has made about Britain's "dirty tricks" in Ireland have been refuted by the UK government.

Holroyd has written a book about his saga in the Six Counties entitled, *War Without Honor* (Medium, England, 1989).

His appearance was sponsored by the Irish National Caucus, a Washington, D.C.-based lobbying group working for peace and justice in a united Ireland.

Holroyd plans to continue his fight for justice in Ireland. "I believe," he said, "that once the British security forces cross the barrier-the law-then they are no better than the terrorists. I believe it is possible to fight a counter insurgency campaign within the law."

# 5. Ode to PATCO & the American Labor Movement
## August 13, 1981

Fellow Citizens of our Glorious Republic, mark ye well the brave men and women of the Professional Air Traffic Controllers Union (PATCO) and their families. You are bearing witness in 1981 to a rare phenomenon on the American labor scene.

No one tells his own government to shove it with such finesse, grace and courage as Americans do, especially when they get their Yankee-Doodle-Dandy up for it.

The only problem is that Ronald Wilson Reagan is now our president and "Big Business" never had a truer or stronger friend in the White

House. The battle lines are drawn. The issues formed. The conflict ensues and the blood, symbolically only I hope, will run. Chances are if does for real, that it will run from the red veins of honest union men and union women.

Union members are again going to jail for what they believe in, to wit: the right to strike over the conditions of their employment. "Expeditiously" is the only word to describe how quickly our esteemed government puts union members behind bars.

My goodness, they usually don't even do that in the US District Court in Baltimore to our ethnic type defendants. At least, they wait until after they have given them a full trial on the merits. And then, of course, the court doesn't hesitate to incarcerate the deserving rascals, usually for long periods of time.

It helps our elitist ruling class in the Greenspring and Hunt Valleys to feel safe at night. It also helps them sleep with only one cocktail before bed time, instead of the usual two. They need the lift to ease their social consciences, warped from reading too many labor biased editorials in the *Baltimore Morning Sunpapers.*

PATCO members are letting it all hang out in front: their jobs, pensions, future rights of employment with the US Government, possible severe individual and group civil penalties and the heavy burden of criminal sanctions. Our behavior scientists have a name for this kind of brazen conduct. It's called "Risk-Taking."

Studies on totalitarian regimes indicate how the great mass of workers were rather easy for the ruling elite to control. The ordinary laborer had a deep fear of losing his "pension, life insurance, the security of the family. Such a man was ready," a researcher insisted, "to sacrifice his beliefs, his honor and even his human dignity for the cause."

The lack of docility on the part of PATCO members should be taken as a sign of a healthy work force in a vibrant America. Quite honestly, it takes a lot of guts to do what PATCO is doing.

It has been a long, long time, since anyone in the "American Labor Movement" acted in such a manner. It rekindle thoughts about the idealism, vision and courage, that was once properly the earned heritage of American Labor. It look like I was wrong. American Labor is still alive and, indeed, kicking if you please.

If there is one person, who can take full credit for unwittingly radicalizing PATCO, it's our simpleminded US Secretary of Transportation, Drew Lewis. It appears Mr. Lewis, with his head buried deep in the false piety of Washington, DC, would rather be right, than have this business finished.

Mr. Lewis likes to shoot off his mouth about the supremacy of the law dealing with strikes by public service employees. He prefers to do that, than utilize his efforts to reach an amicable settlement fair to all the parties, including the traveling and taxpaying public.

A just settlement should acknowledge the real long term concerns PATCO has about: the lack of communication with FAA management, stress on the jobs, and a need for a shorter work week.

The true national interest demands that the US Secretary of Transportation come down from his Mount St. Helens now, before he causes more trouble with his discredited union-busting attitude.

That kind of mind set belongs back in the "Robber Baron" era of 1890. Mr. Drew Lewis, if he doesn't watch out may even perform what some consider a miracle of sorts. He might just awaken the sleeping giant out there. It has been dozing off, since they put the old radical and social dreamer, Eugene Debs, in his cold grave.

That sleeping giant is something, that we nostalgia buffs reverentially refer to as "The American Labor Movement."

*     *     *

# 6. Judge Thomas Ward: A Man of Classic Virtues
## September 9, 1982

He authored the city's first "Minimum Wage Act." At age 55, and after an illustrious 29 year career as a trial attorney and public servant, he is running for the lofty elected position of judge of the Supreme Bench of Baltimore City.

Long associated with conservation and environmental groups, he co-founded and wrote the corporate charters for the Fells Point, the Federal Hill Preservation Society, and the Mt. Vernon Belvedere Association.

His name is Thomas Ward.

"I feel like I am gone to win this judicial election. I have widespread political support in all areas of the city, and especially on the southside, where I have developed many lasting and true friendships over the years," Ward explained.

"The endorsement of the Baltimore Council of the AFL-CIO of my candidacy was very meaningful and important to me since I have I have always been such a staunch union man all of my life," Ward emphasized. The record shows that Ward has belonged to four different unions, including as a reporter for the *Baltimore Sun,* membership in the prestigious Newspaper's Guild.

Married to the former Joyce McCartney, the Wards have four, fine children who have all been very active in their dad's campaign. They are Kathleen, Patrick, Tracy and Meagan. Insiders day that nobody had worked harder in this grueling 18-hour-a-day contest, then Joyce McCartney Ward. Candidate Ward conceded, "I could not do it without Joyce, and the kids being behind me 100 percent."

The Bolton Hill resident had long been active in politics and co-founded and became a leader of the Mount Royal Democratic Club.

A member of *Corpus Christi* Roman Catholic parish, Ward named Presidents Franklin D. Roosevelt and Harry Truman, and the late Governor of Illinois, Adlai Stevenson, as some of his personal heroes.

"I worked at the Maryland Drydock and Shipbuilding yard back in 1947, right after I got out of the US Army", continued the ex-parachute veteran. "What a terrific learning experience that was for me as a young man," he said proudly.

Elected to the City Council from the 2nd district, Ward sponsored legislation to create the "Parking Lot Control Act," the Architectural and Historical Commission, and a tree planting program, which resulted in over 25,000 trees being planted throughout "Charm City."

"In the presidential election of 1980, I received 97,900 votes in my quest for a judgeship. This is my third try for that high office. There are three positions open on the ballot and eight candidates. I believe because of my overall citywide strength, past campaign experience, and my professional qualifications, that I will finish first this time," Ward concluded.

      *            *            *

*Author's Note-Thomas Ward won election to the Supreme Bench (renamed the Circuit Court for Baltimore City) in the 1982 electoral battle. He was later reelected after his first fifteen years term to another comparable period in office. Ward just recently retired from the Bench. He is an exceptional individual, who was known as one of the hardest working judges on the Baltimore court.

It is beyond dispute, that Ward was the single most important individual in stopping the federal government from routing Interstate 95 (I-95) through Baltimore City and destroying the neighborhoods of Federal Hill, Little Italy, and Fells Point (see, related Article 38, "Did Sen. Barbara Mikulski Inflate her Resume'?").

In every way, he is an outstanding citizen, devoted family man, and a first rate public servant. The City of Baltimore could use more public servants, like the Hon. Thomas Ward.

      *            *            *

# 7. "Viva Peter Angelos!": CEO of the Baltimore Orioles
## April 5, 1999

"Viva Peter Angelos!" From his modern day Acropolis (read Camden Yards), he took his Baltimore Orioles south to Fidel Castro's Cuba. Not only did his baseball team win by a 3-2 count, but Angelos scored a diplomatic coup as well.

An American major league baseball team hadn't played a game in Havana in over 40 years. The last time it happened, the military thug Fulgencio Batista was in power in Cuba, and the notorious mobster Meyer Lansky was his bagman.

A Capitol Hill wit wagged over the success of the Oriole event: "Will Serbia be next on Angelos's foreign policy agenda?" Even the *Sun's* columnist Michael Olesker tried to get into the act. He excitedly announced that the trip meant, "The Cold War is over." Coming after more than ten years of detente and the Mikhail Gorbachev era, his crack made me wonder, "What planet has this guy been living on?"

Nevertheless, some half-brights at the hawkish State Department didn't want the Oriole boss to take such a bold initiative. But, Angelos is his own man. He proved that during the last strike by major league baseball players. Instead of joining forces with the other fat cat owners and denouncing the players, Angelos sympathized with their demands and the dispute was settled.

The truth is that he is proud of his long association with organized labor, particularly the Building & Construction Trades Council of Baltimore. Labor hasn't forgotten him either. How many millionaires do you know that have won a "Social Justice Award" from the AFL-CIO? Well, Angelos has one in his collection.

I first remember him when he was a feisty City Councilman from the Irish-dominated 3rd District, where he served from 1959-63. Then, his family had a popular restaurant and bar on Harford Road, just south of

Clifton Park. Former Mayor William Donald Schaefer was in the Council during those halcyon days, serving with two other political legends, the great civil rights advocates, Walter Dixon and Jacob Edelman.

I used to attend the Council's Monday night meetings with my political mentor, south side Councilman Michael "Iron Mike" McHale. Like today, when the 3rd District's fiery Martin O'Malley squares off with the 1st's "Battling Nick" D'Adamo, the public sessions are the best, totally unrehearsed, free show in town.

For whatever reasons, Angelos and Sol Liss, a councilman from the 5th District, regularly would go at it in no-holds-barred verbal contests. It was like watching an organized brawl. Liss, now deceased, was an accomplished public speaker, who later went on to a distinguished career as a state jurist.

Angelos, a budding young lawyer, however, would always rise to the occasion. He was more than equal to Liss' skills in that robust give and take public forum. And, why shouldn't he have been? His brilliant Greek ancestors invented debating, politics and democracy.

As an attorney, he has also left his mark in the successful trial of civil cases representing plaintiffs, who have sustained serious personal injuries from long exposure to asbestos. Many of these individuals had worked in the maritime industry.

The indefatigable Angelos has won hard fought victories, on their behalf, at both the circuit and appellant court levels. He also set precedents for other similarly injured workers to follow.

However, it is in another very important arena, philanthropy, that Angelos has shown his remarkable leadership ability. His name repeatedly shows up in the first ranks of givers, whether the cause is the Baltimore Symphony Orchestra; Baltimore Opera Co.; U. of Baltimore; Babe Ruth Museum; House of Ruth; Leon Day Park (formerly Bloomingdale Oval Park); Kennedy Krieger Institute; or some other worthy charitable, social and educational project.

Baltimore has been blessed over the years by fantastically successful entrepreneurs, who strongly believed in giving back to the community. I mean the word "community" here in its widest possible sense.

Some of the generous individuals, who have endowed our city with their beneficence over the years, include: Johns Hopkins, Enoch Pratt, George Peabody, Henry Waters, Dr. John S. Goucher, Yale and Peggy Gordon, and Joseph Meyerhoff.

Angelos, without fanfare, has continued this splendid tradition of *noblesse oblige.*

This leaves only one last thing to say about him: "Viva Peter Angelos!"

*          *          *

## 8. The Smearing of the Rev. Jesse Jackson
**May 17, 1999**

What does a guy have to do to get some respect? The Rev. Jesse Jackson must be asking himself that question. His successful retrieval of three American soldiers from war-torn Yugoslavia is his latest coup. It was simply put-brilliant!

Most Americans rejoiced in his daring rescue. Instead, however, of bringing him applause from Washington, it has brought him undeserved brickbats from Madeline Albright.

Bill Clinton's Secretary of State insists Jackson's humanitarian concerns have caused "terrible problems." She believes the picture of him praying with Slobodan Milosevic "enhanced" the Yugoslavian president's position in the global community and hurt U.S. efforts to end the war. What "efforts," outside of bombing the Serbs, is she talking about?

Somebody should tell Albright, "The Mad Bomber," that her incompetent conduct of foreign policy, which includes threats, temper tantrums and name calling, embarrasses America.

It makes many of us long for the days of one of her predecessors, the great George C. Marshall, and to wonder aloud, "How in God's holy name did this horrid little woman, a Dr. Strangelove clone, ever get appointed Secretary of State?"

Richard Cohen, a pseudo-liberal pundit for the *Washington Post* also got on Jackson's case. He unfairly accused him of helping to free the three U.S. POWs by utilizing "maximum publicity" and "moral obtuseness." Cohen thinks Jackson played into Milosevic's hands by calling for a "bombing pause." Like other myopic commentators of his ilk, he believes a settlement can only be reached in Kosovo via the military route.

Neo-conservative scribe Michael Kelly was even harder on Jackson. He lambasted the Chicago-based justice seeker for "giving aid and comfort to the enemy, for grandstanding on a grand and gross scale, and for leading the freed soldiers to chant, in a supremely revolting moment, 'Free at last, free at last, thank God Almighty, free at last.'" The only thing appropriate about Kelly's off-the-wall rant was that it appeared in one of media mogul Rupert Murdock's rags, the *New York Post.*

Herb Block, the shamelessly over-praised cartoonist, for the *Washington Post,* also got into the bashing Jackson act. He demonized him by depicting a vulture flying over a wasted Kosovo carrying a sign which said, "Give Peace a Chance." Above the cartoon, the mean-spirited Block wrote, "The Jesse Jackson-Milosevic Call For Nato To Stop The Bombing."

I believe all the criticism of Jackson is unfounded. He wasn't born yesterday and has dealt with controversial figures, like Milosevic before. These naysayers forget that in 1984, it was the intrepid Jackson who talked Syrian President Hafez Assad into releasing Lt. Robert Goodman, a Navy pilot, whose plane was shot down over Lebanon. Not long after that uplifting victory, he was successful in securing the release of 22 Americans and 26 Cuban political prisoners from Fidel Castro's jails.

One of Jackson's most marvelous accomplishments came in 1990. That year, he persuaded Iraq's Saddam Hussein to release 700 foreign women and children, who were detained as human shields during the Gulf War.

In none of these circumstances did Jackson's splendid intervention cause any change in U.S. foreign policy. It is highly unlikely, especially with Albright in power, that it will towards Yugoslavia either. So what is all this smearing of the civil rights champion really about?

Jackson has demonstrated again and again the importance of keeping a door open to our supposed enemies. The leader of the "Rainbow Coalition" is a national asset and he has exhibited the qualities that many people in the world still associate with America: compassion, decency and justice.

This may be hard for some to believe, but there are many wirepullers in the Establishment who find such laudable virtues threatening to their position. To prove my point, look at the virulent reaction of the Clinton administration to the noble efforts of some Congressional lawmakers, who are supporting a bipartisan Kosovo peace plan drawn up with the help of the Russian *Duma* (Parliament).

One rabid Clintonite, Rep. Sam Gejdenson (D-CT), viciously described the proposal as "treason."

Well, peacemaking has never come easy. Fortunately, Jackson is undeterred by the venom of his critics. He is now urging Democrats in Congress to abandon the U.S. air war in Yugoslavia in favor of diplomacy.

If Bill Clinton has any sense left, he should begin listening to Jackson. In fact, Clinton should go even further. He should immediately dump Albright as his Secretary of State before she does what Germany's Adolf Hitler and Japan's Hideki Tojo couldn't do to America: destroy it!

*   *   *

# 9. Nelson Mandela: A Noble Spirit
## June 8, 1999

Nelson Mandela is fading into the sunset. Almost 81 years of age, the heroic symbol of resistance to *Apartheid* and respected international statesman has turned over the reigns of power in South Africa to his African National Congress (ANC) party successor, Thabo Mbeki.

Jumping at the opportunity to praise Mandela, the *Baltimore Sun* pulled out all the stops. Keep in mind, this is the very same newspaper, that not only condoned his cruel 28 years in prison at the hands of a racist regime, but for a long time also remained silent about *Apartheid*.

*The Sun* (06/04/99) called the recent election won by the ANC party, "a triumph for Mandela." It went on to compare him to George Washington, whose greatest service to his country was "after exercising power, cheerfully leaving it." Retracing Mandela's political career, the *Sun* said, "He took to the gun in 1960." It didn't elaborate, and for good reasons, on that aspect of the revered rebel's life.

What is so appalling about the *Sun's* editorial is its rank hypocrisy. The ivory tower types at 501 N. Calvert St. failed to come clean about their shady role in disparaging the ANC, Mandela, and the legitimate aspirations of the black majority in South Africa to freedom.

For example, in 1988, the administration of Ronald Reagan came out with an infamous document entitled, "Terrorist Group Profile." It wrongly labeled the freedom fighter Mandela, as a "terrorist," and the ANC as a "terrorist group." *The Sun*, which not only endorsed Reagan for president twice, also regularly went along with his nutty views on foreign policy. *The Sun* failed to challenge the justification for such profiling.

The Reganites also did everything they could to discourage human rights groups in this country, like "TransAfrica," that championed Mandela's cause. One of the purposes of the "Terrorist Profile" gimmick was that it gave ammunition to pro-apartheid forces who were unfairly denouncing advocates for Mandela and the ANC as "supporters of terrorism."

Mandela believed that as long as *Apartheid* persisted, the black majority of 22 million in a country with only 5 million whites, had a right to resist its rule by armed struggle. The Reaganites, aided by extreme right wing idealogues, like Jeanne Kirkpatrick, disagreed. They strongly supported the fascist government in South Africa and blasted any resistance to it. In 1982, Reagan endorsed a $1.1 billion IMF loan to prop up the South African regime, without one word of dissent from the *Sun*.

Absent the great work done in this country by activists, like the splendid Randall Robinson, former Rep. Parren J. Mitchell (D-MD), Rep. Ron Dellums (D-CA), Rep. Charles Rangel (D-NY), and others, to spotlight the evils of *Apartheid*, the *Sun* probably would have never seen the light. It was only after Mandela was released from prison in 1990, that the *Sun* began to change its tune about him.

Last summer, we had a friend, a physician, who was born in South Africa stay with us for a few days. This young lady's father was Jewish and her mother was of Dutch stock. She had grown up in Johannesburg.

Our friend told us that Mandela projected "a nobility of spirit," which was strongly evidenced by the fact he had invited as a special guest to his 1994 presidential inauguration, one of his white guards from the notorious Robben Island prison. The white community, she added, generally saw Mandela as a "man of principles," who despite his harsh treatment by the *Apartheid* regime, did not have any hatred in his own heart. Instead, she underscored, "He had love."

She refused to romanize about the monumental problems any new government in South Africa must face. Our friend indicated the great disparity in wealth between the rich and the poor there, was "striking," and that fear of crime was driving some white South Africans to leave.

As the new day dawns in South Africa, many in America will be wishing the government of Mbeki success in addressing the serious challenges that confront it.

And, although the *Sun* is now saluting Mandela and his "final achieve-ment," history will show that it only jumped on the ANC victory train after it had arrived in the station.

*      *      *

# 10. Will Lee Spike Clinton's Hate Crime Law?
## June 3, 1999

Spike Lee, the brilliant film maker, may just save us from Bill Clinton's "Hate Crime" law. Recently, Lee said, "Somebody should shoot him," and he was talking about actor and National Rifle Association honcho, Charlton Heston.

Lee claimed he was only joking, in response to a question about whether Hollywood was to blame for the recent rash of school shootings. "The problem," he underscored, "is guns." Heston was mostly amused. He feels Lee was being "foolish."

In this age of political correctness, however, some are demanding Lee's scalp. They insist his "joke," if made by Heston about Lee would have constituted a "Hate Crime." They want Attorney General Janet Reno to prosecute Lee.

Meanwhile, President "Bubba Bill" Clinton, when he's not busy bomb-ing Belgrade, is looking to further federalize the "Hate Crime" scheme. His proposed legislation (S. 622) will enforce tolerance by outlawing hatred. Punishment will be stiffened for thugs, who pick out victims because of their race, religion, sex or national origins.

The bill will also dole out grants to local cops to learn how to probe for possible lawbreakers. Can the witch hunts far behind?

Mystery novelist, and sometimes U.S. Senator, Barbara Mikulski, is one of S. 622's co-sponsors. More resume' inflating, I suppose. The big problem with this latest Washington brainstorm is that only in totalitarian societies are people penalized for their ideas.

For instance, in the Third Reich, snickering at Adolf Hitler's mustache lead right to Gestapo headquarters; in Red China, too, during the Cultural Revolution, disagreeing with Mao's "Red Book," was a one way ticket to prison; and, when *Apartheid* reigned in South Africa, blacks were jailed for the slightest objection to the ruling clique. Will bad-mouthing Clinton, while protesting the Balkan war, be added to this list?

Lee's *faux pas* came after other celebrated First Amendment controversies concerning politico Jesse Jackson, talking head Jimmy "The Greek", and sports team owner Marge Schott. As punishment for speaking their minds (read gaffes), Jackson was demonized; "The Greek" lost his TV job; and they're still trying to take Schott's Cincinnati Reds' baseball team away from her. Just imagine, losing your property, in America, for being silly.

What's next? The rehabilitation camps of the *Gulag?*

Let's pause to consider this: Have we lost our sense of the absurd? Will we continue to permit the political clout of a few to split our society? Do we really want Orwell's "Big Brother?"

Clinton also should be reminded, that if you punish crimes against only some favored groups, you make a mockery out of the notion of equality before the law. There are already more than enough laws on the books to guide people's behavior, including my favorite, "The Ten Commandments," and especially the one that says, "Thou Shalt Not Kill."

Offensive ideas, I believe, should be rebutted in the public arena not by criminalizing someone's thoughts. For example, all murders and assaults are hate crimes. We don't need to single out one despicable act for "special" treatment. We do, however, need to punish "all" of them, and to do so without fear or favor. Remember, when the Mafia kills someone, it usually rationalizes, "It's only business." So, that's better than killing a gay or a black or a Latino for hate? Huh?

The truth is "Hate Crime" laws are well intended but totally unnecessary. And the notion that there has been a plague of bias-related crimes, as claimed in S. 622, is bogus. A recent study, "Hate Crimes: Criminal Law and Identity Politics," by James Jacobs and Kimberly Potter, concluded that so called "hate crimes" constituted about one thousandth of all violent attacks.

In ancient Greece, anyone who wished to propose a new law had to do so with a rope around his neck. If his motion failed, he might be hanged with deliberate speed. Too bad, the U.S. Senate doesn't have such a rule.

Also, philosopher Benedict Spinoza's statement seems to ring true today: "The real disturbers of the peace are those who, in a free state, seek to curtail the liberty of judgment which they are unable to tyrannize over."

What we should cultivate, instead of a "Big Brother" mentality are more characters, like Lee. He reminds us that this is America, where citizens have the right to Free Speech, and the right, too, to be foolish.

> \*       \*       \*

# 11. Dale Anderson: Unrepentant Populist
## January 26, 1983

Dale Anderson is back!

At a well-preserved 66 years of age, and after eight years away from politics, the crusty, salty, plain-spoken former two-term Baltimore County Executive took the oath of office on January 12, 1983, as a freshman delegate. He will be representing the sprawling 8th district of his own northeast Baltimore county.

"There is no criminal justice system in the federal courts," Anderson insists. "There is a system, but it sure as hell isn't justice. It's a horrible things to look back on what happened to me, knowing that it shouldn't have ever happened in the first place and that it was strictly political."

In March of 1974, Anderson was convicted in U.S. District Court, after a sensational 10-week jury trial, on 32 counts of extortion, conspiracy and tax evasion. The case centered around a scheme of payoffs from engineers and contractors in exchange for receiving county contracts.

According to the government's view of the evidence at the trial, William "Bill" Fornoff, a former administrative officer to Anderson, served as Anderson's "bag man." Anderson was sentenced to five years in prison by Judge Joseph Young, and in fact, served 13 months of that time at Allenwood. The balance of his sentence was suspended and he was placed on parole.

"There were politicians in this state, who saw me after I helped defeat the (proposed) Constitution, helped defeat Joe Tydings, who was a member of my own party, but who was an unmitigated snob, who went to Washington as a playboy, and paid no attention to his constituents," recalls the balding, chain-smoking Anderson. "And the voters showed they knew it by kicking the hell out of him.

"The politicians realized at the time, that I was the strongest Democratic office holder in the state," Anderson continued. "They knew if they had to move ahead in the state, they had to get rid of me. And they did an extremely good job of it. they wiped me out completely.

For the decade of the 70s, the state of Maryland held the dubious title of the "Political Crime Capital of the U.S.A." Even hardened New York, New Jersey and Pennsylvania politicos were taken aback by our home-made, shocking and sordid scandals.

The political landscape was littered with the corpses of the once and mighty public office holders and their cohorts: Spiro T. Agnew, Marvin Mandel, and I. H. (Bud) Hammerman; Irv Kovens; Dale Hess and Bill and Harry Rodgers; Joseph Alton; Ottavio Grande; George Santoni; and of course, Dale Anderson, were among the washed up debris flushed out by the long arm of the U.S. Attorney's Office in Baltimore from the whirlwind of corruption trials.

"If the U.S. Attorney or the people in that office aren't out to get you, you aren't gone to be gotten, continued Anderson, in a gravelly voice, while seated in his new delegate's office, in the Thomas Hunter Lowe Building, in Annapolis.

"There are many extreme weaknesses in the criminal justice system, which I call the federal injustice system. For instance, corroborating evidence isn't necessary in a federal case. So, there were 17 admitted felons given immunity to testify against me. But no corroboration of any of it, and, in no court in the world would that stand up, except in the Federal Court of the United States."

Anderson started his heady rise up the political ladder in 1958, when with the help of the machine of the late boss, Mike Birmingham, he was elected to the County Council. He served as the chairman of the council from 1958-1962, and served another term as a Council member from 1962-1966.

In 1966, he was elected County Executive and served two four-year terms in that office. Most sources, including even his worst political enemies, considered Anderson as a strong, gutsy, effective and conservative leader in his role as County Executive.

"I have never in my lifetime had anybody approach me and talk to me as if they thought I was a crook. Never! I have never had anybody say to me, 'You are a crook,'" says Anderson. "The people in Baltimore County know that I took a terrific beating. What happened to me was not justice at all, it was injustice. They knew it. They sincerely believed it. And therefore, they put me back in office."

Anderson finished second in the Democratic primary and third in a field of six in the November, 1982 general election, polling 12,481 votes. Anderson added that the electoral victory brought him "considerable satisfaction" and that he was anxious to get back in office.

One observer of Baltimore County politics gave this view of the Anderson brouhaha: "The liberal ilk wanted urban renewal and subsidized housing for Baltimore County. It was their money-making thing. But, Dale said it just wouldn't wash with his people. He refused to go along. So, they started painting him as a dumb redneck, an 'Archie Bunker' type.

Hell, the truth was Anderson was a real populist, right out of the mid-western states, where he was actually born and raised. They crucified old Dale on a cross of progress, and the cross was made up of give-away-fed-eral-taxpayers' dollars."

As for what kept him going during his eight-year ordeal, Anderson explained, "That some people call it intestinal fortitude, but among politi-cians it's usually referred to as balls. I think I have always had enough intestinal fortitude to fight for anything I wanted; for my family; or the people in Baltimore County; or the people in this state. I think I am still as capable as I use to be, and if I am, you will see it in the next four years."

Anderson then turned to one of his favorite topics. "The *Sunpapers* referred to me as a racist. Of course, they condemned me as soon as I was indicted, a long time before the trial, and they have continued to do so since. I took the true story to them, after I came home, the manuscript that I had written. I think it was about 70 pages, typewritten. It was a nice, neat manuscript, easy to read, and they wouldn't print it, because they said it isn't news anymore.

Nevertheless, every time they print something about me, they make the statement that I was a convicted criminal, that I went to Allenwood and served time. It's news when they want it to be news. But, when I wanted them to print the truth, they wouldn't do it. They are just a bunch of no good bastards in that *Sunpapers*."

Anderson feels very strongly that he "had won the case, unquestion-ably." And, that if his judge, "had the intestinal fortitude that a judge should have," his case wouldn't have gone to the jury. Anderson insisted that "in a state court, a judge would have thrown the case out immediately.

No question about it." Anderson concluded, "It was just a bunch of liars out there."

*   *   *

# 12. Mary Avara: First Lady of the Maryland Censor Board
## June, 1985

Mary Avara is now seventy-three years old.

But from 1961 to 1982, she was a member of the controversial Maryland Censor Board that licensed movies in the "Free State."

For part of that time, Avara was the chairperson of the agency, and gained for herself an enduring reputation as a person who "tells it like it is."

Before the Censor Board was legislated out of existence by a Governor Harry Hughes-dominated General Assembly, Avara became the champion of that segment of our population that despised the hard-core porn movies, and strongly resisted having them shown in our cinemas.

During her career as a regulator, Avara made guest appearances on the Dick Cavett, Johnny Carson and Merv Griffin television shows.

She was a big hit with the national audiences because of her folksy delivery, family- oriented philosophy, honesty, and knack for story telling.

From a family of 16 children, Avara was widowed at an early age with four young children.

She went into the bail bond business, and became an instant success.

Active in democratic politics, Avara was closely aligned with the late boss of the 6th district, the beloved Julian "Fats" Carrick and City Councilman, Michael "Iron Mike' McHale.

Governor J. Millard Tawes also held Avara in the highest regard for her winning precinct work on his behalf in the '60s. Avara believed that movies with explicit sex scenes, gratuitous violence, and obscene language gave "America a bad name."

She made no bones about the fact that she thought, like many celluloid critics, that John Waters' movies were "simply trash."

Devoted to her church, St. Peter the Apostle, and her southside community, Mary Avara, in every respect, has been a magnificent woman and civic leader.

She has brought great credit to herself, her Sicilian heritage, her city, and to her family.

*                *                *

*Author's Note-Mary Avara died on Aug. 9, 2000, at the age of 90. On August 16, 2000, *Baltimore Sun* columnist Dan Rodricks ran this item:... and another thing! A Mary "The Censor Lady" Avara memory, from Baltimore attorney Billy Hughes:

"In the late '50s, I was working on the docks in Locust Point with the late Michael "Iron Mike" McHale (Del. Brian McHale's father). McHale was a popular city councilman from the 6th District. One night, Mike took me to a political meeting over in Southwest Baltimore, by Hollins Market. We had to climb up a steep flight of stairs. When we got to the top, a half-inebriated character came up to McHale and started bad-mouthing him in a very loud and hostile manner. Before he could respond, this smallish woman, with coal-black hair, rushed out of the shadows. She grabbed the drunk by his coat lapels, shook him as hard as any stevedore could and yelled in his face: "Don't you dare insult Mr. McHale! He's my guest!' The drunk wisely nodded his compliance and slid back into the crowd. McHale then turned to me-by then my jaw had nearly dropped to the floor-and said, "Billy, I want you to meet Mary Avara!"

*                *                *

# 13. Frank J. Battaglia: Baltimore's Top Cop
## May 25, 1983.

"The biggest menace you have today in the country is narcotics. It is very profitable. It is hard to get to them. I have always said it is our number one problem. I have put together a 60-member squad to fight it. Just the other night, we made 33 arrests and confiscated 11 guns. We have had over 17,000 narcotics-related arrests in Baltimore City, since I took office 20 months ago. We're trying to put a dent in this narcotics business, because it is such a terrible thing."

Thus, Frank J. Battaglia, the 70-years old Police Commissioner of Baltimore City, began a recent interview.

Raised within the shadows of the Baltimore and Ohio Railroad's Camden Street Station, (now the location of the Camden Yards baseball park), Battaglia is truly a policeman's policeman.

Over a distinguished 43-year public service career, he rose slowly and diligently through the ranks of the men in blue, from the position of foot patrolman to Baltimore's top cop.

The son of a Sicilian immigrant, Santo Battaglia, and an American-born mother, Katherine DiMarco, he has received 14 official commendations for his police work, and he is acknowledged by experts in the field to be one of the country's leading authorities on civil disturbances.

"I always had a great desire to be a policeman. My grandparents had a little confectionery store down around Camden Station. They called it the 'B & 0.' The policemen would always come in, and naturally they would sit down and have a cup of coffee. I became quite friendly with them, and I use to walk around the post with them at night. I built up a great admiration for the police department. One day, one of the police officers, Edward McCarron, he's now retired, said to me, 'Why don't you come on and be a police officer?' So, I got the application and that's it," continued the soft-spoken Battaglia, while sitting in his office, on the eighth floor of the Police Department's headquarters, in down town Baltimore.

In the early 50s, there were 22 taverns located in the blue collar Southside peninsula of Locust Point. During the long dog days of summer, before the coming of the air conditioning culture, each tavern would keep all its doors and windows wide open and allow the juke box to blare away, even past the 2 a.m. closing time. The naive natives, this commentator included, thought that was the way it was supposed to be.

"I made the taverns down there close up on time and also either to shut their juke boxes all together, turn them down, or keep their doors and windows firmly shut," Battaglia recalled from his early no-nonsense days as a sergeant from the Southern District.

"Some of the other sergeants didn't bother the tavern owners, because they had become quite friendly with them. I wanted to be friendly with them, too, but I also wanted them to adhere to the law. I would go in the tavern and say, 'It's 2 o' clock, close up.' One of the owners decided to try me out. He said he wasn't going to close up. I believe he had some kind of connection to a publishing company. So I said to him, 'O.K.' I simply went in and took down the guy's liquor license number. He contined to give me a hard time about it, but I ignored him. I then prepared a case against the owner before the Liquor Board for staying open after hours. The Liquor Board agreed with me and found the owner guilty of violating the law. I never had any more trouble with that owner, or others, after that incident. The message went out that when it's 2 o'clock, it means you close up. I told him, you can sell all the wiskey you want to up until 2 o'clock, but after that, it's time to close," Battaglia said.

In the late 50s, Battaglia came to the public's attention with his adoption of a controversial plan in the Southwestern District of stopping automobiles at random in order to check out the driver's compliance with the State's motor vehicle registration and licensing requirements. The novel scheme created a strong police presence in the high crime area. But, it also brought a storm of protest by civil libertarians because of its patent infringements on civil and constitutional rights.

The so-called *Battaglia Plan*, although well-intended by its creator to protect the public's safety, was eventually discarded by the department. The State Police's present campaign of stopping automobiles at selected road blocks to detect possible drunk drivers undoubtedly has its geneses in the Battaglia Plan of that earlier era.

"I remember the first night I went out on the street as a rookie policeman. I never had any training handling a gun-no practice shots at all. In those days, when you were appointed to the force, they gave you a gun and your keys. You were in the Police Academy during the day, but two or three nights a week, you were out on the streets.

"It was a terrible thing to do. I remember we got a call to the Crescent Candy Company about a possible breaking and entry. The lieutenant told me to take the back and he would take the front of the building. I knew the area very well, but it was very dark and isolated. I went back there, in the alley, and here comes this black man out the back door of the building. I had my gun out and I was shaking. I didn't know what to do, I was so green. I didn't want to shoot the man. And, it was lucky that I didn't shoot him, because he turned out to be the company's night watchman."

"I was so grateful that the Lord didn't let me fire that gun, because I would have killed that man. The company was in fact robbed and we did pick one of the suspects up that night a couple of blocks away from the building. We cleared up a lot of good cases with that arrest. The robbers were a gang operating out of the State of Pennsylvania," Battaglia reminisced.

In 1940, when Battaglia first put on a uniform, there were only 28 automobiles in the entire department's fleet. Today, there are 436 marked police vehicles in a total fleet of 816. Manpower-wise, the growth has been just as significant from a uniformed force of under 1000 members in 1940, to over 3,500 today. In addition, there are presently over 700 civilian personnel assigned to the department, supported by the most sophisticated crime fighting equipment available, including an award-winning helicopter unit.

Battaglia said the department is presently in full compliance with all federal court decrees, dealing with past racial and sexual discrimination on the police force. "We are going to be fair with all people. We are striving to work together. We are all one. That is the way I always wanted to work," Battaglia emphasized.

The recent flap, deliberately hyped by the Establishment media, over mayoral candidate Billy Murphy's comments regarding a need in the future to have a black police commissioner in a city with a 55 percent majority black population, was brushed aside by Battaglia. He called it a "political issue," and said that he will finish out his term of office.

Battaglia fondly remembered the late Alexander Emerson, the legendary door-busting hater of pimps and sleazy gambling czars, and the then head of the "Vice Squad," as the policeman he "most admired." Battaglia characterized Captain Emerson as a "honest, hard-working, good man."

In order to be promoted to captain himself, Battaglia recalled that the late Police Commissioner James M. Hepbron, (who held that post from 1951-1961), literally put him on trial. Hepbron told him that if he wanted the job, he would have to go ahead and clean up the Southwestern District. At that time, it was the most corrupt and most crime-ridden district in the city. If he didn't succeed, Hepbron said that not only wouldn't he keep the promotion, but that his future on the force was over.

Battaglia not only cleaned the area out, (including throwing some unsavory bondsmen out of the local court house), but he was cited by the commissioner as "one of the best captains I ever made."

Battaglia added with obvious pride that he would like the people of Baltimore to know that, "In the present difficult fight against crime, that we have one of the best police forces in the country. I think we have got some of the top men and women-good, hard-working and dedicated. We are practically free of organized crime in this community am committed to keeping it that way."

Unlike his flamboyant predecessor in office, Frank J. Battaglia doesn't ride on a white horse at the front of a full-dressed parade. This self-effacing man of unimpeachable integrity is one of the most respected and beloved Italian-Americans in the nation.

He is, in my considered opinion, the finest commissioner in the modern history of the city's police deparment.

# Chapter Two

## The Reality-Challenged

### 14. Earth to Al Gore
### June 19, 1999

No surprise! Al Gore wants to be president. What is shocking though is just how fast he is running away from the White House's present occupant, Bill Clinton. Years of scandals has taken its toll on their cozy relationship. Maybe running isn't the right word. Try speeding!

Gore, a "President-in-Waiting," made his announcement for the high office on June 16, in front of the courthouse in his supposed home town of Carthage, Tennessee. Politicians usually go back to their roots when launching an important campaign. For example, Sen. Barbara Mikulski

(D MD) likes to do her campaign launching thing from Fells Point, even though she rarely visits the area nowadays. It shows she cares about people.

History isn't much help to Gore's lofty aspirations either. Sure, George Bush, Sr. rode Ronald Reagan's coat tails into the White House, but V.P. Hubert Humphrey went down in flames because of his attachment to Lyndon B. Johnson and the Vietnam War. And, Dan Quayle is living proof that any simpleton can be elected Vice-President of the United Sates.

Gore was a bland congressman from Tennessee for four terms and a senator for one undistinguished six year term, before "Bubba Bill" selected him as his running mate on the 1992 Democratic ticket. Gore even has a failed bid for the presidency in 1988, on his dismal resume'.

Now 51, Gore has lived most of his life in and around Washington, D.C. Nothing wrong with that. Conservative firebrand Pat Buchanan, also a presidential candidate, is from Washington, too, but he doesn't try to hide it. Gore does! He did spend some of his summer years growing up back at Carthage, but little else. Why all this fakery over origins?

Gore's late father, Al Gore, Sr., was a very powerful senator from Tennessee and later an ambassador and fat cat lobbyist. He was so close to Armand Hammer, a shadowy international-based tycoon, that the late business man helped to pay young Gore's way through college and also to jump start his national political career in 1988.

Washington D.C., and not the farming community of Carthage, Tennessee, is home to Al Gore, Jr.

Swanky hotels, like Washington's former Ritz Carlton, is where Gore spent most of his sheltered childhood. He also went to an elite private school, St. Alban's, for the children of rich kids in the district. Then he went off to Harvard in 1969 and on to the Vanderbilt Law School.

In his mostly boring campaign spiel to the locals, Gore mentioned his moral and family values theme 27 times. If he would have hit 28, he would have passed a record set by the Rev. Pat Robertson in a recent TV sermon.

On the night of June 16, on ABC's "20/20" program, Gore called Clinton's affair with intern Monica Lewinsky, "inexcusable." He indicated the president had lied to him about the nature and extent of the liaison. (It would be nice, too, to see Ann F. Lewis, Clinton's mouthy Director of Communications, come clean about her shameless shilling for Clinton on this issue, but don't hold your breath waiting for that to happen.)

On the "20/20" show, host Diane Sawyer (a graduate of the Barbara Walters' School of Fluffy Journalism) was careful not to press Gore on his own sordid scandals, like those involving fund raising at a Buddhist Temple and from Chinese businessmen with suspected ties to Red China.

Some in the Congress believe that there is a connection between the fund raising Gore did in the Chinese community and the serious lapses in security, involving alleged assets for Red China, at the Los Alamos nuclear research facility. Gore, however, insists there is no connection and that, "No security breaches have occurred on Clinton's watch."

One of Gore's most irritating flaws is his tendency to want to be on both sides of an issue. For instance, at the 1996 Democratic Convention, he recounted, with teary eyes, how his sister had died of lung cancer from being an habitual cigarette smoker. However, in 1990, he boasted how the family farm in Carthage grew tobacco for big firms that make products like Marlboro and Camel cigarettes. In 1990, too, he was accepting lucrative campaign contributions from tobacco companies.

Gore's talking out of both sides of his mouth on critical questions won't fly anymore. If he wants to be considered as a serious candidate for president, he has to cut the nonsense out. The time for fairy tales is over.

*     *     *

## 15. Book Review: Malachy McCourt's *A Monk Swimming*
### September 6, 2000

"…A silly tale told by a stage Irishman."

This bore of a book is a huge disappointment to me. I thought it might be both funny and insightful. It was neither. I had met Malachy McCourt in New York City, in the 90s. At the time, I was doing a weekly commentary for WBAI's *Radio Free Eireann* (RFE). He would turn up on the show as an occasional guest doing a light comedy routine.

Initially, I was shocked that McCourt didn't plug the RFE's boy-oh, Johnny "Bob" McDonagh, in his acknowledgments. McDonagh, a champion of Irish freedom, had been very good to him, allowing him plenty of free mike time on the popular left-of-center station. Instead, McCourt paid tribute to Adrian Flannelly, a host of a NYC-based Irish radio show, mostly known for its politically conservative and pro-Dublin slant.

The hard truth is that McCourt's yarn belongs more in a dysfunctional family medical journal. It's a sickening case study about him boozing it up, loathing the memory of his father, wildly hating the Roman Catholic Church, and playing at life with air-headed blue bloods, rugby players, and card carrying alcoholics.

Interestingly, he just loves all the Jews he meets. Now, this sounded just a little bit contrived to me. Especially, since McCourt also made it a point, without a shred of evidence, to brand the members of the New York Athletic Club as "Hitlereans." Mean stuff, coming from an impoverished foreigner, who ate, slept, and drank freely thanks to many generous Manhattanites.

Predictably, McCourt blasted the Brits every chance he got in his feeble tome, but that also rang false. When he had an opportunity to picket the NYC visit of Queen Elizabeth and Prince Philip, as others did, he declined. McCourt, however, did appear at an exclusive reception for the royal couple, along with his Tory cronies, where he had a public chat with Prince

Philip. Did he use that rare opportunity to protest British rule in Ireland that he pretends to care so passionately about? No, our pseudo rebel hero didn't. Instead, he tried to ingratiate himself with the Britannic duo.

I think the pandering scene with the royals said more about his true character then anything else. What a windbag this reformed drunk is! It all made me believe that Ireland, and America, too, would have been better off if McCourt had never stopped his notorious boozing!

After 290 pages of his mindless drivel, I no longer cared what happened to him. In fact, I felt deeply sorry for his poor parents for having brought him into the world and for the good people of Limerick, and NYC, too, for having to put up with him all these whiskey-soaked, bad-mouthing years.

Finally, what is to be said about this dubious memoir?

I think this: It's a silly tale told by a stage Irishman.

*     *     *

# 16. Father Healy & Margaret Thatcher: A "Special Place" in Hell
### February 10, 1981

Maryland Irish National Caucus, Inc.
110 Bosley Avenue. Cockeysville, Md. 21030

Rev. Dr. Timothy S. Healy, S.J.
President, Georgetown University
Washington, D.C. 20057

Dear Father Healy:

Our organization is very unhappy over the fact that you plan to bestow on British P.M. Margaret Thatcher on February 27, 1981 an Award for Humanitarian Service from Georgetown University. We wish to strongly protest such action on your part as giving moral comfort to a leader of a country that treats Irishmen and Irishwomen as less than full human beings.

Margaret Thatcher is the head of an elitist imperial government, the United Kingdom, that believes it is proper to continue their criminal, violence producing hegemony over the Irish People in the six gerrymandered counties of northeastern Ireland. Northern Ireland is a bloody British police state maintained by brute military force that denies by fear and terror the natural and lawful right of the Irish People to full self-determination within the framework of a 32 county federated Irish State.

We realize with regret that historically the Church as an institution, both in this country and especially in Ireland, has tended to support the political and economic status quo. It appears the Church's primary objective has been to have a protected status in such a society for itself. (Footnote 1)

We acknowledge that institutions, like Georgetown, the well known Jesuit founded institution, must compete for dwindling financial support from both the public and private sector with similarly situated schools of higher learning. We know that such fund raising efforts place additional pressures on even the ablest of administrators and you are certainly an able administrator.

We believe the ethical issue is crystal clear. It would be morally wrong for you and your school, under the present oppressive colonial situation in Ireland to in anyway honor Margaret Thatcher or by implication, her government. To do so would be to give your stamp of approval on British crimes in Ireland and condone the vicious cycle of colonial violence that the British propaganda machine very skillfully blames on its Irish victims.

Your silence on the Irish Question in the past has been shamefully noted. Your intended course of conduct is inexcusable and indefensible. (Footnote 2)

We submit that you should immediately rescind any such invitation to Margaret Thatcher for any type honorary award from Georgetown as being improvidently granted.

To paraphrase your illustrious and saintly founder, St. Ignatius of Loyola, "What does it profit Georgetown if it gains the favor of Margaret Thatcher of Great Britain and the anglophile World and loses its moral base as a Catholic institution of higher learning all at the immediate expense of the beleaguered nationalist minority in Northern Ireland?"

Respectfully,

William Hughes
State Chairman, Maryland Chapter of Irish National Caucus
Baltimore, Maryland

1. S. Dangerfeld, *The Damnable Question,* (Atlantic, Little, Brown &;Co. 1976).
2. Hannah Arendt, *Eichmann Jerusalem: (A Report on the Banality of Evil),* N. Y., The Viking Press, 1965 Ed.

cc: Concerned Parties

        *             *             *

*Author's Note-Father Healy ignored all the objections of the human rights activist community. He arrogantly went ahead and granted an "Honorary Degree" to Margaret Thatcher. I remember him sending me, in response to my letter, a copy of the bogus "degree" that he had awarded to the notorious Brit. To add insult to injury, the document was written in Latin! I recall, in anger, tearing it into a thousand little pieces. In the spring of 1981, the Jesuit-approved Thatcher (the UK's Augusto Pinochet) allowed ten brave Irishmen to die on hunger strikes over the issue of their status as political prisoners. History,

I'm convinced, history will judge the tyrant Thatcher and Healy harshly. One of the great "Fathers of Christianity" was the legendary

Ambrose (339-97 A.D.), Bishop of Milan. He believed that the Church had a civic duty to obey the lawful ruler, but that it must also be the "conscience of the state," ready to chastise rulers for wrongdoing. It is beyond cavil that in this matter, Father Healy, (now deceased), miserably failed both his duty to his fellow man and to his God. As late as 1996, another Jesuit institution, Boston College, announced plans to again honor Thatcher. As a result, however, of a firestorm of protest from outraged American activists, the Jesuits at Boston College abandoned the ill-advised project.

*            *            *

## 17. Wecoming Queen Elizabeth to "Charm City"
## May, 1991

The Baltimore Orioles have announced that the British monarch, Queen Elizabeth II, will attend a night game at Memorial Stadium on Wednesday, May 15.

The Queen has been a staunch supporter of maintaining England's connection to the disputed six northeastern counties of Ireland (Northern Ireland). Local supporters of Irish freedom believe she has regularly condoned the excesses of her security forces in the strife-torn colony. They are unduly irate over her planned visit to "Charm City."

During her visit to the U.S., the Queen is also expected to address a joint session of the Congress.

After "Bloody Sunday" in British occupied Derry in 1972, (where 14 Irish nationalists, 7 of them children, were killed in a civil rights march), the Queen's publicly decorated the paratroopers responsible for the indiscriminate slaughter.

Gail Sheehy, the celebrated author of *Passages*, was in Derry on that tragic day. She referred to the barbaric incident in the first chapter of her best selling book. An independent inquiry labeled the conduct of the troops that days as "unadulterated murder."

Under the British constitutional system, the Queen is both the legal head of state and of the worldwide Anglican Church. She is reported to have amassed a personal fortune of nearly $13 billion dollars. Since the halcyon days of King George III, it has been well-documented that much of the wealth of the British Crown has been accumulated by unsavory means. These methods have included: illegal confiscation of the property of colonialists people; slave ownership and trading; exploitation of Third World workers; opium running; and outright piracy.

The Queen's visit is being seized on by Irish Americans as an occasion during which they will state their case for Irish freedom. Protest plans are now being formulated by activists from Irish Northern Aid (INA), and other leading Irish-American organizations, peace and justice groups, and labor unions in the Baltimore, Washington, D.C., and Philadelphia areas.

Anti-British feelings are running high as a result of the well publicized injustices inflicted on "The Birmingham Six," the biased British judicial system. The six Irishmen served 17 years in a British prison for crimes for which they were framed.

A recent rash of brutal murders of unarmed Nationalists in the Six Counties by Loyalist death squads (believed to be in collusion with the security forces), have only added to the outrage. The patent hypocrisy of the U.S. standing with the British to "liberate" Kuwait, while Northern Ireland remains under England's ruthless control, is also beginning to hit home.

There are presently over 400 Irish Republicans languishing in British jails. Many are serving indeterminate sentences for crimes that they did not commit.

The Irish, of course, aren't the only ethnic group with a strong resentment against the British elite. Latin Americans were also incensed over the British conduct in the war over the Malvinas (Falkland) Islands. This included the cruel decision of Prime Minister Margaret Thatcher to order the sinking of the Argentinean vessel *General Belgrado*. The vessel was torpedoed, without any warning, outside the prescribed war zone. Over 380 Argentinean naval personnel lost their lives in that debacle.

Many Jews, too, have reason not to applaud the appearance of the Queen. During WWII, while the holocaust was raging in Europe, British officials adamantly refused permission to Jews to emigrate to Palestine. British policy at that time was geared to placating the Arab world and the grasping interest of their own prospering oil cartels. Hitler's death factories, and the fate of the trapped Jews, were outside their tunnel vision.

The Orioles will be playing the Oakland A's on May 15. It will be the first and only time the Queen has attended an American baseball game. She was invited by the Orioles' owner and will be sitting in his private mezzanine box along the third base side of home plate. It is unlikely she will stay for the entire game.

The Queen's trip to Baltimore, which appears on the surface to be a harmless news item for "Entertainment Tonight," is more than it seems. It is a calculated act of deception by the well-oiled British propaganda machine. Its main purpose is to mesmerize the American masses into accepting the Queen ( and Britain itself, as an extension), as a lovable, trusting and fun-loving country incapable of barbarism.

The last thing the clever British p.r. apparatus wants is for the starstruck Yanks to see behind its carefully-crafted-Disney-Worldesque Royal Family persona. The Queen's controlled appearance fortifies and perpetuates that fairy tale-like view of reality. The media coverage promises to be extensive.

It is not known, at this time, whether President George Bush will accompany the Queen to the baseball contest, though the present British Ambassador to the U.S., Antony Acland, will most certainly be one of her escorts.

Acland recently boasted how the "Gulf crisis" had brought the two countries closer together. Acland, true to his beastly upper-class instincts, made no mention, however, of the awesome human casualties, especially to the Kurdish refugees, caused by the blood and mindless conflict.

The Queen will travel to the game from the British Ambassador's residence in D.C., via helicopter, landing near Lake Montebello, about a mile east of the stadium. She will then join up with a motorcade. Security will be extremely tight.

According to a reliable Capitol Hill source, the Queen will be in D.C. the night before the game. She will be the honoree at a very exclusive White House function. Only high rollers in the national Republican Party, connected plutocrats, Nancy Reagan apologists, and prominent blue bloods from the Anglo-American community can expect invitations. Ex-U.S. Charles "Mac" Mathias, who voted in 1986 to gut the political exception clause from the Extradition Treaty with the United Kingdom, will head the guest list of flaming British-Firsters.

Mathias is now a fat cat lobbyist for Red China, the "Butchers of Tienanmen Square". After leaving the Congress, Mathias was given an honorary knighthood by Queen Elizabeth II.

There is some irony of the Queen coming to Baltimore more than 170 years after the historic "Battle of Fort McHenry". Just prior to attempting to seize our city, the British imperial forces had wasted Washington, D.C. and torched our beloved White House to the ground.

When the British soldiers were inside our nation's Capitol, they actually took a mock vote to burn it. Absent the heroic defense of Baltimore on September 12 to 14, 1814, Americans might still be living under the British yoke. And, the fabled "Star-Spangled Banner," our national anthem, may never have been written by the immortal Francis Scott Key.

The revered "stadium," dedicated to the sacred memories of the valiant Baltimoreans, who died fighting the fascists in WWII, holds around 60,000 fans. Because of the massive publicity hype surrounding the Queen's sojourn, it can reasonably be expected to be a sold-out game.

*         *         *

*Author's Note-This protest, from a p.r. perspective, was one of the most successful in the history of Irish American activism. The media coverage was extremely positive in its focus towards the human rights agenda of the protesters. Their action received worldwide publicity.

*     *     *

## 18. Spiro T. Agnew: A Fall From Grace
## May, 1984

"The mere happening of an accident does not justify an inference of negligence," said the handsome-looking, strong-voiced Adjunct Professor of Tort Law, at the University of Baltimore Law School.

It was in the early fall of 1962, and I was in my first year of Law School. Spiro T. "Ted" Agnew was one of my instructors, and at the time, he was the on-the- move County Executive (1962-1966) of sprawling Baltimore County.

Political events were to catapult this son of a Greek-born father into the governorship of Maryland, and then into seven years as Richard M. Nixon's Vice-President (1968- 1973).

His fall from national power was, however, to be just as sudden, and ended in his public disgrace, with his forced resignation from office on October 11, 1973, after pleading "no contest" to a federal charge of tax evasion before US. Judge Walter E. Hoffman.

Disbarred from the practice of law, Agnew has moved to the west coast of the country, and is reported to be acting as some kind of international business consultant.

Hollywood insiders insist that of all of Agnew's former fair-weather buddies, only the crooner, Frank Sinatra, has remained his most faithful and trusted ally.

The tragedy of Agnew is itself out of the pathos of Greek mythology. Our Maryland Court of Appeals called his behavior nothing less than, "morally obtuse." It can be argued that the Gods have claimed yet another noted victim of man's insatiable ability to deceive himself.

\*         \*         \*

*By way of full disclosure, I thought Agnew was a wonderful teacher and very enthusiastic. And, at all times, he conducted himself in the class room as a gentleman and a scholar. I received an "A" for the course from him and I am very proud of that fact.

Although, I am a life long Democrat, I also felt very bad, on a personal level, for Agnew when he eventually fell from power. I couldn't help but notice how many of his former colleagues here in Maryland quickly abandoned him after he was forced out of office and how others were so fast to "rat him out" to the Feds.

\*         \*         \*

## 19. Galway's Bishop Eamon Casey Fouls Out
### May 25, 1992

Some would call it a double standard. The lusting Eamon Casey, Bishop of the all-too-trusting Galwayians, liked to pry into this parishioners private affairs, but he didn't want them knowing anything about his own philandering-even if they were subsidizing it.

Casey, an arch reactionary on issues of morals, himself excluded, has been "found out" as having a mistress, Ms. Annie Murphy, to whom he has paid over $115,000 in child support. These once-secret payments went on for over 15 years.

Casey, now 65-years-old, has resigned over the sensational scandal. He gave "personal reasons" as the cause. Ms. Murphy has gone public; TV, radio and print media; with her side of the story. She now lives in Connecticut and has a son Peter, age 17, that she says is Casey's love child. Murphy described her early relationship with Bishop Casey as a time of "magical love."

Irish Church leaders, on the supposed orders of Cardinal Cathal Daly, have closed ranks around the embattled Casey and are now stonewalling the press and also the shell-shocked Irish Catholic peasantry about all the sordid details.

Ponder this fact: At the height of the brutal British policy of "Internment" of Irish rebels in Northern Ireland in 1973, Bishop Casey was beginning his illicit affair with Ms. Murphy. At that time, he held the sinecure of Bishop of Kerry in his ecclesiastical career. Although Casey had spoken out in the past about human rights abuses in the Third World, he was careful to parrot Cardinal Daly's blame-the-Irish-victims line of the North.

The West of Ireland, more Catholic than Rome itself, is reeling from the titillating disclosures. Not since the great Charles Stewart Parnell was publicly castigated by the spiteful bishops for his love for Kitty O'Shea, has a sexual escapade so stirred the Irish masses and shaken their blind faith in their God-like Church leaders.

The bishop's fall from grace avenges the church's despicable role in the merciless sacking of Parnell in the last century. He was a Protestant of Anglo-Irish stock and a gallant leader of the "Home Rule Movement" and regarded by many nationalists as "Ireland's Uncrowned King."

Bishop Casey plans to go into "mission work" in order to redeem what is left of his honor. Whether he will be assigned by Cardinal Daly to the British occupied Six Counties isn't clear at the moment.

In Ireland, north and south, many of the bishops, including Casey, came to power during the blood-stained reigns of Heath, Wilson or Thatcher in the United Kingdom. Almost to a man, they have adopted a see-no-evil policy with respect to the British domination of the six northeastern counties of Ireland. Within the last year alone, the UK government has been cited by three respected organizations for violating the human rights of the nationalist minority in Northern Ireland.

Rona M. Fields, in her landmark study on British terror tactics, *Northern Ireland, Society Under Siege,* described in cogent terms the *modus operandi* of many of the clerics. She wrote, "The clergy and church hierarchies are apologists, who sustain the social system even while they interminably moralize and condemn violence, which in the final analysis only serves to desensitize the listeners to its real horrors."

The playwright Sean O'Casey said, "The clergy were always in the stream of things going against Ireland. They fought the men of "Forty Eight," the Fenians, and then Parnell."

During the desperate famine years, 1845-50, there wasn't one recorded case of a member of the Catholic clergy dying from the great hunger (See, *Paddy's Lament* by Thomas Gallagher). While the Quakers were trying to feed the starving Irish peasants, the Vatican was busy plotting to defeat the Italian drive for national independence and unity.

In fact, the "Land League," founded by Michael Davitt to combat unfair evictions of tenants by absentee British landlords, and rent gouging, made its first stand against an estate in County Mayo on April 20, 1879. It was administered by an Irish Catholic priest, Canon Burke *(Bold Fenian Men* by Robert Kee.)

The damage some of the bishops, and the church, have done to Ireland and to its people is incalculable. There are, of course, brave exceptions within the church's hierarchy, and in the ranks of ordinary priests and nuns. Some have stood loyally over the last two decades with the besieged Republican Movement. But they are such a rare dissident breed that their numbers can be counted on the fingers of two hands.

It does my heart good to see God's just law of retribution working to level the Irish bishops-one of the most oppressive, unjust and authoritarian bodies of the Modern Age.

How pseudo-liberals, and defenders of the bishops, like Conor Cruise O'Brien, will respond to the Casey expose' is unclear. The likely spin by the Dublin establishment is to target the practice of celibacy and paint Bishop Casey as a "vulnerable, lonely and overworked cleric."

According to my Galway City sources, these are the main questions being raised by the shocked populace over this disgraceful affair: First, what was the source of the $115,000 that Bishop Casey used to buy Ms. Murphy's silence?; Second, did Bishop Casey have more than one mistress?; Third, is Bishop Casey's seamy hidden life an aberration or the norm within the ranks of the over-privileged bishops?; Fourth, will the Church allow the financial books of the Bishops to be open to an outside audit by an independent agency in order to ensure that there isn't any other type of hanky panky going on?; Fifth, will Bishop Casey come clean with the people about his gross deception and state for the record whether any other of the clergy helped him coverup this insufferable violation of their code of ethics?

Like the moral hypocrite Bishop Eamon Casey, many of the bishops have been systematically betraying the Irish race and the nationalist cause since the notorious "Treaty of Maynooth" in 1792.

Now, with the ignoble Casey affair, one of them has also betrayed his calling and his God.

*          *          *

# 20. Did Sen. Barbara Mikulski Inflate Her Political Resume'?
## May 22, 1999

According to a colorful tourist marker located in Fells Point, at the corner of Broadway and Thames St., Barbara Mikulski, now a U.S. Senator, attended a protest rally in the late 60s opposing the controversial "East West Expressway" project. The ill-conceived juggernaut, if completed as planned, would have gutted both the Federal Hill and the Fells Point waterfront areas of the city.

Supposedly, Mikulski shouted out, "The British couldn't take Fells Point, the termites couldn't take Fells Point, and the State Road Commission couldn't take Fells Point."

Fortunately for her rebel image, someone at the rally took down her rant, which reads like it was authored by a p.r. flake. Keep in mind that this is the same politico, who voted on the Senate floor not to dismiss the impeach charges against President Bill Clinton. When her blunder was pointed out, she changed her vote.

The inscription on the marker gives the impression that Mikulski played a leading part in opposing the roadway and that she stood up for the then mostly blue collar neighborhood. No other local activists are mentioned. Mikulski's campaign literature also has regularly boasted of her supposedly significant role in the "East-West Expressway" brouhaha.

No doubt this is good for her bulldog persona, but I've talked with several people who were intimately involved in blocking the "East-West Expressway," and none of them can remember Mikulski doing anything to stop the project during the critical 60s period.

When the highway enterprise came up before the City Council for final approval only one Councilman had the courage to vote against it: Tom Ward of the 2nd district!

Today, he is a highly respected judge, now recently retired, of the Circuit Court for Baltimore city. Ward emphasized, "Mikulski didn't write any letters, speak out, attend any City Council meetings, or work on the project. I know this because I was there. The key people in that battle were Lucretia Fisher and Robert Eney, and, of course, many others were involved. My short list of splendid anti-expressway activists would also include Roland Reed, Larry Mullen, Charley and Libby Duff, Coard Simpler, Margaret Dougherty, Mary Geeson, Jane Springer, Shirley Doda and the late Jack Gleason."

Ward forced the Council (1) to repeatedly vote on the measure by demanding the city get the prior approval of municipal agencies and (2) to file an environmental impact statement on the planned project. His delaying tactics, and an effective court case, turned out to be pivotal.

According to Ward, the roadway was finally stopped by the legal strategy of having the Fells Point area designated as a Registered Historic District. "Mikulski," he added, "had absolutely nothing to do with that effort either." Federal law prohibits a federally funded highway from being built through such an area. Eventually, the "East-West Expressway", (now part of "I-95"), was completed along the south side of Locust Point, leading to the Fort McHenry tunnel.

Mikulski was born in the Highlandtown section of East Baltimore. During most of the 60s, she lived in Towson and worked in the city as a social worker. In fact, she didn't move back to the city until around 1967. She first resided in the Bolton Hill area, then moved to East Baltimore, and ran for the City Council from there in 1971, and won.

Thanks mostly to the emerging Feminist Movement, Mikulski has been successful in her electoral pursuits. In 1976, she went from the City Council job to Congress as a member of the House, representing the 3rd District; and in 1986, she won a seat in the U.S. Senate. Mikulski was reelected to that post in 1992.

In light of Vice President Al Gore's recent outrageous claim that he "invented" the Internet, isn't time for the public to investigate questionable claims made by political personalities?

Does Mikulski's name really deserve to be on that tourist marker in Fells Point? Or, has she over the years inflated her role in opposing the East-West Expressway? If she did inflate her political resume', isn't it time for her to, finally, come clean about it?

\*　　　　　\*　　　　　\*

## 21. Rep. Edward A. Garmatz: "Ah Dud Congressman!"
### January, 1985

He was a very poor public speaker, who habitually slurred his words. An electrician by trade and ex-police magistrate, Edward A. Garmatz, served in the U.S. Congress from Baltimore City's 3rd District from 1947-1973.

"It is simply amazing that a man, like Garmatz, with his obviously limited skills could rise in the Congress to such heights of power and become chairman of the influential Merchant Marine and Fisheries Committee. But, in that stifled bygone era, seniority, not talent, ruled, and Garmatz was pushed to the top," recalled one Capitol Hill insider.

To his credit, Garmatz championed the shipbuilding industry that brought a lot of government and private work to the Port of Baltimore.

An LBJ-styled Democrat, Garmatz deserved strong censure, however, for his knee-jerk support of Johnson's mindless Vietnam War policy. A longtime crony of labor fakers, Garmatz, who fashioned being saluted as "Mr. Chairman," was a product of Thommy (The Elder) D'Alesandro's political machine.

When Garmatz voluntarily left the congress, his salary was a mere $42,500. For a short period, he did some lobbying in Washington, D.C. for the Baltimore Gas & Electric Co.

According to the *Washington Post*, his annual federal pension, because of cost-of-living increases, is now a staggering $61,000. He lives part time on Florida's "Gold Coast."

No doubt, Garmatz, now 73, remains forever grateful for his lucky political star.

\*     \*     \*

# 22. Sen. Charles "Mac" Mathias & the Johns Hopkins' Scholars
## May, 22, 1986

Scholars at the Johns Hopkins University are in for a real academic treat. Republican U.S. Sen. Charles "Mac" Mathias, who is retiring after three terms in the Senate, is donating all of his public papers-going back to his salad days in the Maryland House of Delegates-to that prestigious center of higher learning.

At first glance, I felt sorry for the Hopkins intellectuals, but, who knows, some good might come out of their probing efforts. In studying Mac's heady documents, copies of his computer printout letters to his constituents, and inestimable expense vouchers, the social scientists may be able to tell us, if having a U.S. Senate is necessary to the preservation of our democracy.

There are a lot of cynics, who feel the Senate should be abolished, since it's mostly an expensive debating society for millionaire politicos. These Ambrose Bierce types theorize all power is actually exercised by the president, as a mindless agent, of the big plantation owners; like the Rockefellers, Mellons, DuPonts and Harrimans. This is silly, treasonable nonsense. Naturally, I don't believe a word of it. I just want to be fair, and tell you both sides of the issue.

In any event, assuming they can stay awake, the scholars will find a treasure trove of information in Mac's papers. Mac just loved traveling around the world as a US Senator, at the taxpayers' expense, of course. In fact, he was one of the leaders in the senate in that costly category. He was also a leader, in recent years, at having one of the worse attendance records for that body. Mac has a talent for going to the front of the line-any line!

Most of his career, Mac acted like he was an unappointed Secretary of State for our country. And invariably, after returning from the exotic capitals of the globe, Mac would write about it in an Op Ed piece for the *Baltimore Sunpapers*. For the longest period, I mistakenly thought Mac was the travel editor for *The Sun*. I didn't realize he was our elected senator, until I saw him on a television debate sponsored by the League of Women's Voters.

If anything, Mac's papers can be valuable as a tourist guide for future elected officials to ponder. His restaurant selections, alone, will make his material worthy of historic preservation. Hopefully, his restaurant rating system is not in the realm of "classified government information." Now, that would be a dirty trick.

Some citizens will anxiously await Mac's inside story of his countless meetings with the great leaders of our war-torn planet. Since, so often, many of them, unfortunately, don't survive in office very long; like the low life Ferdinand Marcos, "Baby Doc" Duvalier and Spiro Agnew. Mac's scholars must work quickly.

Mac was also an unrepentant leader in giving outside speeches to trade associations, corporate groups, and private clubs around the country. Most of the time, which is the lawful custom, he received a fee for his golden throat services. On one particular day, he actually gave three speeches, and got $5,000 back for his troubles. It will be interesting to see if Mac's popularity as a public speaker continues after he leaves the US Senate.

There will be some, who will contemptuously criticize Mac for turning his papers over to Hopkins. They will say things, like "Who cares?", and, "Isn't it a publicity stunt-anyway?"

But, you will never hear me complain. Because as long as those public papers are at Hopkins, it means Charles "Mac" Mathias isn't writing a book!

*           *           *

From the, Baltimore *News-American* newspaper, Letters to Editor section, March 25, 1982

Re:The Golden Throat of Sen. Mathias

Dear Editor:

Thank you for printing the remarks of Sen. Charles Mathias (R-MD).,
on the issue of nuclear weapons. (The *News American*, March 22). The last
time anybody here in South Baltimore heard about the good senator was
when we read in *The Washington Post* of Feb. 28, that Sen. Mathias had
been labeled a "golden throat senator." The reason for that nickname was
that the senator, according to the *Post* account, had made $40,300 from
outside speaking engagements in 1981. In fact, the *Post* documented the
fact that Sen. Mathias made $5000 for making three speeches in
Minneapolis on Aug. 1, 1980. Now at the rate of $5000 a day, I figure
that the senator could earn about $1,825,000 a year, depending on how
successful his booking agent was. The senator presently earns $60,662.50
salary a year as a U.S. senator.

Since no one in South Baltimore could ever afford to hear the senator
speak in public, we would greatly appreciate if the next time you publish
comments on Sen. Charles Mathias, you also publish his photograph, so
that we at least know what he looks like.

William Hughes
South Baltimore

# Chapter Three

## Taking on the Establishment

### 23. The Chesapeake Bay: Death by Democracy
### July 17, 1986

Democracy can be a real killer. Just any true friend of the once pristine Chesapeake Bay. The bay is dying a slow, miserable death by toxic poisoning. Every single day, thousands of tons of the worse kind of industrial waste, heavy metals, biological material, municipal sewage, and chemical runoffs from 24,000 farms are dumped into this unique life sources.

The Irish bard, Oscar Wilde, wrote in the *Ballad of Reading Gaol*, that "all men kill the thing they love." It is difficult for rational people to actually believe that there are situations where love isn't enough to save some-

58

one you care about. But, the bay, and our flawed relationship to it, is a case on deadly point.

You see, our Congress, in your good name, was deeply concerned about the bay, and the 50 major tributaries that feed into her. In 1972, they passed a well-intended law. They called this law the "Clean Water Act". Their fondest hopes was that by 1985 all the pollution of the nation's waterways would be finally halted. Under the act's visionary permit system, limits were to be placed on the amount of pollutants that could be discharged into any body of water from whatever source.

Now, Victoria Churchville, in a recent expose' in the *Washington Post* worthy of a Pulitzer prize, tells us the permit system doesn't work. Churchville revealed that permit users regularly exceeded their legal level of discharge in one or more pollutants. None of this means the regulators don't care about the bay. They honestly do. The understaffed state and federal bureaucrats are doing their very best to enforce the law, but a let's-be-fair-to-everyone law can't fix the bay.

If not one more finger is lifted to save the bay, four trillion gallons of waste water will be poured into her each year. Imagine your bay, 64,000 square miles of it, being treated like an open sink and all of our human garbage, and you get the picture. Robbed of needed oxygen, the bay's once abundant aquatic life is beginning to disappear. The more than 2,000 species of plants and animals that inhabit the bay and its shorelines are also threatened with eventual extinction.

The scientists are enamored, too, of this national treasure. Since 1970, there have been over 4,000 studies of this 200 mile long waterway. This noble work hasn't eased one iota the pain of the death-watch-for the-bay by the grieving environmentalists. The wake has already begun.

We are learning from our terrible mistakes, but time is running out for this *cause celebre*. Preserving the bay is not about love. It never has been. It is not about passing laws that balance cost to the polluters with benefits to the bay. This was just another example of our solve-it-with equal treatment illusions. It is also not about public posturing from do gooder politicians, or finding bad guys for some pundit to kick around. At its core, it's simply about being responsible for an irreplaceable natural asset.

This is an emergency situation! An extraordinary remedy is now necessary. The challenge to saving the bay must be put on a wartime crisis basis. There are precedents, like in the courageous World War II "Manhattan Project". All excuses were laid aside, at that heroic time, for the building of the first atomic weapon by our country, in order to end that tragic global conflict.

Congress should immediately create a "Chesapeake Bay Authority" and delegate plenary authority to czar-like director with a clear mandate to get the job done. In the mold of the late U.S. Administrator, Robert Moses of parks, parkway and World Fair fame. The director would be granted sweeping powers to rule by decree over any and all issues touching on the viability of the bay. The only standard, subject to constitutional limitations, is for the director to act in the best interest of the bay.

Wilde said the coward kills the thing the loves "with a kiss". We have watched with genuine love, of course, as the waterfowl, rock fish, oysters, shad and soft-shelled clams were greatly reduced in the bay over the years. We have openly shed a tear or two over the sharp decline of the commercial fishing industry. To our shame, we have even passively stood by as the bay has been sullied, tainted, abused and gagged with millions of tons of explosive debris.

In the name of our shared humanity and common heritage, now is the time for us to take decisive action. Democracy is killing our friend. Freedom for the equal opportunity polluters means a certain death sentence for the bay.

Only your commitment today to excellence, discipline, tradition and authority, can avoid this grim forecast. Tomorrow it may be too late to save a priceless estuary-the largest of is kind in the country.

*        *        *

# 24. Warhawks at 501 North Calvert Street
## May 5, 1999

Last week, I was standing in the checkout line at Eddie's Market in Charles Village. I noticed a legal size pad lying next to the front window, with a long list of signatures on it. So, I picked it up. The paper was entitled, "Petition." It was a earnest plea by the local citizens to the City Council to find the money to reopen a local Enoch Pratt Free Library branch. It had been closed because of lack of public funding.

On the corner, as I headed homeward, I couldn't help but stare at the banner newspaper headlines in a long row of boxes. They told of the continuing carnage in the Balkans and of the U.S. role in it. The experts say this war may cost more than $100 billion to win, and that American troops might be in the Balkans for "another 30 years" to keep the peace.

What a contrast! Baltimoreans are rightly upset that a library branch has been shut down for fiscal reasons. But, where is their outrage over an undeclared military conflict, that is killing innocent civilians, aggravating a monumental "ethnic cleansing" problem, and sending our tax dollars to evaporate in an orgy of black smoke in the Balkans?

Congress has not declared war on Yugoslavia, a sovereign nation. Nor does the civil war there pose a threat to our national interest. Yet, Bill Clinton, and Madeline "The Mad Bomber" Albright, have targeted Serbia for a trip back to the Stone Age. It was Albright's State Department that in 1998, listed the Kosovo Liberation Army (KLA), a separatist movement, as a "terrorist organization." The KLA is suspected of bankrolling its operations from proceeds from the international heroin trade. Now Albright, because of politics, wants to arm them.

How does Clinton and his gang, get away with such patently unlawful conduct? What explanation is there for the gross indifference of so many citizens, including the clergy, to this situation? Well, it sure helps to have on your side a complicit press, such as *The Baltimore Sun*.

Since U.S. bombs first began falling on Yugoslavia, *The Sun* has utilized all its editorial muscle aiding and abetting Clinton's amoral and reckless military intervention. The propaganda coming from the computer desktops of the warhawks at 501 N. Calvert Street has been nonstop, despite the fact there isn't any legal basis for such an aggressive attack. Humanitarian concerns for the refugees doesn't cut it. Sen. Russell D. Feingold (D-WI), put it best when he said, "I'm really perplexed how genocide and tragedy of this proportion requires our action, but do not require our action in Sierra Leone, Rwanda, Sudan and East Timor."

Also, just imagine the outcry, if during our civil war, Great Britain would have invaded the North to "punish" Abraham Lincoln for his militant defense of the Union. Kosovo is a part of Yugoslavia and Belgrade has every right to defend its national borders. This does not excuse the excesses of Slobodan Milosevic, but he's Europe's problem, not America's. However, none of these arguments have penetrated the skulls of *The Sun's* geopolitically-impaired warhawks.

On April 28, the House of Representatives voted against funding ground troops in the conflict. To their credit, Baltimore's Rep. Ben Cardin (D-3rd) and Rep. Elijah Cummings (D-7th) have demanded Clinton get their approval before making that kind of military commitment.

Cardin said, "I have serious concerns about ground troops. If the president believes it is necessary to use ground troops, I believe he must come to the Congress in compliance with the 'War Powers Resolution.'" The House also, on April 28, voted by a 472-2 margin "against declaring war."

*The Sun* responded on April 30, by mocking the independence and integrity of the House members and barking that it "gets a failing grade." The warhawks claimed the lawmakers are, "not coming to grips with the problem, merely pointing blame in a contradictory manner."

*The Sun* also let loose its cartoonist Mike Lane, to ridicule the congressmen. He portrayed the courageous vote of House members, like Cardin and Cummings, as giving a "comfort basket" to Milosevic. If anyone is waiting for Lane to criticize the drug running KLA, in the same vicious guilt-by-association manner, don't hold your breath.

I hope *The Sun's* warhawks don't prevail on this issue. Americans don't deserve to again witness their fallen heroes returning to the Dover, Delaware Air Force base in body bags. One Vietnam is one too many.

As the great Martin Luther King once said, "Spirit of God, forgive our pride in being so well adjusted to life that we fail to be maladjusted to the tragic effects of physical violence and to tragic militarism."

Finally, Baltimoreans are entitled to a free and vibrant public library system, without petitioning to higher powers.

Let the brass at the Pentagon, for a change, go the solicitation route to get its funding.

*　　　　*　　　　*

## 25. *Black Book of Communism: Crimes, Terror, Repression,* by Stephane Courtois, et. al. (Cambridge, MA, Harvard U., 1999) 858 pp.; hardback $37.50.
## July-August, 2001.

A Book Review

This extensive tome is a ringing indictment of Communist governments over the last century as "criminal enterprises." Its condemnation is supported by archival documents that reveal crimes that cost the lives of 100 millions victims: 65 million in China, 25 million in the Soviet Union, 2 million in Cambodia, and millions more in Vietnam, North Korea, Latin America, Angola, Ethiopia, and Eastern Europe.

It traces the history of militant Communism from the ideologue Karl Marx, through the blood stained regimes of Lenin, Stalin, Chairman

Mao, Ho Chi Minh, Pol Pot, Kim Il Sung, Nicolae Ceausescu, and many others.

Most victims of the "Red Terror" were chosen on the basis of class distinction. Sometimes, like in the Soviet Union, they were even picked to fill "a quota;" or in Cambodia, because they unfortunately lived in a city. The supposed enemy was initially dehumanized, then he was exterminated.

First published in France, this best seller, authored by six respected scholars, caused a firestorm of protest. Its chief editor, Stephane Courtois, morally equated the evils of Communism with Nazism. For this act of conspicuous bravery, and political incorrectness, he was falsely denounced as "anti-Semitic" by *Le Monde*, a Paris newspaper.

The intrepid Courtois, who was careful not to denigrate the immense suffering of the Jewish people during its holocaust, had dared to write: "The deliberate starvation of a child of a Ukrainian Kulak as a result of famine caused by Stalin's regime is 'equal to' the starvation of a Jewish child in the Warsaw ghetto as a result of famine caused by the Nazi regime." Famine, Courtois, insisted was "used as a weapon" by the Kremlin, especially, in the Ukraine, 1932-33, where 6 million peasants, mostly Christians, were starved to death for resisting collectivism.

Courtois wondered, too, why Communist excesses have been ignored by history. Heinrich Himmler's name is recognized for barbarism, but the Bolshevik monster, Feliks Dzerzhinsky, a Jew, who was a mass murderer, too, and head of the dreaded Soviet's *Cheka*, languishes "in obscurity."

This book is thoroughly researched and raises profound questions that challenge our historical perspective on militant Communism.

It is a worthy chronicle of a deadly scourge that still haunts our planet.

*       *       *

# 26. Latino Free Speech & Mayor Schmoke
## May 1, 1999

Calling Mayor Kurt Schmoke!

Mr. Mayor, where are you? I hope you're still not up at the Charles Theater watching your favorite movie, "The Godfather".

We all know the Maryland Film Festival ended last weekend and that the mayor was one of the celebrity presenters at the gala event. But it's now time for new business. Mayor Schmoke, please speak out on the controversy steaming towards Camden Yards on Monday, May 3rd.

The Latino community wants to protest at the Orioles-Cuban nationals game. The Orioles's brass and Major League Baseball officials are pulling out all the stops to restrict their efforts.

One of the Latino leaders is the highly-respected Rep. Bob Menendez, D-NJ, a long time opponent of the Fidel Castro government. He has accused the Orioles's Peter Angelos and Major League Baseball of acting "like Castro" in their proposed ban on any demonstration.

Our mayor knows all about protesting. He took and passed "Civil Rights 101." He is the same irate politico who, a few years back, ordered the flag of South African taken down from the lobby of the World Trade Center. That was his way of objecting to the evil of *Apartheid*. Most Baltimoreans were proud of him for taking that action.

Well, now it's time for the mayor to speak out about the right of others to dissent. This doesn't mean he has to agree with their political opinion, but only with their First Amendment right to express it.

Now, we know if gadfly "Battling Bob" Kaufman were our mayor, there wouldn't be any question where he would stand on this issue. Candidate Kaufman has been in more picket lines than Kweisi Mfume has passed fire hydrants. Kaufman would see to it that all the draconian restrictions being imposed on the anti-Castro activists-such as limiting political banners, flags, musical instruments and chanting at the game-were lifted. Kaufman would also insist strongly on the right of pro-Castro activists to counter-demonstrate at the event.

Incidentally, the planned Latino demonstration for May 3rd won't be the first at an Oriole baseball game. There is a precedent.

Back on May 15, 1991, human rights activists spearheaded a large protest action against the appearance of British Queen Elizabeth at a Baltimore Orioles baseball game played at Memorial Stadium on 33rd St. Naturally, the editorial scribes at the *Baltimore Sun* objected, but no one with a brain paid any attention to their Tory-like rantings.

Leading the demonstration against the British monarch that evening were Irish Americans outraged over the brutality of British rule in the occupied six northeastern counties of Ireland. They were aided in their effort by leaders from local community groups, labor unions, and peace and justice organizations from as far away as New York City.

That protest was accomplished in an orderly manner, both inside and outside the facility. The same strict regulations that the Orioles and Major League Baseball are trying to enforce against the Latino community were on the books then. Management, and the police, however, wisely decided to look the other way. Just before the game started, a chorus began singing, "God Save the Queen". The protesters, mostly seated in right field section, simply turned their backs to the playing field.

During the afternoon of the game, one activist even hired an airplane to fly over the Inner Harbor for one hour. The plane hauled a long banner which read, "England Out of Ireland". Advertising by airplane was forbidden by federal authorities over the stadium for the baseball game because of the appearance of both President George Bush and the Queen.

I think leadership from City Hall is required for the May 3rd event. Silence won't cut it. Nor will issuing a press release that sounds like it was written by a nerd. Mayor Schmoke does have enormous authority in this matter under the city charter and he has a duty to use it.

Let's not forget what the great Dante said about those that remain neutral on important questions of the day. He wrote in the "Divine Comedy," that such individuals deserve a special place in hell for "standing apart." Well, I think Dante's penalty might be a little too harsh under the present circumstances. But, if the ACLU plans to give out any awards in the future for defending our constitutional rights, Schmoke should be overlooked.

Unless, of course, he now acts decisively to uphold the right of the Latino demonstrators to free speech.

*          *          *

Author's Note-Two good books that attempt to set the record straight about Hispanic Culture are: *The Black Legends and Catholic Hispanic Culture,* Antonio Caponnetto, St. Martin de Porres Lay Dominica Community, New Hope, KY, (1991); and, *Tree of Hate: Proaganda & Prejudices Affecting U.S. Relations with the Hispanic World,* Philip Wayne Powell, Ross House Books, Vallecito, CA, (1985).

# 27. What About Political Profiling?
## July 6, 1999

It's not a pleasant feeling to be singled out for "special treatment" by law enforcement officials, whether it's a cop on the highway pulling you over and insisting on looking into your car, or a custom official at an airport, searching through all your belongings. People are often subjected to this humiliating practice on the basis of "racial profiling," which targets mostly blacks and minorities.

Racial profiling was so bad in New Jersey, that the governor there fired the head of the state police.

On the national level, President Bill Clinton has demanded the Custom Service justify its disputed conduct. There is, however, another kind of profiling that you haven't heard too much about-"political profiling."

Let me tell you of my experiences with it: One occurred in Israel and the other in the United Kingdom.

My first shocker came on December 3,1977, when I was visiting the "Holy Land." At the Ben Gurion airport, outside Tel Aviv, I was subjected to a demeaning strip search. Despite the fact, I was traveling with a Zionist-sponsored Baltimore group, I was treated like a suspected terrorist. At the time, I was working in the City Solicitor's office and my politics were slightly to the right of then-Mayor William Donald Schaefer.

My passport, however, showed that I had made visits in the early 70s to Ireland. When I was questioned by the Israeli official, I politely told him that my mother (God bless her memory) was Irish born and that I have relatives living there. I also pointed out that I was in Israel because I wanted to see the Christian sites the nuns at Locust Point's Our Lady of Good Counsel R.C. school had so often told me about. He was unimpressed.

Well, I can only speculate on the real reason for my "special treatment" in Tel Aviv. By the late 70s, I had already done some writing on the Irish cause, including a presentation on that issue to the Platform Committee of the National Democratic Party in NYC, in July, 1976. I also had letters published on that topic in the *Baltimore Sun,* the *Irish People* newspaper, and the now defunct Baltimore *News-American.*

I believe the Israeli custom official was fully aware of my activism and thought to himself, "If this guy is sympathetic to the Irish cause, then he might also be sympathetic to the Palestinians." The truth is that at that time, I was totally clueless about the Palestinian. It was only much later that I began to understand their plight.

In the summer of 1990, my experience with "political profiling" was further broadened. I was part of a group of Americans who were making a fact-finding mission to the north of Ireland. We were investigating human rights abuses there that had been documented by other organizations, like Amnesty International. In Derry City, a vehicle in which I was a passenger was stopped at a roadblock by a British Army patrol. I was instructed, at the point of a rifle, "to step out of the car."

After I identified myself as an American and explained to the army officer the purpose of my visit, I thought he would let me pass. Wrong! I was searched, along with all my luggage. It was a very scary episode. I'm now sure that "my" politics, perfectly legal in the "land of the free," made me a target for harassment in a United Kingdom, then dominated by the bellicose Margaret Thatcher.

Both of my targeting experiences proved another point to me: Ideas are important and governments tend to fear them, sometimes to the point of paranoia. I think political profiling occurs in this country, too.

On March 29, I chronicled for *Baltimore Press* readers the saga of Marshall "Eddie" Conway. For over 29 years, he has been languishing in a Maryland prison cell, a victim of the federal government's deliberate targeting of his political party, the Black Panthers.

The stories of the victims of "political profiling," like those of the victims of racial profiling, also deserve to be told.

*　　　　　*　　　　　*

# 28. Who Put that Dagger into the Heart of Black America?
## June 10, 1999

A few years ago, I traveled up to Allenwood, in central Pennsylvania, to visit a friend of mine who was incarcerated in a federal prison there. The facility, "Allenwood FCI," was new, spacious, and state of the art.

I was shocked to find out from him that most of the inmates housed there weren't white, like him, but were mainly poor blacks from the inner cities of America. He told me, "The blacks don't belong in here. It's a disgrace. They are all little fishes who were caught up in a federal net, while the sharks, the major cocaine importers, are still on the loose."

I later learned that, in order to appear tough on crime, the Congress had enacted mandatory minimum sentences for certain drug and gun offenses. For instance, for selling crack cocaine anyone convicted of even a first offense will get 10 years in a federal slammer. The judge has absolutely no discretion in the matter.

According to the latest statistics, the U.S. is second only to (gasp) Russia in the proportion of its population behind bars.

There are almost 2 million Americans in prison, and the states and the federal government are spending $31 billion a year on corrections.

The Justice Department reports that the number of prisoners nationwide has more than tripled, from 500,000 to 1.8 million, over the past 20 years. Of that number, 1.1 million were locked up for nonviolent crimes, mostly drug-related.

Syndicated columnist Muriel Dobbin says, "One in four blacks faces the possibility of spending time behind bars in their lifetime. Almost one in three black males in the 20-29 age group is in prison, on probation or parole, representing 74 percent of prison sentences for drug offenses."

But when a federal commission in the 80s recommended tough sentences for corporate and white collar-criminals, Ronald Reagan's Attorney General Richard Thornburgh dropped the report down the "Memory Hole." And, the blowhard law and order lawmakers could have cared less.

All of the above gives some explanation to why there are so many blacks languishing in the federal prisons today. But, how did the dangerous drug crack cocaine end up being sold on America's streets?

To find the answer to that question, I attended a presentation at the Central Pratt Library on Wednesday evening, June 9. The guest speaker was the prizewinning, investigative journalist Gary Webb, formerly of the *San Jose Mercury News*. He is the author of the

controversial book, *Dark Alliance: The CIA, The Contras, and the Crack Cocaine Explosion.*

"The crack cocaine epidemic began in South Central Los Angeles in 1982, and then spread across the country,"

said Webb. An LA street dealer, Ricky "Freeway" Ross, got the powered cocaine from a drug ring ran by officials of the Contras, who also were "protected assets of the CIA," he continued. "The street dealers baked the cocaine into crack and then sold it," he underscored, making multimillionaires out of the sellers.

The Contras were a right wing organization which was attempting in the 80s, with the support of the Reagan-Bush administration to overthrow the Sandinistas-led government of Nicaragua. Webb said, the profits from the cocaine deals "were funneled back to the Contras" to finance their campaign of terror against the official government.

As the result of a sordid 1982 secret agreement between the CIA and the Justice Department, there was supposedly "no responsibility" on the part of the CIA to report on the "drug trafficking" of their assets. In other words, Webb emphasized, there was a sleazy deal for thirteen years "to look the other way" while imported cocaine was dumped on our inner cities. This allowed the CIA to claim in its recent self-serving report, that there was "no evidence" of Contra/CIA drug trafficking.

Webb's courageous investigative reporting has cost him his job at the *Mercury News*. It has also allowed enemies of his expose' to paint him as a "conspiracy nutcase." Nevertheless, his riveting book *Dark Alliance* warrants reading by every citizen concerned about his government.

The crack cocaine explosion is a dagger plunged into the heart of Black America. It has brought death, terror and misery to many thousands of innocent lives, both black and white alike.

The American people have every right to ask: Who put that dagger there?

*         *         *

## 29. Has the *Baltimore Sun* Lost Its Moral Compass?
## March 23, 1999.

Like many Baltimoreans, I was shocked to read that a *Baltimore Sun* editorialist was shamelessly hawking his book to fat cat Annapolis lobbyists and lawmakers. What is this world coming to?

According to Eileen Murphy, a feisty columnist for the *City Paper*, (03/17/99), Barry Rascovar, the *Sun's* scribe in question, was pushing his rarified ramblings, entitled, *The Great Game of Maryland Politics*, at a recent breakfast gig, held in Annapolis.

The gala affair was hosted by power broker Alan Rifkin, a well connected attorney and lobbyist. Rascovar, the invited speaker, was seen signing copies of his tome for the select politicos and the deep pocket lobbyists, like Rifkin.

This might be a "great game" for a political insider such as Rascovar, but it will be harder for others, who believe the press should be above such lowly, incestuous back scratching, to stomach.

Talk about a cozy relationship! Who, if anyone, is drawing the ethical lines here? No one, it would appear. *The Sun* , a media monopoly, is supposed to "cover" Annapolis, and the workings of the General Assembly, not have its pundits end up in bed with the old boys? network.

What is also disturbing about this event, other than the obvious, is that Rascovar is the same holier-than-thou pundit who recently took Governor Parris Glendening to task, (03/17/99), for not giving the store away fast enough to the hotel chain, Marriott Inc.

In a sweetheart deal, the state will give Marriott, a giant multinational and the largest hotel operator in this country, $22 million in tax credits to keep its national headquarters in Montgomery County. Rascovar panned the governor for being asleep at the switch and claimed his "inattentive" conduct towards Marriott?s needs was nearly an economic disaster. What rubbish!

Marriott, a corporate behemoth, has been threatening to move to Virginia and cause the loss of jobs for over 8,500 local employees. By playing Maryland off against Virginia, it was able to squeeze our state for every last penny in a so-called "economic incentive package."

What Rascovar failed to mention in his puffy pro-corporate spiel, is that by granting a massive tax break to Marriott, the state simply shifted the tax burden on to the backs of others, notably the individual and small business taxpayers, who can least afford it. This all sounds to me like a brutal shakedown by a big corporate bully. I say enough is enough.

I would like to know what the difference is between members of the International Olympic Committee demanding gifts in order to name Salt Lake City the winner of the "2002 Winter Games," and a entity, like Marriott, leaning hard on Governor Glendening to bleed tax credits from our treasury? The Marriott's gambit may be legal, but it still smells.

While all of this was going down, it was revealed the Racing Industry in Maryland had spent $500,000 of its promotional budget last year on political ads boosting a pro-slots agenda. The industry is also receiving substantial tax assistance, close to $1 million in 1999.

It's true that economic development is important to our state, but this is not the way to do it. The practice of playing one state off against another must be stopped. It?s shady and sleazy and un-American. Federal legislation should be enacted immediately to end this sordid maneuvering, that stains our state's reputation and robs its taxpayers. Under no circumstances can this kind of predatory procedure be said "to provide for the general welfare."

If you want to create jobs for our fading middle class, then stop the "Free Trade" policy madness. You can look around you and see that it doesn't work. How many plant closings, like Proctor & Gamble in South Baltimore, do there have to be before the people finally wake up? The "Free Trade" insanity only favors the grasping global financial speculators, like Mayor Kurt Schmoke's crony, George Soros. It does nothing to build or strengthen the industrial foundation or long range economic well being of the nation.

In fact, "Free Trade" is destroying the middle class, the very element that is absolutely essential to maintaining a thriving democracy.

As for the Rascovar's book-pushing brouhaha, it should force the know-it-all honchos at 501 N. Calvert Street to answer this compelling question: "Has the *Baltimore Sun* lost its moral compass?

*     *     *

## 30. Michael Olesker & The Ten Commandments
### June 24, 1999

We all should be grateful the *Baltimore Sun's* Michael Olesker decided to be a columnist and not a history teacher. Recently, (06/22/99) he did an article with one of the longest titles in the annals of print media, "God Shouldn't be a Plank in a Political Platform."

Olesker made it clear that he wasn't against God, but only that "faith should be private." He related how he had called on God to help him pass a deep water swimming test when he was just a young believer.

Drawing on his vast powers of recovered memories, Olesker told how God had almost let him drown in a Camp Airy swimming pool in Western Maryland almost 43 years ago. He was only eleven years old at the time of his spiritual awakening.

What has presently drawn Olesker's ire is the fact that some in Congress want to pass a law requiring the "Ten Commandments" to be posted in every school room.

Presidential candidates, like George W. Bush, Elizabeth Dole and Al Gore have endorsed the lofty idea. Most of them feel that posting the "Ten Commandments" in classrooms would be better for children than guns, drugs and killings. Backers argue that the "Ten Commandments," of ancient Jewish origins, do not promote any particular religion and serve a broad secular purpose by instilling in youngsters an appreciation for history, morals and law.

Olesker, also a budding theologian, strongly believes it is wrong "to invoke God in a political forum." He says, "God deserves better than easy, one-dimensional sound bites, and so does the country." That sounds anti religious to me.

I hope no one tells Olesker about the motto found on all U.S. coins of "In God We Trust." That will really ruin his day, plus, I'm afraid, be the source of even more religion-challenging articles from him. And what about all our cities named after saints, like San Francisco, St. Louis and St. Paul? Will he demand their illustrious names be changed and go the way of prayers in the public class rooms?

Olesker insisted the Founding Fathers understood the dangers of "mixing politics and theology, carefully omitted all references to God when they wrote the Constitution." Well, how does historian Olesker explain how those same Founding Fathers, in our Declaration of Independence, invoked God's name on four different occasions? In fact, our gallant revolutionary leaders' appeal for justice and separation from imperial Great Britain relied on the protection of "Divine Providence." Who does he think they were talking about? George Lucas's Jedi warrior?

There are a lot of huge misconceptions about the Founding Fathers and religion, which I'm afraid Olesker's spiel reinforces.

The First Amendment was directed at the Congress (the national government) and prohibited it, in part, from establishing a national church. Just as importantly, it mandated that it make no law to disestablish any church created by state and local governments. In 1789, at least six states, including Maryland, with its Anglican majority, had government-supported churches (See, Akhil Reed Amar's *The Bill of Rights*). **Now does this give the impression the Founding Fathers were hostile to religion? I don't think so.**

We have sure come along way when a pundit can be irked by the mere mentioning of God's name. When this state, Maryland, was first settled back in 1633, two Jesuit priests, who accompanied the English colonists, "erected a large cross and celebrated mass" (*The First Freedoms,* Thomas J. Curry). The happy clerics were publicly giving thanks to the almighty for their safe journey across the Atlantic.

When the great war time leader, and later president, Dwight D. Eisenhower, launched the WWII Allied invasion of Normandy on D-Day, June 6, 1944, he invoked God's name in his message to the soldiers, sailors and airmen under his command. In fact, his riveting book about the defeat of Nazi Germany, had a religious tone to it, too. Eisenhower called it, *Crusade in Europe.*

And, it wasn't too long ago also that the Supreme Court said, in speaking of America, "We are a religious people, who presuppose a belief in a supreme deity."

Question: When does one's First Amendment views cross the line and become anti-religious?

Olesker is constitutionally entitled to his opinions on religion, history and the Ten Commandments, and, by God, I reserve the right to disagree with him on each and every one of them.

*       *       *

# 31. Beware the Dark Force of "Boss Sun"
## June 1, 1999

Since the turn of the century, Baltimore City elections have been dominated mostly by machine politics. At the top of that juggernaut, peopled by precinct workers and ward captains, has been the "Boss."

Fitting that rank have been the likes of Sonny Mahon, Willie Curran, James H. (Jack) Pollack and Irv Kovens. Kovens, who died in the 80s, however, was the last of the true citywide leaders.

In our hi tech age of p.r. specialists, political strategists, and mass mailings, the political "boss" is a relic. He has sadly gone the way of the dodo bird.

Yet, another powerful player on the local political scene has never stopped trying to dictate who voters should elect to public offices. I'm talking about that bossy, anti-populist, pro-big business dark force itself, the *Baltimore Sun!* If anybody was responsible for shoving that "B" film actor Ronald Reagan, (and his co-presidency wife Nancy), down the throats of Baltimoreans, it was the perpetual "Wind Machine" at 501 N. Calvert St.

For years, when *The Sun* was owned by the Black family, a well connected landed gentry clan, it regularly railed against candidates, mostly Democrats, who had close ties to the working and middle class communities. At election time, it invariably endorsed a Republican for mayor. Only white male candidates who lived in Roland Park or Guilford, read the King James version of the Bible, and wore pin stripes suits, with a vest, needed apply. Since The *Sun* was taken over by the media conglomerate, *Times-Mirror*, there have been some cosmetic changes, but its arrogant, elitist attitude is still irritatingly visible.

Take for example, *The Sun's* rant, (05/26/99), "Who Will Step Up in Mayor's Race?" Following the decision of Kweisi Mfume not to run for mayor, the Calvert St. boy-ohs tried to give the impression that Lawrence Bell and Carl Stokes were the only candidates worth mentioning left in the race. Then, it turned right around and jumped Bell and Stokes for failing to define themselves. *The Sun* roared, "They must do better."

*The Sun's* reaction was peculiar for a number of reason. First, as of May 26, Bell has still not officially filed for the office of mayor. Secondly, the editorial didn't even deign to cite mayoralty candidate

"Battling Bob" Kaufman, who has already nearly worn out one pair of shoes canvassing the voters. Third, *The Sun* totally overlooked candidate Mary Conway, who just happens to hold one of the most important elected offices in the city, Register of Wills. Nor, did it even have the decency to name the other six aspirants, who have tossed their hats into the ring.

What was so appalling, too, about the editorial was the fact that it is *The Sun* itself, which is primarily responsible for the other declared mayoralty candidates not having what it calls, "compelling political identities."

Almost from the beginning of the supra glitzy "Draft Mfume 2000" movement, *The Sun* has acted liked one of its promoters and has deliberately chosen to marginalize the official candidates. Its pages have been filled with one puff piece after another about either how great the "Draft Mfume" committee was, or how the confused Mfume himself was going to ride in on a white horse and save the city from perdition.

For instance, on May 17, *The Sun* ran a flattering article on the "Draft Mfume" committee. Its campaign manager was the subject of the piece. It read like one of Barbara Walters' celebrity-type interviews. No hard ball questions were asked of the manager by *The Sun's* reporter.

I'm sure many Baltimoreans wanted to know relevant things like: "Where did all that money come from to finance the committee's efforts?" And also, "Exactly how much money had been raised as of that date to persuade Mfume to get into the race?"

Well, *The Sun's* feature was silent on that kind of important information. But instead, we did find out that the committee had done a terrific job, and that, "If that support holds, Mfume will have a strong following going into the election."

In his May 27th column, *The Sun's* wordsmith, Michael Olesker, also pretended that Bell and Stokes were the only candidates worth writing about in the mayor's race. The awful truth is that it is *The Sun,* and not the candidates, who "must do better."

Meanwhile, let's us all be grateful that it is the voters of Baltimore, who will have the final say about the coming election, and not the dark force itself, "Boss Sun."

                 \*                     \*                     \*

## 32. Rep. Michael D. Barnes: Human Rights in Central America
### January, 1985

"The best friend the communists have in Central America are the right-wing thugs, many of them in the military, who believe the way to fight communism is to murder labor organizers, nuns and moderate politicians," said a clearly incensed Rep. Michael D. Barnes (D) from Maryland's sprawling 8th district.

Only 41, Barnes was elected by his colleagues as chairman of the Inter-American Affairs subcommittee of the House of Representatives. That role, plus the fact he served as a Senior Counselor to the Kissinger Commission, makes Barnes a pivotal figure in the shaping of U.S. foreign policy for the 80s.

Headed by former Secretary of State Henry Kissinger, the Kissinger Commission is a bipartisan group that recently completed a fact-finding report and recommendation to President Reagan and the Congress on social and governmental conditions in Central America.

Barnes's committee has held over 25 hearings on Central American matters, and the congressman has made many visits to the strife-torn area. As a result, he is of the strong opinion that unless fundamental shifts are made in U.S. policy, the region will be headed for "a major confrontation."

Barnes's own dreary appraisal of the present situation was summed up by a comment of a companion on a recent return flight home from

Central America. The friend had said that Central America in 1983 had reminded him of Europe in 1938—with an air of inevitability of war.

The Kissinger Commission, according to Barnes, "missed an opportunity," to put more emphasis on the diplomatic and political aspects of the crisis. Substantial military assistance to the area, support of the covert war against Nicaragua, and toleration for widespread human rights violations are seen by Barnes as a failed and doomed policy.

In only his 3rd term in the Congress, the Montgomery County lawmaker receives high marks for his skills on Capitol Hill. Speaker Thomas (Tip) O'Neill considers Barnes an expert on human rights matters, and calls him "the key Congressman as far as Latin-American Affairs are concerned."

Former Special U.S. Ambassador Robert Strauss, a member of the Kissinger Commission, refers to Barnes as "a splendid representative" and added, "The nation is better off for his service, as are his constituents."

In 1984, primarily because of his outstanding work as committee chairman, Barnes was ranked by the prestigious *Almanac of American Politics* as one of the "most influential congressman."

U.S. long range interests, Barnes urged, would be better served if our country supported an end to the terrorism carried out by some of these Central American countries against "their own people."

He has consistently underscored the necessity for our country "to step back and allow the Latins themselves to find solutions to their problems." The principle of nonintervention is as important to Latin America as "democracy is to us," Barnes emphasized.

The mild-mannered, Kensington resident said that his committee would continue to be a forum for "responsible debate and discussion of U.S. policy in the Western Hemisphere."

It is time for the U.S. to deal with Central America "as partners, as equals; something we haven't done in the past," concluded Barnes.

\*　　　　　\*　　　　　\*

## 33. *The Road to Terror: Stalin and the Self-Destruction of the Bolsheviks,* 1932-1939 by J. Arch Getty and Oleg V. Naumov (New Haven-London: Yale U. Press, 1999) 635 pp.; hardback $35.00.
July 18, 2000
**Book Review**

Unlike other mass murderers, the Bolsheviks left a paper trail detailing their horrific criminal deeds.

Naturally, dictator Josef Stalin is prominently cited in the formerly top secret transcripts of the Soviet's Central Committee. Others, however, like his *nomenklatura* henchmen; Lazar Kaganovich, a Jew and rabid Christian hater; Vyacheslav Molotov; Lavrenti Beria; and Genrikh Yagoda, were just as complicit as him.

The historian, H. R. Trevor-Roper put it well, "Great massacres may be commanded by tyrants, but they are imposed by people."

The authors conservatively estimate that "1.5 million" Communist Party members were killed during the "Great Terror" purges of the 1930s. The majority were shot to death, others died in the *Gulag* camps, originally established by the fanatical Bolshevik thug, Vladimir I. Lenin.

This riveting story opens by telling the sad tale of one Alexander Yulevich Tivel. It is typical of what happened to many of Marxism's true believers.

A hack propagandist for *Pravda,* Tivel was shot as an "enemy of the people" on March 7, 1937, in Moscow, after a perfunctory trial. He was also a Zionist, who had made the fatal mistake of knowing Grigory Zinoviev and Karl Radek. Like Tivel, they were all Jews, who were suspected by the Kremlin elite of plotting with its arch rival, the exiled zealot, Lew Davinovich Bronstein, a/k/a Leon Trotsky.

The Tivel drama didn't end there. His wife was sent to Siberia and she wasn't freed until 1953. Their young son was placed in an orphanage for being a "member of the family of a traitor of the Motherland."

In this book, too, surprisingly, you will find the modern seeds of the dubious "Hate Crime" concept, championed by Sen. Charles Schumer (D-NY). Stalin, in a rant about the putative enemies of his Communist hell hole, is quoted in October, 1937, as saying, "Anyone who by his actions, thoughts, yes thoughts, and encroaches on the unity of the socialist state, we will destroy them and their kin." I'm sure Schumer, a pompous windbag, will deny the alien-based connection to his legislative scheme.

This is an authoritative book that exposes the unspeakable crimes of Stalin's Bolshevik gang against its own party faithful.

It should be a sobering lesson to anyone who tends to believe in extremist solutions.

*   *   *

# 34. Is "Big Brother" Watching You?
## September, 1993 issue

Are you being watched?

Is information about your First Amendment activities being sent covertly to alien intelligence agencies? Have secret files been compiled on you?

A major scandal, centered around ex-San Francisco Police Inspector Tom Gerard, a shadowy character named Roy Bullock, and the Anti-Defamation League of B'nai B'rith (ADL) suggests that American liberals, and others, may be under surveillance. Evidence seized by the police indicates that numerous progressive activists, newspapers, elected officials, and labor unions-are the targets of a domestic snooping operation.

Its legality, and scope, are now being tested and examined in a civil rights case filed in a state court in San Francisco.

Gerard has been charged in San Francisco with theft of government property and conspiracy. He is suspected of having collected privileged material on many residents and organizations in the Bay Area. He turned the information over to Bullock.

Gerard was introduced to Bullock in the San Francisco office of the ADL. An antique dealer, Bullock, has been the ADL's top "investigator" for more than three decades. The ADL paid him over $170,000 between 1985 and 1992 for his cloak-and-dagger work.

Bullock liked to pick through the garbage of his victims, and once infiltrated an Arab-American delegation that visited Rep. Nancy Pelosi (D-CA) in her Washington, D.C. Office. (Pelosi is the daughter of Baltimore's late Mayor Thomas J. D'Alesandro, Sr.)

According to a *Los Angeles Times* article (04/09/93), Bullock worked as a paid informant for the FBI, as well as the ADL. On April 8, 1993, police carried out a five hour raid of the ADL offices in San Francisco and Los Angeles. They discovered the ADL had copies of computer files on 12,000 Americans and more than 950 groups.

According to police reports and court documents, Bullock acknowledged he obtained the information from Gerard, who traded police files, criminal histories and license plate numbers in exchange for Bullock's data on so-called extremist groups. It is feared by some that this confidential information may have been filtered to spook networks in Israel, South Africa, and the United Kingdom. Gerard had tied earlier in his career to the CIA.

The ADL boasts of keeping its eye on extreme right-wing groups, like the Skinheads, the Klu Klux Klan, and Aryan Nation. Their role in this mess indicates they may have reached too far in search for "Anti-Semites."

Police found files on the African National Congress: the ACLU: Irish Americans; the United Auto Workers; AIDS activist groups like ACT-UP; *Mother Jones* magazine; Pacifica News Network; Lesbian Agenda for

Action; Greenpeace; Christic Institute; Rep. Roy Dellums (D-CA); the National Lawyers Guild; NAACP; CISPES; Carpenters Local 22; Jews for Jesus; and many Arab and Palestinian individuals and organizations.

The ADL had denied any wrongdoing in the growing scandal. Gerard has pleaded "not guilty" and released on $20,000 bail. Bullock has not been charged. The probe is continuing.

Abraham Foxman, the head of the ADL, lashed out at the San Francisco district attorney for "trying us in the media," according to an interview he gave to the Northern California Bulletin, a local Jewish weekly. Foxman said the ADL would continue to monitor people or groups that "pose a threat to Jews" and defended the organization's probe of the African National Congress on grounds the ANC "were violent, they were anti-Semitic, they were pro-PLO, and they were anti-Israel." (See *The Washington Report on the Middle East* magazine,08/93).

The ADL was founded in 1913 for the declared purpose of defending Jews against "defamation." For the most part, their record over the years has been a laudable one. During the Reagan years, however, the ADL made a noticeable turn to the Right.

Dr. Alfred M. Lilienthal, a respected author and anti-Zionist, said, "What exactly constitutes anti-semitism was to receive continually different interpretations. With the creation of Israel in 1948, the meaning of the word was broadened and eventually, totally distorted." (*The Washington Report on Middle East Affairs,* 07/93).

Irwin Suall presently runs the ADL's "fact finding" division out of their national office at the United Nations Plaza in Manhattan. It operates in all 50 states and has 31 regional offices, and it works closely with state and federal police forces. It has over 400 employees and an annual budget of around $32 million.

In a memo dated July, 1992, Suall praised Roy Bullock as "our number one investigator." He was also quoted as saying that the real enemies of the Jews are on the "American Left." (Robert I. Friedman's 'The Enemy Within', *Village Voice*, 05/11/93).

On April 8, 1993, a detailed report on this brouhaha was presented on ABC's "Nightly News" before a national audience estimated at over 18 million. This expose first ran in the print media in the *San Francisco Examiner* and was later taken up by the *Los Angeles Times*.

Alexander Cockburn has been doing a running and biting commentary on it in the pages of *The Nation*. In his riveting account of the affair, Friedman made this damning statement: "Once a proud human rights organization, the ADL had become the Jewish Thought Police."

The ADL sharply disagrees with that assessment. They see themselves as an altruistic human rights organization dedicated to watching out for the kooks and fringe groups in our society.

Ex-US Rep. Pete McCloskey (R-CA) has filed a class action lawsuit in a California court against the ADL, charging invasion of privacy. His name also appears in the data base, along with that of his wife. McCloskey has been a persistent critic of Israel's brutal suppression of the 1.8 million Palestinians languishing in the occupied West Bank and Gaza.

The son of the former Israeli Defense Minister Moshe Arens, Yigal Arens, is also a plaintiff in the suit. Arens supports a two-state solution to the Israeli-Palestinian conflict. "The ADL believes,"said Arens, "that anyone who is an Arab-American or who speaks politically against Israel is at least a closet anti-semite. (See also, *The Washington Report on Middle East Affairs*, (06/93).

The civil suit claims that the ADL collected information on opponents of the Israeli and South African government policies and passed it on to those countries. The ADL has denied all the charges in the suit and has promised a vigorous defense. It says it does not condone illegal methods of obtaining information.

Bullock had his computer-based data divided into four categories: "Right Wing", "Pinkos", "Arab and Skinhead" organizations. About 4,000 of the files are on Arab-Americans; the rest are on groups and individuals as diverse as the Assembly of Jesus; Boycott Coke; Black United Fund; the Weatherman Underground; and the United Farm Workers. Bullock admits to selling some of his ADL files on anti-apartheid opponents to South African intelligence agents. He also had ties to a group of informants across the country with code names, like "Scumbag", "Ironside", and "Flipper".

Attorney Marc Van de Hout of the National Lawyers Guild, which is listed in the ADL's files, said, "I am a Jew myself, and when I see the breath of the organizations in these files that the ADL has conducted surveillance on, it is very clear that they have sort of lost touch with reality in terms of organizations that are engaged in real anti-Semitic activity." (See *Washington Report,* 08/93).

As Doug Struck's recent insightful reporting in the *Baltimore Sun* amply demonstrates, the Israeli crackdown in the occupied territories has resulted in gross abuses of human rights, including the "torture of Palestinian prisoners."

Americans should have the right to complain about Israeli wrongdoing, about their huge annual raids on our national treasury ($11.3 billion in 1993), or their controversial trial of John Demjanjuk, without ending up in a file of the ADL or under surveillance. I think it is wrong for the ADL, or any other private group, to appoint itself as the pseudo-guardian of our civil liberties.

The ADL, however, like any other defendant, is entitled to its day in court and to present its side of this mounting controversy to an objective fact finder.

\*              \*              \*

*Author's Note-A partial settlement has been reached to resolve the very important civil rights suit mentioned above that was brought in the federal district court in Central California by the feisty American-Arab Anti-Discrimination Committee against the Anti-Defamation League

(ADL). At this writing, according to the Center for Constitutional Rights (CCR), Fall 1998 Docket, the ADL has agreed not to engage in such unlawful spying activity "in the future". The ADL has also agreed "to the establishment of a complicated system of oversight, including the appointment of a special referee, to purge certain confidential information. The plaintiffs agreed to waive general damages, except in cases where job loss or other injury occurred."

The CCR, located at 666 Broadway, 7th floor, NY, NY 10012, (email at CCR@igc.apc.org), is part of the outstanding legal team representing civil rights and social justice groups and individuals in this lawsuit to vindicate the rights of American activists against the illegal over reaching of the ADL's national surveillance network.

On Sept. 28, 1999, U.S. District Court Judge Richard Paez approved a final settlement in the above described 6-year old case, "ordering the ADL permanently enjoined from engaging in any illegal information gathering and saying it had to provide an annual statement to its legal counsel for the next four years explaining the steps it has taken to remain in compliance." (Source, *Washington Times,* 09/28/99.)

\*          \*          \*

# 35. El Salvador: Horrors of the Civil War
## November 26, 1981

The country of El Salvador in Central America is at war. But the war is not against a neighboring nation. The war is against its own people and the Roman Catholic Church.

Since 1979, 22,000 of its citizens have died in a blood bath unprecedented by even Latin America's grisly standards. Among the dead have been one Roman Catholic Archbishop, 10 priests and four nuns. None of the murderers of the religionists have been brought to the Bar of Justice by the State authorities.

The Catholic Church's "crime" in El Salvador has been that she has fully identified with plight of the beleaguered poor. According to the *Sojourner's Magazine.* El Salvador is "both the smallest and most densely populated country in Latin America, with 4.8 million people living in an area the size of Massachusetts. Two percent of its population owns 60 percent of the land, with 75 percent of export earnings in the hands of 200 families. Unemployment is at 50 percent, and is the highest on the continent; 90 percent of the people make below $100 per year."

One of my earliest memories of my childhood was attending Our Lady of Good Counsel School, in Locust Point, in South Baltimore. It was there that I learned of the fine missionary work being done in Central and South America by the Maryknoll Order.

Recently, at a sparsely-attended public meeting, held at St. Mary's Star of the Sea Parish hall, (also in South Baltimore,) I listened to Sister Joan Petrik, a Maryknoll nun. She recounted her moving and painful experiences as result of her eight years of toiling in the vineyards of El Salvador. She worked there with the indigenous peasant population in the areas of literacy, health, community welfare and political education.

"I knew I had a missionary's vocation, while I was still in grade school in Overlea," said the 53 year-old nun. She was a 1946 graduate of Seaton High School. Her hair is starting to turn white. She stands a little over five feet, five inches tall, on an evenly proportioned frame. Her eyes are light and blue.

Sister Petrik spoke softly, but with deep feelings of her recent memories. Her face is full of character and expressive of her committed Christian love for all of God's children. Of Bohemian ancestry, she has witnessed the effects of the violence of the right wing death squads and the absolute terror of a country truly under siege from its own military forces.

In the ongoing battle between the political Right and the Left, Sister Petrik says, "There is no middle ground." She was a friend of the four female missionaries, who were brutally slain on December 2, 1980, as well as the late Archbishop Oscar Romero, and the Jesuit Father Rutilio Grande, the first priest slain in El Salvador.

Sister Petrik recalled, with admiration, how the courageous Archbishop Romero "spoke out about the repression, the atrocities by the military. Even though, he knew he was signing his own life away, when he wrote the then-President Jimmy Carter urging him to cut off all military aid to the Junta running the country."

She continued, "If we ignore those, who suffer, then we will be condemned for it. The people of El Salvador don't want to sell their country to the Russians, but they do want to establish their own identity as a people."

Sister Petrik believes our own country is making a serious foreign policy mistake by seeking a military solution to a problem, that is really political and economic. In 1981, despite the continuing cruel repression, the administration of Ronald Reagan approved $5.7 million in military assistance to the *Junta*.

The distinguished former U.S. Ambassador to the El Salvador, Robert White, who was fired by Secretary of State Alexander Haig, also thinks our policy is a mistake. According to the *New York Times* (03/08/81), he labeled some of the militarists in El Salvador as "the most out of control, violent, blood thirsty men in the world."

A prestigious international study group, headed by Willy Brandt, ex-Chancellor of West Germany, has recently called for the U.S. to end all military aid to the *Junta* and for a negotiated end to the hostilities.

Archbishop Romero prophesied, just before his assassination,while saying Mass at a hospital, "If I am killed, I will rise again in the people of El Salvador."

When I heard the words of Sister Petrik, I was proud to be a Catholic and of the noble struggle of the Church. I am confident the vision of that great martyred churchman will indeed live on after him.

I also believe that an awakened and outraged American people will demand an end to our discredited and immoral foreign policy towards El Salvador and its embattled people.

*           *           *

## 36. Exposing State Terrorism
### February, 1992

"State Terrorism is responsible for ninety-nine percent of the acts of violence that we call terrorism," said Ramsey Clark, the Attorney General during the Johnson administration. "While the United States was labeling the black African National Congress a terrorist organization, the white *apartheid* government of South Africa was using more violence against its black population than any other repressive regime in the world."

Clark, a champion of human rights, was the keynote speaker. at a symposium entitled, "The Politics and Imagery of Terrorism." It featured prominent scholars, activists and media critics, like *The Nation's* Alexander Cockburn.

The two-day affair was held on January 24 and 25 at the Maryland Institute, College of Art.

Clark defined terrorism as "the use of fear to compel the conduct of others." He said this is why police states use torture on their opponents and leave "the victim of their death squads for the community to see in order to intentionally terrorize the people".

A multi-dimensional exhibition of the works of 39 artists, "Beyond Glory: Re-Presenting Terrorism". It was launched at the same time as the symposium. It contains powerful imagery that examined terrorism as "a global issue". It also challenged, on political and philosophical grounds, the term "terrorism" as normally used by governments and parroted by a complicit media.

As soon as you entered the exhibition area, you were confronted by a wall filled with boiler-plate expressions that are endemic to apologists for state terrorists. The disinformation experts for governmental wrong-doers immediately came to my mind.

"It is very difficult to verify these alleged atrocities; "These are unpleasant, but inevitable facts of life"; "Certain things are beyond our control"; and "Nothing is merely black or white." These were just some of the Orwellian-like cliches presented.

Mel Chin's "Jilavia Prison Bed," 1982, a sculpture of steel and cotton, stunningly represents the Romanian government's use of covert action and bitter religious persecution under the late tyrant Nicolae Ceausescu.

Luis Cruz Azaceta's 14-foot-long painting "Latin American Victims of Dictators" (1987), reveals a tortured body. It cries out for God's justice and mercy in a land long dominated by the greedy and selfish few. In a dazzling three-dimensional animation, Grey Barsamian's "Putti" shows "Cupid" being transformed into a military helicopter-thus raising questions about perception, relationship and change.

Insightful works by Belfast's talent Rita Duffy, Derry's Willie Doherty and England's Paul Graham helped to focus attention on the battered landscape and brutalized lives of the nationalists people in the British-occupied six counties of northeastern Ireland. Duffy has portrayed in one drawing a British soldier with a monster gas mask covering his face and British pound signs painted on his trousers.

In her "Free State General 1981," she created a grotesque figure of a military goon, who obviously lacks all sense of genuine honor or true patriotism.

In "Same Difference", Doherty displayed a hugh photograph of an imprisoned IRA freedom fighter on a TV screen. Under it, he alternately flashed the neutral word "volunteer," with damning characterizations like "fanatic" or "murderer."

Graham's four-color photographs captured scenes as varied, as graffiti around the "Turf Lodge" area of Belfast, to a long red brick wall painted with the slogan, "Support the Hunger Strikers. They are IPOW."

Doherty's earlier photographs "Fixed Parameter," "The Other Side," and "Closed Circuit," dealing with the inescapable evils of Northern Ireland, won praise from the Manhattan-based critic Gary Nickard. Writing in *Afterimage* (April, 1991), Nickard described Doherty's efforts as forcing "the viewer to realize that in the North of Ireland nothing is innocent, everything is emblematic."

Another symposium speaker, Edward Herman, coauthor of the expose' *The Terrorism Industry* (along with Gerry O'Sullivan), explained how governments use their enormous powers to depict their enemies as terrorists, in order to dehumanize and destroy them. The politicalization of the word is aided by a mostly-sycophantic media that "assumes the government means well" and by influential think tanks connected to the Pentagon, the CIA, the British and Israeli governments, or funded by corporations.

One of the alleged "experts" on terrorism, Maurice Tugwell, spent the greater part of his adult life as an intelligence officer and propagandist for the British army," according to the authors. Paul Wilkinson, another mouthpiece for the Western line, is described in the book as "an apologist for low-intensity warfare in Northern Ireland, which includes the use of outright torture and murder. He works In the counterinsurgency tradition of Sir Robert Thompson, Richard Clutterbuck, Frank Kitson and Maurice Tugwell."

Herman said the Reagan/Bush Administration "supported the corrupt Salvadorean ruling clique under an anti-terrorism law, while that clique was butchering 700 to 1,000 innocent civilians a month. Rebels are generally called "terrorists," with the notable exception of Ronald Reagan's 'Contras', but governments are always anti-terrorists. This is a gross misrepresentation of the truth and must be resisted.

Unfortunately," he added," most establishment columnists don't work to combat this kind of insidious propaganda."

Statistically, Herman demonstrated, the victims of state terror, over the last three decades alone, ran into the millions, while the numbers actually killed by so-called terrorist individuals or groups were "only around 3,500."

The editor of the hell-raising *Lies of our Times,* Bill Schaap, pointed out numerous examples of how governments have utilized the "Big Lie" technique.

Angela Sanbrano told how opponents of U.S. policies in Central America have been constantly "harassed by the FBI and labeled as subversives."

Randall Robinson, an articulate advocate for a free South Africa, accused the DeKlerk regime of undermining the present peace negotiations by deploying British-styled "pseudo-terrorists" to create a pervasive climate of violence.

President George Bush's "Ace-in-the-Hole" during this tough election year, may be "a military strike at Libya, Cuba or Iraq," offered writer John Stockwelt, an ex-CIA agent. Ward Churchill of the American Indian Movement (AIM) revealed how the oppression of our native population, especially on the "Pine Ridge Reservation," continues to this day.

Author Michael Parenti said that the media is not "dumb, stupid or foolish. It is simply an instrument of government policy on terrorism. It acts in lock-step," Parenti insisted, "because it is controlled by the same class interests that own the country."

Margaret Randall, a poet, emphasized the importance of "art, images and words helping to bring community together."

When he was growing up in Ireland, Alexander Cockburn said the British regularly "demonized the Irish for their opposition to their rule." Most of the media are "into self-censorship," Cockburn suggested, and this is why the "engineering of consent" among the populace is successful and "so demented." He gave as an example the herd-like reaction of Americans to "Operation Desert Storm."

Chris Bratton and Annie Goldson's award-winning video documentary "Counterterror," ended the program. It examined how the label "terrorism" has been used to criminalize political dissent in Northern Ireland, the West Bank and Gaza, Puerto Rico, and in this country. Bratton said Claire Sterling's wacko thesis of a Soviet plot to destroy Western Civilization, by funding international terrorism, was used to justify suppression around the globe.

Their "Framing the Panthers" is a damning indictment of FBI tactics used against African-American activists during the '60s and '70s. Goldson spoke encouragingly of the development of a national cable system, "Deep Dish," with public access for community use. This communication process, she predicted, "could potentially reach an audience of over 12 million viewers."

When the co-curators of this precedent-setting and courageous project, David J. Brown and Nina Felshin, envisioned presenting it, they were mostly seeking to investigate the reasons for "terrorism" and for the public's general misunderstanding of the term. They were moved also by the deaths of two of their students in the terrorist bombing of Pan Am Flight 103 over Lockerbie, Scotland.

They wanted to create a "unique dialogue with both visual and verbal components." Brown wrote of their plans, "The intent is to critically explore the misunderstanding of terrorism, the widespread use of violence and other repressive means, usually for political ends, and the media's representation of these activities."

By any standard; political, artistic or philosophical, the exhibit/symposium was a smashing success.

\*     \*     \*

*Author's Note-I believe that the death of one innocent human being is one too many for humanity, irrespective of whether the wrongdoer is from the extreme political Right or the Left. As to the role of critics of any regime, it is important to keep in mind the proposition championed by the legendary French intellectual, Roger Garaudy. The courageous WWII hero said, "History cannot begin from an unchallenged *a priori* any more than the sciences can."

# Chapter Four

## Clubhouse Politics

### 37. Lights, Camera, Inaction: A City Council Meeting
### April 28, 1983.

Show time is 5 p.m.

But, on this Monday in mid-April, 1983, there were only three city council cast members on stage. It's going to be another late curtain for the regular weekly meeting of the Baltimore City Council.

It's not what you would describe as a Cecil B. DeMille production. There are only 18 members in the ongoing drama-plus a director, who also doubles as the president of the assembly.

It is 5:05 p.m.

The scene is the large, ornate chamber room of the City Hall. Center stage is the president's rostrum. Stage right is a desk filled wtih mayoral aides. Stage left are seen council staff people and press types. In front of the rostrum and immediately under it are the clerks of the council. There is a center aisle that divides the chamber in half. On each side are two rows of seats for nine of the cast members. There is a railing that separates the cast and the stage from the audience. I am seated on the railing and have a critic's view of the proceedings.

It is 5:10 p.m.

Tim Murphy (D-6th) is being interviewed at his desk by a radio reporter. The TV people are next in line to talk with him. The glib Mr. Murphy is fast becoming the Barbara "Babs" Walters of the city council.

Victorine Adams (D-4th) is teacher-like at her desk, reading the night's three page agenda.

Ed Johnson (D-2nd) is his friendly self as he sweeps by the railing heading for his berth on the wide right.

Kweisi Mfume (D-5th) dances through the press corps and splits towards his place on the extreme left.

It is 5:15 p.m.

Mary Pat Clarke (D-2nd) makes a twirling, Loretta Young-styled appearance. She goes swingingly to her desk and promptly lights herself a cigarette. And, then she deftly pirouettes and heads cater-corner across the room towards a mayoralty aide.

The new councilwoman from the 5th, Iris Reeves, comes in wearing a big, yellow button, which reads, "Do It-Register And Vote."

Tom Waxter (D-5th) strolls in with both hands in his suit pockets.

Don Hammen (D-1st) crosses the council's threshold with the permanent grimace on his face and the usual cigarette in his mouth. It is 5:20 p.m.

Banker Joe DiBlasi (D-6th) takes his seat on the extreme left, next to the dean of the council, and unofficial mayor of Brooklyn, Willie Myers (D-6th). It is Mr. Myers' 79th birthday.

And, Nathaniel McFadden (D-2nd), standing head and shoulders above them, moves quickly to his place right. It is now 5:25 p.m.

Rikkie Spector (D-5th) makes the scene and exchanges pleasantries with Iris Reeves, who sits directly behind her.

The audience is now completely full. The TV cameras are set up and ready to roll. The tensions mounts as Frank Gallagher (D-3rd) posts. Mr. Gallagher emerges from a crowd of spectators to take his seat next to Mary Fitzgerald (D-3rd). Mrs. Fitzgerald is dressed in a bright, cardinal red suit that clashes with Mr. Gallagher's dark, blue pin-stripped suit.

It is 5:32 p.m.

The director and president, Clarence (Du) Burns, appears Alfred Hitchcock-like, out of nowhere. A muldoonish clerk greets the tardy director with a servile, "Hi chief!"

The president takes a long, last, deep drag on his cigarette and mumbles an incoherent answer. The director, without escort, takes the rostrum to perform his presidential duties. It is exactly 5:35 p.m. on the large walk clock. The curtain rises.

Action!

The president offers no explanation or apology for the late curtain. Michael Mitchell (D-4th) is absent from the meeting. Joan Bereska, the mayor's *gray eminence* is also missing from her usual seat, stage right. It is a harbinger of yet another totally dull and boring city council meeting.

Mary Pat Clarke rises to address the seminal issue of "rehab housing" in Baltimore. Almost on cue, one-half of the cast members start jabbering with the other half. Absolutely no one on the stage is paying any attention to Ms. Clarke. If Federico Fellini were directing, he would yell at this point- "Print It!."

Mr. DiBlasi stands to defend voter registration as a gesture of patriotism. A lonely cast member gives the novice mocking applause for his *chutzpah*.

At 5:58 p.m, the president mercifully adjourns the meeting.

The curtain falls.

In 23 minutes, the 18 elected and appointed cast/council members at $19,500 a year salaries, and a president/director at $39,500 a year, have played out the most expensive amateur act in town-the weekly meeting of the Baltimore City Council.

I could laugh. But, as a taxpayer, I remind myself that I am paying for this weekly God-awful performance.

*       *       *

# 38. The Gov. Mandel Affair: The Federal Mail Fraud Case
## December, 1984

Five days a week his familiar and friendly voice can be heard on the popular "Morning Magazine" talk show of Annapolis radio station WNAV-AM (1430).

At age 64, Marvin Mandel, the former embattled governor of the state of Maryland, is making a courageous attempt at an Elba-like return to full public life.

"I really enjoy the radio show," began Mandel while puffing away on his ubiquitous pipe. "I am on for one hour a day from 9:30 AM. to 10:30 AM. discussing a relevant news topic usually with a guest, sometimes it's politics, but not politics exclusively."

Mandel also spends a lot of his time working as a business consultant out of a Severna Park office. Whether Mandel can figuratively duplicate the spectacular feat of France's Napoleon, in February, 1815, (where the deposed Emperor escaped from exile on the island of Elba and returned in glory to Paris to rule for a hundred days), and regain some measure of his former prestige and political power he lost as a result of his running afoul of the draconian federal laws dealing with mail fraud in the late 70's, remains to be seen.

In retrospect, Mandel's tangled legal problems can only be described as a hellish decade of nightmares worthy of the pen of the immortal Prague-born writer, Franz Kafka, and the hapless defendant in his novel, *The Trial.*

Although one may desire to censure Mandel for his less than virtuous conduct during that period, by any standard of reasonableness, it was inherently wrong and morally objectionable for the machinery of justice to be misused to brand the former governor and his close associates as common criminals.

In 1977, after two protracted and sensational jury trials, Mandel and five codefendants, were finally convicted in U.S. District Court in Baltimore City on the controversial mail fraud and racketeering charges. The legal theories of the government's case were so complex and difficult to sustain that a panel of appellate court judges in Richmond, Virginia, voted two to one to reverse the lower court conviction and order a new trial.

Even one of the original jurors in the case who had voted Mandel "guilty," said he thought the ex-governor was really innocent and that the case against him was "very weak." The juror, unlearned in the ways of the law, naively believed that the appeal court would simply dismiss the case and that Mandel would be freed. Unfortunately for the plight of Mandel, the sympathetic juror was wrong.

The full Appellate Court in July, 1979 was evenly divided on deciding the merits of the case and voted four to four, with one jurist abstaining, to uphold the lower court verdict. Despite the passionate plea of Judge Francis Murnaghan of Baltimore that a great injustice was being done by the court by not deciding the case by a majority vote, a rehearing was denied. The Supreme Court denied review of the case and the original conviction stood.

Mandel began serving a harsh four year sentence at the Elgin Detention Center in Florida. His experiences there were not unlike those endured by the great Irish bard, Oscar Wilde, as expressed in his memorable *Ballad of Reading Jail.*

Wilde had written of his own prison travail in the British-made *gulag*, "I know not whether laws be right, or whether lows be wrong; all that we know who lie in jail, is that the wall is strong; and that each day is like a year, a year whose days are long."

Despite an unblemished record as a strong chief executive, Mandel was forced, under the strict terms of the state's Constitution, to forfeit the "Office of Governor," and was also eventually disbarred from the practice of law. Mandel has persisted, in an unrepentant manner, in his unshaken belief in his own innocence. He believes that he will be finally vindicated of all charges placed against him.

According to a reliable legal source close to the case, this is what the mail charge against Mandel came down to: Mandel didn't tell the legislature that some of his friends, who had made gifts to him, had financial interests in Marlboro and Bowie race tracks and might benefit from laws the General Assembly was passing. One of the glaring ironies in this entire travesty of federal justice was that the parties in the case had stipulated as an undisputed fact before the jury that Mandel's alleged conduct was not considered a crime under Maryland law.

Like many governors before him, Mandel had friends with whom he had a mutually beneficial relationship. He contended that he had always acted in the state's best interest and that there was simply no connection between his official acts and his business relationships with his friends and codefendants.

The federal authorities, however, in an indictment reminiscent of a "Rube Goldberg invention," created a corruption theory out of Mandel's long time political, business and social relationships with his friends. They christened those otherwise innocent relationships "a scheme," and said they violated the mail fraud and racketeering statutes, and that they also deprived the citizens of Maryland of their intangible right to Mandel's loyal services.

The local editorial writers fulsomely praised the prosecutors for their legal ingenuity, while blistering Mandel as a putative liar and fraud. The mail fraud counts, a classic and unconscionable example of the law being abused to punish a popular governor, would become Mandel's Waterloo.

The government's corruption theory, nevertheless, had some holes in it. For starters, the evidence at the trial showed that Mandel had no direct pecuniary interests in any of the race tracks. He also had no obligation by virtue of his public office to disclose information about third parties' interest in Maryland race tracks. None of his codefendants were public officials. And, there was no state law requiring any of them to disclose that kind of ownership information. And, finally, there were no victims in this matter as in the traditional sense of a properly or economic crime.

The Maryland Law Review, published by the University of Maryland Law School, is one of the most prestigious journals of its kind in the country. In a learned treatise entitled, *United States vs. Mandel,* Volume 40, 1981, the author reviewed the case against Mandel and his associates. It condemned in the sharpest terms, the fairness and justice of the entire judicial proceedings.

The article made the following damning assessment: It raised doubts whether the defendants received a fair trial; questioned whether they had been unjustly convicted; stated that the Court seemed to ignore its responsibility to the public and the defendants; assailed the fact that the defendants were jailed after half the Appeal Court voted to reverse their conviction; and, that it was patently wrong for the Trial Judge not to instruct the jury on what constituted bribery under federal law.

All during the gubernatorial reign of Mandel (1969-1979), South Baltimore's Harry J. McGuirk was an influential member of the State Senate and chairman of its Economic Affairs Committee. An avowed Mandel partisan and conceded master of the legislative process, McGuirk is still painfully troubled by his friend's conviction and subsequent banishment from the helmsmanship of state government.

"I am still in a quandary," McGuirk said, "as to exactly what Mandel was supposed to have done wrong. As far as his ability to control every vote in the legislature, that was simply impossible. And, yet, that is what the prosecuting attorney seemed to indicate. And, the fact that when he mailed the minutes of the Board of Public Works to another institution, it ended up being the basis for his being charged under the mail fraud statute."

"As time goes by," Mandel underscored, "more and more people in this State are beginning to understand the nature of the criminal action that was brought against me." Recently, a codefendant convicted in the Mandel case, an attorney from Southern Maryland, was readmitted to practice before the Maryland Bar. Mandel calmly emphasized, "At the appropriate time, I also intend to file for readmission to the Bar of Maryland."

In December of 1982, thanks to the noble and creative efforts of celebrated Annapolis lawyer and lobbyist, Bruce Bereano, Mandel won a full pardon from Republican President Ronald Reagan. "It simply came down to enough was enough," recalled the talented Bereano. "All over this state, there was a tremendous groundswell, broadly based, for Mandel's early release from prison. The people felt he had suffered enough. It took me a year to work on the pardon petition and it was worth it," remembered Bereano.

The U.S. Parole Commission required Mandel to serve three years of his original four year sentence. As a result of the presidential pardon, however, Mandel actually served only two years in the federal penal system.

"I enjoyed my ten years in office and making government work for the people," Mandel said. "It makes me feel good now to reflect on the massive school construction program that I initiated that literally saved some of our cities and counties from fiscal disaster." The former Speaker of the House of Delegates also mentioned, with obvious pride, his efforts to reorganize the state government, the creation of a cabinet-level executive system, judicial reform, the building of the highly praised $50 million Convention Center in Baltimore City, a Public Defender system, and a Mass-Transit agency.

With respect to Bradford "Brad" Jacobs, an editorial writer on sabbatical leave from the *Baltimore Sunpapers,* who had written an historically-oriented book focusing on the Mandel trial, the ex-governor became slightly flustered. The book entitled, *Thimbleriggers: the Law Versus Governor Mandel,* was released in late September by Hopkins Press. It takes a strictly pro-government view of the case.

"My wife and I met with Mr. Jacobs a couple of years ago, when he said he was going to do a book on me. And, I told him straight-out," Mandel recalled, "if there is anyone I thought who couldn't write an objective book about me it was him. I simply refused to cooperate with him." Jacobs, in a telephone interview, responded to Mandel's comment by saying, "It's interesting that the governor would say that without having first read my book."

A scion of inherited wealth, Jacobs lives in fashionable Stevenson, a bastion for the landed gentry, located in Baltimore County. Jacobs is also a direct lineal descendant of Maryland Governor Augustus W. Bradford (1862-1866). It is one of the great ironies of the Mandel saga that a relative of Governor Bradford would write a book criticizing another Maryland governor.

According to H.W. Buckholz's chronicle of the *Governors of Maryland* (W & W Co., 1980), Bradford, a candidate on the Unionist ticket, won his election "by intimidation and through the unlawful use of soldiery. The only fault to be found with him, therefore, is his pretension that he had been chosen by the free vote of the people."

"There definitely is a double standard at *The Sun*," a Mandel associate told me. "In the Mandel affair, *The Sun* deliberately created a news climate of hysteria and of guilt before the trial. But with respect to the Watergate-related disclosure that Republican Richard M. Nixon had bartered thirty-one ambassadorships to well-healed WASP contributors, including one to a Hunt Valley type for a secret $100,000 campaign contribution, *The Sun* gave us its silence."

One of the private irritations that continues to cut away at Mandel is the fact that present governor Harry Hughes appears to go out of his way not to be seen with Mandel at any public gatherings. A Mandel confidant told me that the ex-governor is deeply hurt over the continuing snubs from the present occupier of the state's mansion.

What rubs the salt in Mandel's wound is the fact that in the early '70s, Mandel made Hughes, after much importuning that he needed a job, his first "Secretary of Transportation". He even gave Hughes a hefty raise when he pleaded he couldn't live off his then state salary. "It's the gross ingratitude," added the confidant, "that literally drives Mandel up the wall."

Since Maryland's earliest days as a prosperous British colony, religious and ethnic rivalries have tainted the state's "Free State" image. Originally, Maryland was founded by George Calvert of England, the first "Lord Baltimore," and a Roman Catholic. In 1649, under Calvert's benevolent influence, Maryland passed a "Religious Toleration Act".

In 1654, the Protestant bigot, William Claiborne, gained hegemony in the colony, and immediately began oppressing the Catholic population, barring them from public office, and creating barriers to keep them from participating fully in the political and social life of the growing colony. Although this pernicious condition was eventually ended by the Maryland Provincial Convention, in 1776, it has left deep and lasting scars.

It wasn't until 1826, in Maryland, that a Jew could legally vote and hold office, and our black citizens had to wait until the middle of the 20th century to experience the full benefits of their franchise rights.

In the pre-Civil War period, the state saw the emergence of the anti-Catholic, anti-Jewish, anti-immigrant "Know Nothing Party." This strongly racist group was notorious for its bigotry, corruption and proclivity for violence. Its membership was totally WASP-dominated, primarily from the emerging mercantile class.

The Know-Nothing Party was openly supportive of slavery, the Southern cause for rebellion, and British imperial interests throughout the world. They were so powerful that they were able to elect members as mayors of Baltimore City, Samuel Hinks and Thomas Swann, and even one, Thomas Hicks, in 1857, as governor.

It was only after the Civil War, that the Know-Nothings, as an organized and legal party, went into active decline, and reform Democrats regained control over the state government. It is important for a full understanding of the "Mandel Affair," with all its undercurrents, to understand that Maryland has had, in its recent past, an ugly history of intolerance against minority groups and individuals. It wasn't until 1938, that Maryland elected its first and only Catholic governor, Herbert R. O'Connor.

Mandel has been the first and only member of the Jewish faith to hold that office in the 350 year history of the state.

The stage is now set to discuss "The Letter," keeping in mind, the dictum of Sir Francis Bacon, "Read not to contradict and confute, nor to believe and take for granted, but to weigh and consider."

In 1898, the great French writer, Emile Zola, in a historic pamphlet, *J'accuse*, attacked the army of France for its wrongdoing in the "Dreyfus Affair". On November 7, 1975, Mandel in a last minute attempt to prevent his indictment, sent a 19 page letter to the Justice Department in Washington, D.C.

The letter was a sweeping document alleging the existence, at least since 1970, of a vast conspiracy by some federal officials, and others, to persecute Mandel, or at least destroy him politically. Mandel accused the U.S. prosecutors of a "concerted effort to destroy me almost from the inception of my tenure as governor."

Mandel also cited systematic news leaks as, "the latest examples of a pattern of activities that date back five years; an outrageous, calculated and systematic effort to undermine me politically, to destroy my rights as a citizen, and to poison the minds of those that elected me." He bitterly blasted the I.R.S. for secretly investigating him as far back as 1970, of bugging his telephone, and the U.S. Attorney's Office for the harassment and intimidations of grand jury witnesses.

Mandel insisted that the federal sleuths had a double standard; one for Democrats; and another for Republicans. He pointed out that well-known WASP Republicans, like U.S. Senators J. Glenn Beall and Charles "Mac" Mathias, the late Federal Judge C. Stanley Blair, and the then U.S. Attorney, socialite Jervis S. Finney, had escaped comparable scrutiny for their activities. Mandel pleaded that federal agencies were being misused to embarrass him and that, "U.S. officials were out to get him."

Two weeks after sending this extraordinary letter, Mandel was indicted. The Justice Department, under Assistant Attorney General Richard L. Thornburgh, after a cursory investigation of Mandel's complaint, denied there was any basis for an in-depth investigation.

On another topic, national politics, Mandel thought it "was too early to write-off Fritz Mondale's presidential efforts," although he didn't appear too optimistic about a Democratic victory this fall. Particularly, Mandel contended, since Ronald Reagan is a strong incumbent this election year, as opposed to 1980, when he was the unknown and untested Republican Right-wing candidate from the Far West.

Mandel, an astute political observer, had nothing but generous praise for the achievements of Baltimore City Mayor William Donald Schaefer, calling him, "a great Mayor." Schaefer, like Mandel, has been closely connected to longtime Baltimore City and state political godfather, the legendary kingmaker and wheeler-dealer, one lrv Kovens.

Kovens, who was also convicted in the Mandel trial, now lives in semi-retirement in Florida. But, City Hall insiders insist that his shadowy and powerful influence over Schaefer hasn't diminished, since the lean days of the late 50s when Kovens, then the owner of a nondescript West Baltimore street furniture store, took Schaefer under his near-miraculous, protective wing.

From that fortuitous moment onward, Schaefer's magical personal and political transformation from an otherwise obscure and colorless title searcher to *Esquire Magazine's* (Oct. Issue, 1984) "Best Mayor in America," began in earnest. If Schaefer runs for Governor in '86, which appears almost a dead certainty at this writing, Mandel prophesied, "It would entirely change the context of that race, no matter who the opposition is."

Some Prince George County politicos familiar with Koven's *modus operandi*, are both fearful and openly envious, that if Schaefer does capture the State House in the '86 election, that Kovens will again return to power as his *eminence grise*, and that Mandel will be cast in the supporting role of a surrogate governor.

"The politics of government has always fascinated me," Mandel continued. "If you master the art of listening from just the ordinary people as I have over the years, you will be amazed at what you can learn. Most people in public life, contrary to popular belief, are really interested in doing a good job." During the last few arduous years, after being forced out of the state's highest office, and languishing in a federal prison, the former governor has had an opportunity to reflect long and deep on some of his basic values and beliefs.

As Mandel was pausing to relight his pipe, the words of the poet, William Ernest Henley, from his popular ballad, *Invictus*, came readily to my mind; "It matters now how strait the gate, how charged with punishments the scroll, I am the master of my fate. I am the captain of my soul."

The graying, but always dignified Mandel made this final comment: "I am truly grateful to the people of Maryland for all their kindnesses, faith and considerations they have extended to me and my family over the years. I have learned during my long ordeal, who my true friends are. I value deeply their genuine support, and the support and love given to me by my wife Jeanne and my family."

And, finally, there is the shocking disclosure by William Rodgers, in the *Evening Sun* of October 5, 1984, that Mandel knew absolutely nothing of his friends' secret ownership of the Marlboro race track. Rodgers, a codefendant in the case, who didn't testify at the trial, said he went to see the governor, along with attorney Ernest Cory, Jr., at the State House in December of 1972, eight months after efforts to pass legislation to increase the value of the race track. According to Rodgers' account, which fully supports Mandel's claim of innocence, when Mandel was told who really, secretly owned the track, he replied, "Jesus Christ! How could they do that to me."

Almost nine years after Mandel was first indicted, both *The Sun* and *Evening Sun*, were still condemning, either in their editorials or on their Op-Ed pages, the ex-governor. On September 30, 1984, six excerpts from Jacob's one- dimensional *Thimbleriggers* began running in the *Evening Sun*. One wonders if all the writers of negative Mandel editorials from the local media were collected together, what kind of common profile of the authors would emerge? It appears *The Sun's* unholy and undeclared war against Mandel, like the torments of the damned in Dante's *Divine Comedy*, is without end.

*       *       *

*Author's Note-Not too long after the above article was published, and the other two articles cited below, the case against Marvin Mandel collapsed. It was held to be without any legal merit by a ruling of a Federal Court of Appeals. In 1989, the Supreme Court finally upheld the lower court decision overturning Mandel's conviction. The ex-Governor was fully vindicated by the ruling and eventually readmitted to the practice of law by Maryland's highest court, the Court of Appeals.

As for the two other commentaries that I wrote in support of justice for Mandel, the first appeared in the *Baltimore Enterprise,* on May 22, 1986; and the second, in the *Jeffersonian,* a Towson, Md. newspaper, on July 17, 1986.

On January 23, 1981, my letter in support of a presidential pardon for Mandel was published in the *Washington Post.* It said:

"One of the resurrected quotations from the 1980 (*Metro*, Jan. 1) came from an unnamed precinct official, who claimed supposed allegiance to the Democratic Party in Maryland. The politico is recorded as saying,

`The only place where you'll still find Marvin Mandel's picture is on the wall at his mother's.' That statement is both cruel and untrue.

"Since his halcyon days as Speaker of the House of Delegates in Maryland, the portrait of the Hon. Marvin Mandel has been proudly displayed on the wall of our club. The Stonewall Democratic Club, in the heart of South Baltimore, is the oldest Democratic club in contiuous existence in the State of Maryland.

"We have no intention of removing the portrait of our fallen leader, who was a good, strong, effective governor for all the people of our state during his long tenure in office.

"We are not unmindful that Gov. Mandel is languishing in jail and has been disbarred from his chosen profession because of a tie vote of the highest federal appellate court that reviewed his criminal case.

"We believe that Marvin Mandel, a proud man, has indeed suffered enough, and no useful public interest is served or enhanced by his further unnecessary incarceration.

"We call on President Reagan to mercifully grant Marvin Mandel the parole that has been so callously denied by the outgoing administration."

William Hughes, Counsel
Stonewall Democratic Club
Baltimore, Md.

# 39. A Satirical Look into Baltimore's Political Future
## February 2, 1983

I was sitting (in 1983) in my dimly lit library den, one night, reading one of Jacques Kelly's lively columns in *The News-American*. The article was full of priceless trivia, like the exciting fact that the late movie actress, Joan Crawford, "was never a Horn & Horn waitress." I fell sound asleep after the very first paragraph.

Somehow, I found myself in City Hall. The year was 1995. William Donald Schaefer was still our mayor. I could tell because there was a massive portrait of Hizgreatness hanging from the center of the rotunda.

There were some other noticeable changes at City Hall. The office of "Deputy Mayor" had been created. Joan Bereska, a long-term aide and trusted food taster for Hizgreatness, was now the deputy mayor. Her office was decorated in a devil red motif. And there were two big stuffed dragons stationed outside her office. The fake, but feared beasts, would breathe in and spew out real fire. Above her door was a neon sign, which gave out alternating messages: "No Reporters Admitted," and *The Sun* Lies."

There was a miniature icons of Hizgreatness systematically placed throughout the vastness of City Hall. The mayor's name appeared on all city property, posters, stationery, pencils, and equipment of every kind and description.

Charles Benton, a bouncy 82 years of age, was still the city's Director of Finance. Although he had moved from Anne Arundel County to Allegheny County, and now worked only on Mondays, he also remained a co-trustee of the city's multimillion dollar megabank for economic loans. The bank had assets of nearly $8 billion. Benton, a born-again Christian, had a large poster of a crucified Christ on his office wall.

I notice a group of happy developers leaving Benton's office. They told me they just got an okay for a $100 million loan from the trustees at a one percent interest, with no collateral. They planned to build a gambling entertainment emporium in the Canton-Highlandtown area. One of the smiling wheeler-dealers told me that, "It will create at least 20 new jobs for card dealers and exotic dancers. Naturally, we won' have to pay any city real estate taxes for the first three centuries of its use."

I asked them where they were going to celebrate their deal and they said a fund raiser was being held that night for Hizgreatness at the palatial home of local civic leader and contractor, Mendel Friedman. I found out later that former Harborplace landlord, James Rouse, had been the toast-master for the gala affair. In fact, Rouse had made a special trip back from his latest Harborplace-Bloomingdale project in Nome, Alaska (it's called the "Ice Palace") for the evening's festivities.

Bob Embry, an errand-boy for Rouse during Dr. Milton Eisenhower's "I don't want NCPACK or Senator Sarbanes' flap," was now managing Harborplace. The fundraiser took in about $6 million for Hizgreatness's campaign coffers. If Schaefer wins another term, he will have served 28 years in that office.

There was only one announced serious candidate running against Hizgreatness in 1995. And that candidate was the perennial also-ran, but intrepid, Morgan L. Amaimo. Amaimo, unfortunately was also busy, at the same time, running for U.S. president, congressman, and city councilman from the 3rd district.

Councilman "Mimi" DiPietro (D-1st) was the guest speaker that evening. No one present could recall later one word he spoke. His speech had been written by Councilman Willie Meyers (D-6th). Meyers, a spry 92 years of age, refused to discuss the controversial speech, but he did say that he "supported the mayor 100 percent!"

The city council members' offices were set up according to their fealty to Hizgreatness. (Myers' 100 percent standard was the ultimate test.) Tim "Mirrors" Murphy (D-6th)-who still chaired the Budget and Finance Committee-received the full perks of office. Dissenters, who hadn't been shipped off to Ocean City, were forced to make all their phone calls from a pay phone in the City Hall lobby.

Former City Councilman George Della (D-6th), who had the temerity to suggest that the taxpayers were entitled to twice-a-week garbage collections, was never again allowed, after 1983, to enter City Hall. As a result of Della incurring Hizgreatness's "Divine Temper," the southsider's view of the seat of local government had to be limited to a 20-cent picture postcard of that edifice.

As for the comptroller's office, the City Council had long since declared it defunct. They never bothered to tell Hyman Pressman, the last person to fill the job, who still went around the inner harbor pointing out the life rings, that he forced the mayor into installing.

The new city council president was a young banker from south Baltimore, Joseph DiBlasi. DiBlasi, in order to show his undying gratitude to fast fading Stonewall boss, Harry J. McGuirk, had caused the city council to pass an ordinance rechristening the Key Highway, as "Soft Shoes Drive." McGuirk, still selling the occasional odd piece of real estate, usually keeps to himself, but still talks about how he got "lost in the tall grass," back in 1982.

The governor in 1995 was Mary Ann Willin. Willin was the first female governor of the state and also the first person to wear a loaded sidearm on her person. She had previously served as a deputy state's attorney for the city, under the legendary crime fighter, Billy "The Kid" Swisher. And, for a brief time, she was a crime commission coordinator and czaress for Hizgreatness.

Under her enlightened administration, the state's prison capacity was increased from 11,000 to 50,000. The only problem with that was that there were now 250,000 inmates in the overcrowded penal system, therefore forcing Willin, against her best wishes, to place five inmates in each 6' x 8' cell.

It was at this point that my two English cocker spaniels, "Paul" and "Mac," began chewing on my exposed toenails.

I awoke from the uneasy dream in a panicky sweat.

I continued to read Jacques Kelly's column. There was an interesting item about Joan Blondell, a motion picture actress, who "performed at the Belvedere in 1951."

I started again to fall off to sleep…

         *                *                *

*Author's Note-"Where are they on now?"

Billy "The Kid" Swisher is practicing law, mostly criminal cases, in Baltimore City and Baltimore County.

The Key Highway is still the Key Highway and it is still located in south Baltimore, taking visitors by the thousands daily to Fort McHenry.

Joe DiBlasi is a prosperous banker and business man.

Bob Embry is the highly respected president of the Abell Foundation.

Surprise! Jacques Kelly is writing a column for the *Baltimore Sun.*

Charles Benton is enjoying a well deserved retirement and residing in Prince George's Co. A huge government office building, near the City Hall, has been named in his honor.

Joan Bereska, God bless her kind heart, is also retired from public service and lives in Baltimore City.

Tim Murphy is a distinguished judge on the District Court of Maryland.

George W. Della, Jr. is a very popular state senator, as was his late father, from South Baltimore.

Mary Ann Willin, a longtime and very dedicated public servant, has retired from the public arena.

Mendel Friedman is a highly successful contractor and developer in Baltimore City.

The Stonewall Democratic Club is going as strong as ever down in the 1200 block of south Charles St.

Paul Sarbanes is holding up well, with dignity and considerable talent, one of the posts of U.S. senators from Maryland. He is a neighbor of this author.

Morgan L. Amaimo, Harry J. McGuirk, Willie Meyers, Hyman Pressman, Jim Rouse, Dr. Milton Eisenhower, and "Mimi" DiPietro have all passed on to their final rewards.

Horn & Horn restaurant is history as is the *Baltimore News-American* newspaper, formerly the *Baltimore News-Post,* for which I sold for a dime while growing up in Locust Point.

"Paul" and "Mac," my two treasured English cocker spaniels, (real names, "Loafer" and "Shag"), have also went on to that eternal resting place set aside for man's special four legged friends. They, too, are deeply missed.

Harborplace is a glowing financial and tourist-attracting success and is a fitting tribute to Jim Rouse's splendid tenacity and courageous vision.

The City Hall had a major starring role in the fantastic victory party, on Jan. 30, 2001, for the world champs and NFL kingpins, the celebrated Baltimore Ravens.

Russ Smith, the former co-owner and editor of the Baltimore *City Paper* is the very successful owner-editor of the popular weekly, the *New York Press.* He also writes a lively and controversial political column for it under the *Mugger* byline. His column is so popular that Matt Drudge carries a link to it on his website.

As for the inestimable William Donald Schaefer, he is now the state of Maryland's feisty comptroller, and is 80 years young. According to a *Sunpaper* item of April 5, 2001, he is seriously considering running again (double gasp) for the office of governor of Maryland! If he does, and his health holds up, Schaefer will probably (triple gasp) win! At least, one office tower of a building, a 37 floor hi rise, at 6 St. Paul Place, in Baltimore, is named after Hizgreatness.

By way of full disclosure, I was appointed to the Baltimore City Solicitor's office, as an Assistant City Solicitor, in 1969, by then-Mayor Thomas J. D'Alesandro, Jr. Peter Marudas, who has been Sen. Paul Sarbanes' very capable key aide for years, was then doing the same job for D'Alesandro. He helped to facilitate the process. It was State Sen. Harry J. McGuirk, also President of the Stonewall Democratic Club in South Baltimore, who secured the appointment for me. I became Chief of the Litigation Division for the City Solicitor's Office, in 1977, and served till 1981, when I resigned from the office to return to private practice.

One of the more important cases, that I handled while in the City Solicitor's Office was entitled, *Adler v. City*, Circuit Court, No. 2, File No. 84/A, 379/46221-A. In that case, the plaintiffs, a citizens' group, sought an injunction to permanently enjoin the City of Baltimore from allowing any commercial development in the inner harbor. After a full hearing on the merits, Judge James Perrott, of the Supreme Bench of Baltimore City, on March 13, 1978, denied the plaintiffs' Petition. The first commercial project completed in that disputed area became known as "Harborplace." The rest as they say is history.

I believe it is historically accurate to say that the idea of "Harborplace," began under the mayoralty of Theodore R. McKeldin. And, that it is McKeldin, who deserves the greatest credit for putting forward the concept, that the inner harbor of Baltimore could be developed in a fashion to make it a major tourist attraction. McKeldin's brilliant idea was then pushed and nurtured along by Mayor Thomas "The Elder" D'Alesandro, and later by his son, Mayor Thomas "The Younger" D'Alesandro. The inner harbor finally came into fruition under the long municipal reign of Hizgreatness, William Donald Schaefer.

\*　　　　　　\*　　　　　　\*

# 40. Art Murphy Sees Bell, Stokes As Front Runners
## July 16, 1999

Art Murphy is a consultant with nearly 30 years of experience in the political arena. In the past, he has worked for Political Action Committees associated with the United Automobile Workers (UAW) and the Teamsters (IBT). His political background also includes a stint with the Democratic National Committee, laboring in Chuck Robb's successful bid for governor of Virginia in 1982, and participating in many victorious local congressional, councilmanic, and judicial races.

Last year, the north Baltimore resident gave an interesting talk at a meeting of the New Democratic Club. The topic that night centered on the science of electoral politicking. Murphy recounted how his losing bid for Clerk of the Circuit Court in 1998 had deepened his understanding of the process. I caught up with him recently to get his views on this year's mayoralty race, now filled to the brim with 27 candidates.

Murphy's baptism in the campaign wars dates back to 1970, when he helped to elect his father, William Murphy, Sr., to a judgeship on the now defunct Municipal Court. His family hails from the Cherry Hill area, and his brother, Billy Murphy, is a celebrated criminal defense lawyer.

"The year 1970," Murphy recalled fondly, "was also when Milton Allen became the city's first black State Attorney and Parren J. Mitchell was first elected to the Congress. The breakthrough year, however, for blacks in electoral politics in this city was 1968, when Joe Howard won a seat on the Circuit Court as a judge without any institutional support."

Not since 1971 has Baltimore City had an election for mayor without an incumbent running. "I remember that 1971 contest, too," Murphy said, "since I was managing then City Solicitor George Russell's campaign for mayor. Thommy (The Younger) D'Alesandro in a surprise move decided not to seek reelection. Initially there were six on seven candidates for mayor (including the eventual winner William Donald Schaefer and hundreds of people had filed for the City Council slots, the most ever. It seemed like," Murphy underscored, "everybody and his mother wanted to run for office or upgrade to another spot."

Murphy believes that City Council President Lawrence Bell has an "incredible advantage," in the mayor's race because of his experience as a citywide candidate. He says, "Bell will do whatever it takes to win and he has the team set up to do just that. But, he must continue to look over his shoulder and make sure that (Carl) Stokes doesn't catch up with him." To reinforce Murphy's words, travelers along Erdman Ave., near Belair Road, can't help but notice how Bell's signs already dominate that neighborhood.

Naturally, mayoralty candidate Mary Conaway, the popular Register of Wills, who has run citywide before and won, would disagree with Murphy. In fact, Frank Conaway, who is contending for the City Council President post (and is the husband of Mary) is the incumbent Clerk of the Circuit Court for Baltimore City. If the Conaways (who are veteran politicos) both win this year, they would be the first husband and wife team to ever sit together on the city's important Board of Estimates.

"The black vote generally doesn't split. As the campaign continues, the voters will gravitate towards one candidate," Murphy predicted. "Since the city is almost two thirds black, the challenge for any white candidate, like Councilman Martin O' Malley, is to convince white voters that he can win. It would be wildly atypical for O'Malley to have more than an ice cube's chance in hell to pull this one off. It just doesn't work that way," he emphasized.

Since this is 1999, and not 1971, the energetic O'Malley, I'm sure, isn't buying Murphy's prophecy. Like the other candidates, O'Malley knows this race is unique and that there is a lot of campaigning left to be done before September 14.

Murphy talked about "name recognition," "citywide election experience," "incumbency," "fundraising," as though they were holy mantras. Who knows? Maybe this will be the year when the voters say, "Throw all the bums out. We want someone new in City Hall."

This would be music to the ears of candidate "Battling Bob" Kaufman whose billboard ads now appear on the side of MTA buses.

Or, Murphy could be right.

Stay tuned!

*     *     *

*Author's Note-O'Malley won the electon for mayor in 1999, with 53 percent of the vote in the primary, and a stunning 91 precent majority in the general election.

*      *      *

# 41. Elections Tell of Changing Baltimore
## April 26, 1999

In Baltimore City, municipal elections have always been a reliable barometer of how the place is changing, and, more importantly, of who has the political power. It also shows how class, race, and money are important factors in the life of our great urban center.

Back in the bad old days, when the political process was tightly controlled by the WASP elite, it was rather easy to become mayor if you were white and well-connected. The bosses, sitting around a smoked filled room, like in the then-segregated Maryland Club, would simply anoint one of their own.

This is what they did in 1856, when the loathsome Thomas Swann, a member of the notorious Catholic-hating, immigrant bashing "Know Nothing Party", was given the nod. The only legacy of Swann's tenure that I know of is that there is a small park named after him in south Baltimore, just off Hanover St.

According to Suzanne Ellery Greene's splendid *Illustrated History of Baltimore,* blacks made up about twelve percent of the city's population around this period. Many were freed slaves. The immigrant community, mostly of European origins, made up about 25 percent.

By the middle of this century, however, election politicking went through a momentous change. The bosses, instead of coming out of the corporate board rooms, began emerging out of the working class that was flexing its muscles. The descendants of those formerly despised immigrants of an earlier period had grown in numbers and taken over the political process.

In 1947, Thomas "The Elder" D'Alesandro, the pride of "Little Italy," became mayor, thanks to political king makers with colorful ethnic monikers. Names like, James H. "Jack" Pollack, Willie Curran, Joe Stazak, and the south side dynamic duo of George Della and Joe Wyatt dominated the era. Blacks were 20 percent of the population in this post-WWII period, but still only on the fringe of real political power. D'Alesandro's reign lasted for three terms.

The last hurrah, however, for the ethnic boy-ohs came when City Hall was captured, in 1971, by William Donald Schaefer, a colorful disciple of boss Irv Kovens. After Kovens went to prison in the late 70s, Schaefer fell under the influence of business men, like Jim Rouse, Henry Knott and Henry Rosenberg. It was their patronage that carried him into the State House in Annapolis, in 1987, for two terms as governor.

Meanwhile, beginning in the early 50s, when they comprised about one third of the population, blacks were starting to put their stamp on the city's political landscape. That imprint has lasted down to this day. The election of the first black congressmen, Parren J.

Mitchell; the first black city State's Attorney, Miton Allen; the appointment of the first black mayor, Clarence "Du" Burns; and the election for three terms of Kurt Schmoke, all grew out of this exciting period.

Today, it is estimated that blacks constitute more than sixty percent of the city's 670,000 citizens.

All of the above takes us to the "Draft Mfume 2000 Committee" and an event that is simply unprecedented in our electoral history. On April 19, a full page ad, costing an estimated $30,000, appeared in *The Sun*. It was signed by 200 respected Baltimoreans and pleaded with Kweisi Mfume, head of the NAACP, to run for mayor. The ad, which had a theatre of the absurd aspect to it, claimed the city needed a "national leader" like him to take the helm.

As expected, the other mayoralty candidates expressed outrage over the pricey gimmick and continued to attack the incentives being used to entice Mfume's entry into the race. Recently, the legislature changed the city's residency law to allow Mfume to run. There are also plans to hike the mayor's salary from $110,000 to $150,000, and to permit outside speaking perks to supplement any base pay.

At least one irate voter, a one time Mfume fan, said she felt "manipulated by the media blitz and all the obsequious pandering." She added, "Even Schaefer, with his harborplace-sized ego, never pulled a stunt like this. The city is in a fiscal crisis and Mfume is demanding special privileges. It's hard to stomach. And, if he is so great, then why isn't the NAACP trying to keep him?"

Each mayoralty election has revealed something interesting about our changing city. This one is lining up as Baltimore's unique salute to the new millennium.

*        *        *

# 42. Bush-Cheney Will Win in 2000: Thanks to Lewinsky Scandal
**Aug. 17, 2000**

Mercifully, "Bubba Bill" Clinton will soon ride off into the sunset. When he does, the vast majority of Americans will heave a huge collective sigh of relief. It is beyond cavil that Clinton disgraced the office of the presidency.

His sexual trysts with the portly pepperpot, Monica Lewinsky, inside the oval office of the White House, stained the presidency.

How an air-headed intern, like Lewinsky, could have gained access to the president will probably forever remain a matter of speculation. The

Special Prosecutor, Kenneth Starr, strangely failed to pursue that part of the case.

Clinton was convinced that his conversations with her were being tapped by a foreign power, eager to gain leverage over him. Maybe, Starr's successor, Robert Ray, will find the answers with his new probe.

It's clear to me that the Clinton/Lewinsky vulgarity is the heaviest baggage that Al Gore will carry into the bitter campaign ahead. There is also nothing he can do to change or alter it. Gore, a stiff politico, mistakenly believed that by picking Sen. Joseph Lieberman as his vice presidential mate, he could defect much of the deep resentment throughout America towards "Bubba Bill's" wrongdoing. I'm sorry, but that won't fly. It simply has too many holes in it.

To begin with, Lieberman is just as boring a campaigner as Gore is. In fact, he may be worse, since he has such an inflated opinion of himself. He comes off as a pompous know-it-all. Instead of adding political muscle to the Democrats' bid, Lieberman also will cost Gore support from within the rank and file.

The blacks are very upset with the ticket. They have felt, with justification, that it was long past the time for one of them, like the Rev. Jesse Jackson, to receive the honor of being chosen as vice president. Many in Big Labor, too, particularly the teachers' unions, aren't crazy about Lieberman either. They don't see much difference between his so-called "centrist" views and the union-bashing policies of the GOP.

Lieberman's religion, Judaism, shouldn't be an issue in the campaign. That wouldn't be fair. But, he is a card carrying Zionist and his political beliefs on that controversial issue will be open to debate. Although aid to Israel is popular in the easily-coaxed Congress ($100 billion plus since 1948) that might not necessarily be true in rural and small town America. With urban centers, too, like Baltimore, closing fire houses, libraries and recreation centers, taxpayers are growing more vigilant then ever about exactly where their tax dollars are being spent.

On the other side, the Republican ticket of George W. Bush, Jr. and Dick Cheney is a mixed blessing for the GOP. Young Bush is an intellectual lightweight, whose political resume' was carefully crafted by his father, George W. Bush, Sr., the former president. Nevertheless, he can point to the fact that he has done a relatively good job as governor of Texas, despite his penchant for capital punishment.

Dick Cheney, a clever politico, is however, a big plus for Bush. At age 29, he was chief of staff to President Gerald Ford. Then he became a congressman from Wyoming, and later, a strong Secretary of Defense during the co-presidency of Nancy and Ronald Reagan. In the private sector, Cheney was a CEO at Halliburton, an oil service giant. When he left to join the Bush team, he was given a $28 million retirement package. He is true Washington insider, and, indeed, a wily political strategist.

Another serious minus for the Democrats this year is that two popular candidates will be running on Third Party tickets: Ralph Nader on the Green Party line, and pro-lifer, anti-New Word Order gadfly, Pat Buchanan, heading up the Reform Party slate. They will both divert tons of voters away from the Democrats. Nader will appeal to the liberal/left constituents; and Buchanan to independents and Jeffersonian populists.

For many in the pro-life community, Gore is the ultimate anathema because of his advocacy for the gruesome partial-birth abortion process. Some Democrats have also not forgotten, nor forgiven, "Bubba Bill," and Gore, too, for not permitting the late Robert Casey, then the Democratic governor of Pennsylvania, from speaking at the 1996 Democratic National Convention because he was pro-life. It was a gross insult that will now come back to haunt the Gore-Lieberman camp.

Here's the bottom line: Unless the Democrats can come up with a juicy sex scandal that will stick to Bush (and that appears highly unlikely at this date) the GOP, in effect, will take the White House by default in November.

The Democrats will rightly blame "Bubba Bill" for losing the election. He, in turn, in his heavily-fictionalized memoirs, will simply fault the Secret Service-for not keeping Lewinsky out of the White House!

\*          \*          \*

## 43. For Whom the Bell Tolls?
### April 10, 1999

"Will this be my year?" is the question faced by the young and independent-minded Lawrence A. Bell, III, currently President of the Baltimore City Council.

Incumbent Mayor Kurt Schmoke is finally leaving City Hall after three terms in office. He will be remembered mostly as a decent man, who lacked a passion for the job and made more than a few yearn for a return to the days of Mayor Maximus, William Donald Schaefer. Although it was hard to dislike Schmoke personally, his closeness to the political operative, Ron Shapiro, did turned some citizens off.

Bell, also an African-American, is an ideal candidate to replace Schmoke. He has done an outstanding job in the Council for the last 12 years, almost four of it as its president. He has earned his stripes fighting for property tax cuts, implementing a zero-tolerance attitude towards crime, and struggling to improve the educational system.

In 1993, Bell also impressed many in the human rights community by steering, along with other key players in the Council, the MacBride Principles bill into law. That device, which deals with corporate and pension investment policy, helps to combat religious discrimination against beleaguered Catholics in the north of Ireland. Congress made it a federal law in 1998.

The deadline for filing for mayor is July 6, 1999. Bell, still an unofficial candidate, has reportedly raised "around $400,000" for his war chest to date. The articulate Carl Stokes, a former 2nd District Councilman, has tossed his hat into the ring and his campaign is beginning to get some notice. A. Robert Kaufman, a feisty social justice activist, has filed, too. His bid, at this point, fits into the long shot category. In addition, two other candidates have signed up for the battle on the democratic side, along with one Republican, Roberto Marsili.

A poll by Professor Herb Smith of Western Maryland College, taken in July, 1998, for the Baltimore *African-American* and *Baltimore Times* newspapers, showed that Bell is "by far the most popular elected politician in town." His favorability numbers were high, not only as expected in the black community, but in the white community as well.

Over the last decade, Bell had forged important alliances with leaders in the heavily populated white areas of the city, like Hampden, Locust Point and Highlandtown. With the September 14th election just around the corner, he appeared set as a potential clear front runner. However, as in an Ernest Hemingway novel, at almost the twelfth hour, an antagonist has appeared on the horizon-one Kweisi Mfume!

The head of the respected National Association for the Advancement of Colored People interjected himself into the race for mayor. Mfume didn't do it directly. Cronies of his in the General Assembly, in Annapolis, introduced a bill allowing a potential candidate, like Mfume, now living in Catonsville, to move to the city on a shortened six month residency change. The bill passed.

Then, on March 26, Mfume purchased a luxurious $313,000 condo in the Inner Harbor area of Baltimore. This caused an under employed denizen of Charles Village to ask, "How can I join that NAACP?"

What is most puzzling about a Mfume's candidacy is this: "Why would a man holding a national office, and a powerful one at that, want to run for mayor of Baltimore?" This sounds, on its face, like a step down. Could it be that power brokers within the NAACP are looking to dump Mfume and that this is a clean way for them to do it? Who really knows?

There isn't any doubt Mfume, a former congressman and city council member, is very talented. His excellent work as chair of the Black Caucus in the House of Representatives is especially recalled, but he's not necessarily a universally loved man. One distracter saw him as an "opportunist and windbag." He added Mfume was lucky to follow in the foot steps of a civil rights warrior, like the splendid Parren J. Mitchell, a former 14 term member of the congress from west Baltimore.

My guess is that Bell and Mfume will be the main contenders in the race for mayor. Bell simply can't afford to pass on the opportunity. In the mayoralty campaign, however, Mfume may learn that the city has changed while he was away glad-handing on the national stage. Not everyone is convinced that he's the greatest thing since apple pie.

Baltimoreans should stock up on their crab cakes and draft beer, it's going to be a long hot summer. Let the political fireworks begin!

# Chapter Five

## From the Land of Pleasant Living

### 44. Harry Roe Hughes: Maryland's Caretaker Governor
**November 20, 1986.**

After January 21, 1987, we won't have Harry Roe Hughes to kick around anymore. That's too bad. On that auspicious date, the "Age of William Donald Schaefer" officially begin. (God save the state.)

Harry has been our governor for eight years. It's true old Harry was awfully laid-back, and preferred to let problems solve themselves. This style of passive leadership was not without precedent, since Jimmy "Peanuts" Carter modeled it on a national scale, with disastrous results from 1976 to 1980.

Harry was a good, but not by any stretch of the imagination, a great governor. I am going to give him a "B-" grade for his assignment. He was honest, fair, soft-spoken, worked hard, smoked too many cigarettes, cared about the environment, and always conducted himself as a true gentleman.

Like President Carter, Harry never fully understood how to exercise the power of his high office for necessary political ends. It was like he had graduated *cum laude* from the Adali Stevenson, III, "Wimp School of Politicos."

As far as working to build up the local Democratic Party, forget it. He simply wasn't interested. The patronage game also completely eluded the poor fellow, and to his very last days as first citizen of the state, it remained a deep mystery to his psyche.

If only Harry had read Machiavelli, or was steeped in the memoirs of the great Cardinal Richelieu, or learned his politics at the knee of J. Millard Tawes, Willie Curran, Julian Carrick, or Jack Pollack. His record might have made more of a difference.

He deserves some blame, of course, for the costly Savings & Loan scandal, the simmering prison mess, the shaky competitive position of the port of Baltimore, and the mostly low morale of the faithful and unsung state employees.

I am talking about those thousands of faceless heroes of the bureaucracy, (teachers included), who actually run the machinery of government, and who were royally screwed out of their cost-of-living pension increases by the General Assembly (Mickey Steinberg, please copy).

But, there is one area where Harry is entitled to special kudos from the populace: his appointments to the judiciary. Almost without exception, Harry's many selections for the district, circuit and appellate courts have been excellent, and a credit to him, the justice system, and to the legal profession.

On another level, despite being highly photogenic, Harry never tried to usurp a colleague's photo opportunities by soft shoeing his way into the picture. For this small favor, the people must also be thankful to him. Especially after watching, *ad nauseam,* Sen. Paul S. Sarbanes on election night attempting to hug the spotlight with all the winning Democratic candidates. ( Why didn't someone just step on the senator's foot? It would have served him right.)

After a short dose of the temperamental Schafer's reign of pique, the people may yet yearn for the return of another Harry-like administration. Only time will tell.

It is possible, too, that after a couple of years of anonymity, Harry could make a fortune ending up in one of those American Express "Do You Know Me?" commercials.

Chances are that Harry will just probably fade away into the golden Eastern Shore sunset, and return to his familiar roots as a country lawyer from the sleepy towns of Denton and Easton.

Not a bad ending for a decent man, who will be mostly be remembered as the best kind of two-term caretaker governor.

Good-bye, Harry.

\*　　　　　\*　　　　　\*

# 45. The City Solicitor: George L. Russell, Jr
## August, 1984

"One of the true leaders of the Bar in the State of Maryland in the trial of criminal cases," is how the State's highly respected Public Defender, Allan Murrell, described the excellent reputation for advocacy of George L. Russell, Jr.

The fifty-five year old Russell, a native Baltimorean, has many firsts to his credit. He was the first black appointed to the Circuit Court by the governor; the first black appointed to the Baltimore Civic Center Commission; and, the first man of his race to hold the prestigious position of City Solicitor for Baltimore City (1968-1974).

"He brought a new dimension to policy-making in my administration," recalled former Mayor Thomas J. (The Younger) D'Alesandro.

"Some of my best years at the Bar were spent in the City Solicitor's office," said Russell. "The friends I made there; the comradery we shared; it just had to be the highlight of my legal career."

Although Russell lost to the present incumbent in a gallant bid for the mayoralty in 1978, political pundits gave him high marks for the campaign skills he demonstrated, and for the depths of his electoral following in both the black and white communities of Baltimore City.

Married to Marion Ann Russell, the former U.S. Army veteran (1954-1956) has one son, George, III.

On May 23, 1984, Russell received an Honorary Doctor of Laws degree from the University of Baltimore Law School, and he was also privileged to give the commencement address.

It is clearly within the realm of possibilities that this distinguished trial lawyer could be on the Democratic ballot in 1985 for the high office of Attorney General of Maryland.

He would certainly be fully qualified for that position, and an ideal choice for our citizenry.

*　　　　*　　　　*

# 46. Three Heroes of the African-American Community
## March, 1999

This article will be different from most on the subject of Black History Month.

First, it is from the perspective of a white man, who grew up in a segregated post-WWII Baltimore city; and second, it focuses on three exceptional African-Americans, who I have interviewed and admired over the years.

I believe that their lives have impacted on all Marylanders. The "Civil Rights Movement," that blossomed in the tumultuous 60s was a common theme propelling their storied achievements.

Let's begin with the late, great Henry Parks, Jr. In 1951, he took over an abandoned dairy in 1951, in northwest Baltimore and turned it into one of the biggest success stories in the history of Baltimore: the Parks Sausage Company. The bigoted idea that a black man couldn't compete in the corporate market place was smashed forever by his hard work. Parks' highly-professional "CEO" image also helped to facilitate his entry into local politics.

It was in the 60s, that his considerable talents crystallized to promote the civil rights agenda. Parks served two terms in the City Council from the 4th district. He deserves tremendous credit for spearheading the passage of some of that legislative body's more controversial civil rights laws.

No easy task under even the best of circumstances. Former Mayor Thomas J. D'Alesandro, Jr. praised him for his "solid leadership." Parks finished out his public career as the first African-American President of the City's Fire Board.

The second man I'd like to spotlight was Maryland's first African-American congressmen, Parren J. Mitchell. Beginning in 1970, he ably represented the sprawling 7th Congressional District for 14 terms. From a distinguished family long associated with the struggle of blacks for equal rights, he forged an identity all his own.

An unrepentant champion of human rights, Mitchell opposed America's involvement in the Vietnam War, the crime of *Apartheid* in South African, and British colonialism in the north of Ireland. He also supported the unshakable right of the Palestinian people to self-determination. His position on these controversial issues, and others, did not endear him to the Establishment.

Mitchell served in the Congress under four presidents; Richard Nixon, Gerald Ford, Jimmy Carter and Ronald Reagan. Of the four, he considered Reagan the most hostile to black aspirations. Mitchell was also one of the main driving forces, during this era of momentous social change, for federal legislation that pushed the national government to do more in the area of housing, health care, education and job creation.

Mitchell was then clearly the conscience of the Congress on civil rights. He was also seen by many as the "spiritual leader" of that same movement in the Baltimore area. I can't recall any significant protest action held here without the involvement of his dynamic leadership.

Although Civil Rights laws helped to break the chains of a segregated America, those rights had to be won in hard-fought court room battles.

Enter my third subject, Kenneth Lavon Johnson. In the 70s, he was victorious as an attorney in precedent-setting federal cases that exposed deeply-rooted governmental discrimination against blacks and women. Johnson was particularly successful in his mission to bring racial equality in hiring and promotional practices to the city's Police and Fire Departments.

A fierce advocate for his clients, he was elected, in 1982, as judge to the Circuit Court for Baltimore City. Johnson has served there, too, with great distinction, winning reelection to another 15 year term in 1998.

As African-Americans celebrate, with pride, "Black History Month," they will also recall their painful past. Blacks were originally brought to these shores as slaves in the bottom of British ships. In his seminal book,

*The Slave Trade,* author Hugh Thomas chronicled the miserable bartering in human lives that lasted for over four hundred years.

It is beyond cavil that the crime of black slavery is the greatest holocaust in all of recorded history.

Yet, out of that abyss of unspeakable suffering, descendants of African slaves, like Parks, Mitchell and Johnson, have contributed not only to their own race, but to an evolving, more fair, more democratic, American Republic.

All Marylanders are richer for their splendid accomplishments.

*       *       *

# 47. W. Gregory Halpin: "Mr. Port of Baltimore"
## December 27, 1982

For close to a quarter of a century, his name has been synonymous with the growth, development and promotion of the Port of Baltimore. Governor Harry Hughes says of him, "He is a talented administrator and has been a key factor in the development of the port of Baltimore as one of the finest in the world."

Since June of 1978, he has served as the leader of the Maryland Port Authority (MPA) after diligently working his way up through the ranks. He is W. Gregory Halpin, a native of Brooklyn, New York, who has rightfully earned the sobriquet of "Mr. Port of Baltimore."

"Let's face it," Halpin began, "this used to be nothing more than a railroad-dominated port. Ninety percent of the port facilities back in 1956-the wharves, docks, transit sheds, storage areas, you name it-were owned by the railroads. And, they didn't want to spend the necessary money to improve and develop those facilities. This is why the state had to step in and form the MPA. Today, we are truly, and I say this with some real sense of pride, 'a shipper's port.'"

The fiftyish, balding Halpin was literally present at the creation of the MPA. In 1959, the embryonic agency, in a Manhattan Island type of bargain, purchased from the City of Baltimore 365 acres of prime waterfront property located just southeast of the Broening Highway for a mere $4 million.

Former 6th District Councilman, Mike "Iron Mike" McHale sponsored the ordinance in the council. The site, then called, "Harbor Field," is now the central jewel of the MPA's vast domain, the sprawling Dundalk Marine Terminal. The Dundalk locale now embraces over 545 acres and is one of the largest container facilities of its kind in the world.

Between puffs on his pipe, Halpin glances out the window of his office on the 20th floor of the World Trade Center. The view is spectacular panorama of the southern portion of the city and the port. Halpin pensively adds, "I don't know what we would have done without the Dundalk facility.

"I think our takeover of the Locust Point and Clinton Street Marine Terminal and the changing of our tariff structures to guarantee equal access to both truck and rail service," Halpin continued, "were just some of our other significant innovations over the years."

Presently, over $250 million worth of facilities, including the World Trade Center, are owned or leased by the MPA. The agency employs some 500 personnel, with an annual operating budget of $22 million, including trade development specialists located throughout the United States, Europe and the Far East.

Sigmund Shapiro, a leading foreign freight forwarder in the port, shared this view of Halpin and the MPA. "The Port Authority does a terrific job, but the State of Maryland doesn't know it. Halpin is a very outspoken person and a great salesman. But the port does have its problems."

Bill Detweiler, the President of the Steamship Trade Association of Baltimore (an association of steamship, stevedore and port-related businesses), speaks well of Halpin. "Overall, I am very pleased with his stewardship of the MPA, and I feel that because of him personally there has been a closer liaison with the commercial interest in the port."

The elected leader of the roughly 5000 longshoremen, who work in the port, John Kopp, of the ILA, thinks Halpin "is doing a hell of a job, but I don't agree with his steep increase in the MPA charges for using their equipment and facilities, especially with the world economy being in the bad shape that it is." Detweiler also shares Kopp's reservations about the MPA's recent rate increases.

Halpin does have his critics. One unnamed, but reliable waterfront source, put his complaint this way, "Halpin is just a little bit too much, like Schaefer, too elitist in making decisions; too aloof; at other times; just too damn moody to suit my personal taste. But, of course, there has never been any question about his competency or integrity."

Another source, a stevedore executive, who requested anonymity, says, "I see only one flaw with Halpin's style of leadership and that is that the private sector hasn't been allowed any real input into the MPA's decision-making process. I would like to see that process made more public and to include the views of stevedores, agents, labor and even some kind of citizens' panel. There are just too many significant long range and costly planning decisions being made by the MPA, and I, like my colleagues, don't find out about it until after the fact."

But, Congresswoman Barbara A. Mikulski (D-3rd), an important member of the House subcommittee on Merchant Marine and Fisheries, sees Halpin's role in a more positive light. Mikulski praised Halpin and the MPA as "One of the few agencies to assign a direct liaison with my D.C. office. He has done everything for us from providing legislative advise on harbor dredging to helping arrange, on short notice, a special harbor tour of the port's coal handling facilities."

"We have come, since 1956, and $200 million in port development, from an obsolete to a modern port," Halpin pointed out. "We have created a genuine presence in the world," he added.

A well-circulated economic impact study of the port, prepared and published in March, 1982, by consultants Booz-Allen & Hamilton, showed that nearly 79,000 Maryland jobs are directly related to port activities. And, that in the year 1980, port activities generated $ 1.2 billion in revenues for its users and $1 billion in personal income for Maryland residents. Seventy-three million dollars in taxes were also provided to the state and local governments.

"Halpin has a deserved reputation as a successful advocate for the port industry. His opinion and advice are sought after by government decision-makers in Washington, D.C. I think Baltimore is very lucky to have such a talented administrator for its port," says Peter J. Gatti, counsel to the American Association of Port Authorities.

A noted maritime reporter for the *Journal of Commerce*, and long time MPA watcher, Bill Lalley, says this of Halpin, "He is a very strong administrator, well-versed in the day-to-day affairs of that agency. I think he deserves a lot of credit for picking up the reins of that operation at a critical time in its history and maintaining the port's competitive advantage, stimulating terminal construction, and expanding its trade development."

Halpin acknowledged that "We face strong competition for business from the land-bridge concept, Canadian diversion, and from the ports of the South Atlantic. And, we are still working to resolve the problem of finding funding to dredge our harbor to accommodate the large ore, grain and coal carrying ships of the future.

But the truth is," Halpin concluded, "we are the second largest port on the east coast. By the year 2050, we are prepared to double our present terminal capacity by adding acreage from Seagirt (at the foot of Clinton St. in Canton) and Masonville (Brooklyn) to our operations. I suppose our ultimate mark of success as state agency will be when we go out of business and our functions turned over entirely to the private sector."

\*　　　　　\*　　　　　\*

# 48. Michael Styer & Maryland Public Television June, 1985.

He created and produced many award winning and critically acclaimed programs for over eleven years on Maryland Public Television.

Michael Styer, a Lancaster, Pa. native, has had a fantastic career in both commercial and public television over the last two decades.

He presently serves as director of programming and operations for Md. Public TV, appointed to that post by its energetic executive director, Stephen H. Kimatian, in April, 1984.

"I love my work. I hope I can stay until I retire. It is the position that I have aspired to," says Styer.

The man whose talents sourced the celebrated "Critics' Place" program, Styer called the show, "a very important program.

And, at the time, the only concerted effort in television to do a regular, weekly review of what was going on in the arts, theatre, music and the movies.

Not many stations were willing to take on the expense to make that kind of effort."

Styer has also produced many programs for nationwide distribution by PBS including Diane Johnson's "An Apple, An Orange," Herman Melville's "Bartleby, the Scrivener" and Ring Larder's "A Day with Conrad Green" starring Fred Gwynne, and three music specials with the Baltimore Symphony Orchestra.

Currently, Styer is now producing sixteen specials on Maryland youth and five original dramas for our Maryland Playwrights Theatre.

I have always been a little communicator. Even in my own family," continued Styer, a noted amateur actor in Baltimore's thriving community theaters.

I liked to break the news of what was happening. I enjoy," concluded Styer, "being at the center of activity in an organization that is helping

people; communicating ideas, news, informing; presenting cultural entertainment; and providing good, quality educational projects."

*       *       *

*Author's Note-Michael Styer is presently the highly-respected director
of the Maryland Film Commission. He has done an outstanding job in
that capacity and he is known by the locals as, "Maryland's Mr.
Hollywood".

*       *       *

## 49. Steve Yeager's *On the Block* Film
## Dec. 5, 1990

On December 10,1990, Steve Yeager's first major feature film, *On The
Block*, will make its world premiere at the historic Senator Theatre on York
Road.

Yeager, a native Baltimorean, who grew up in Waverly, will be following
in the illustrious footsteps of other Baltimore film makers, like John
Waters' *Hairspray* and *Cry-Baby*, and Barry Levinson's *Diner*, *Tin Men*,
and *Avalon*. They both chose the Senator as a debut site for some of their
popular productions.

"Howard Rollins, Marilyn Jones, and Blaze Starr will all be there,"
Yeager predicted proudly. "I couldn't have made the movie without them,
especially Rollins. He was the key." Rollins was an Academy Award nomi-
nee for *Ragtime* and is a co-star of the hit television series, "In The Heat of
The Night."

Yeager continued, "Howard has been terrific to me. We go back almost
20 years now, to the local Spotlighter Theatre, where I directed him in his
first play. Once I got Rollins committed to do this film, with his wide

name recognition and acting reputation in the industry, the backers showed up for the project."

*On the Block* has been four years in the making. It centers on downtown Baltimore's infamous red-light district of clubs and striptease joints, located within the shadow of the central police station and City Hall. To devotees of the noir world of neon lights and burlesque queens, it has always been known simply as "The Block."

The focus of the fast-moving plot is a triangular love relationship between a stripper named "Libby", a manic-depressive vice squad lieutenant with a murderous obsession, and Libby's rescuer, a Block outcast.

The Block's subculture of prostitutes, pimps, porno sex shops, quickie sex for sale, hard-boiled club owners, gamblers, loan sharks, and deep-pocket customers looking for a "good time" for a price, are highlighted in the flick.

Blaze Starr, a noted burlesque stripper, plays herself in the movie. She made her reputation as a dancer at the "2 O'Clock Club," one of the Block's most famous emporiums. Later she became one of the club's owners. Star has since retired from the business-a genuine legend in her own time.

"The movie was shot entirely on location," according to Yeager. "We used real Block people and professional actors. The local characters gave it just the right flavor. I wanted everything as authentic as possible. We shot in the night clubs, the "Mission House" for the destitute, the sex bookstore, and at the police station. Some of the lead actors actually researched their parts by spending some time in the strip joint milieu before we began filming."

What inspired Yeager?

"Vittorio DeSica and Roberto Rossellini were two of my favorite film directors. They both belonged to what is known as the 'Italian Neo-Realistic Movement.' That school of film making is defined as 'a concern for people, a use of natural settings and types, with an overwhelming sense of looking at life like it really is.'"

"DeSica had made *Bicycle Thief* and *Shoeshine*, and Rossellini created the memorable *Open City*," Yeager went on.

"I wanted an honest portrayal of the Block and its inhabitants, so I chose to follow the Italian *genre* of film making. I am glad that I did. My movie makes no moral judgment of the characters, their lifestyles, or even of the Block itself, which I admit has a pretty shady rep. The sisterhood and camaraderie of the strippers, however, does come through."

The cable rights to *On the Block* have been sold, along with cassette rights, to H.B.O. The domestic theatrical rights are still being negotiated, although Yeager expects the movie to hit the art circuit first. Locally, that would be places, like the Charles, Key and Towson theaters.

Yeager says there is no sex in the movie, but there is some frontal nudity, and the language is a little rough. He expects an "R" rating for the film.

Yeager, a conscientious student of the art of film making, has labored in the film/video/theatre industry for over fifteen years as a director, editor, cinematographer, and producer. At 40, his work in the realm of industrials, documentaries, and commercials has been well respected for its consistently high levels of artistic achievement.

He has received many honors along the way. In 1982, he won a grand prize for "Best Documentary" at the Houston International Film Festival for *Aquarium*, which was shot at the National Aquarium in Baltimore.

In 1983, he won the Labor Film Festival for *One Voice*, a documentary about early labor practices at Bethlehem Steel.

And, in 1986, Yeager won acclaim from the New York Film and TV Festival for his local spot for *Mary Catherine*, dealing with the Johns Hopkins Children's Cancer Center.

Yeager was quick to credit Linda Chambers for her co-contribution to the screenplay of his new movie, and for her work as an associate producer. The director of photography was Erich Roland, who was also the photography director of the award-winning documentary, *Johnstown*.

Roland was behind the camera on *Clara's Heart, Her Alibi*, and *Driving Miss Daisy.*

Yeager said Roland is a "real artisan." He also had special praise for the actor Robert Redford for his support of the "Sundance Institute," located at Park City, Utah.

Yeager called Sundance "the biggest supporter of independent filmmaking in the country." He added, "Redford is a class act. Few people realize how unassuming this guy is, and the fact that he is making a continuing major contribution to the industry. Sundance has been a big help to my career."

Yeager also paid special tribute to Dick Gillespie, the longtime head of the drama department at Towson State University, from which Yeager received his B.A. in Theatre, in 1960. "Dick Gillespie has been one of the most influential men in my life. He has been my mentor. He has seen all my films and plays."

With such deep roots in the Baltimore community, it seems fitting that Yeager chose the 51-year-old Senator Theatre for his premiere. The 900-seat house, with its fabulous marquee, was built in the classic "Art Deco" style by Frank Durkee, Sr. According to one of its present owners, Tom Kiefaber, it has just been honored by being named to the National Register of Historic Places.

Kiefaber says he has reviewed Yeager's film, and calls it, "quite an achievement." Of the December 10th opening, he says, "It will be a gala Hollywood-styled evening, with all the exciting, fun trimmings. There will be mammoth search lights outside the theatre, limousine service for the stars of the movie, an unveiling ceremony of the handprint-impressed cement block, the presence of local media and political celebrities, and a big bash at the Belvedere Hotel after the screening."

The United Way of Central Maryland, according to Yeager, will be the beneficiary of proceeds from the festivities.

*      *      *

*Author's Note-In the film, *On the Block*, I played the part of Barney, a pub owner. It was my first day player role as a member of the Screen Actors Guild (SAG).

## 50. Delegate Tim Murphy: Lawmaker/Jurist
May, 1984

The grandson of a County Cork, Ireland, barman, Tim Murphy, at age 34, is a member of the Baltimore City Council from the sprawling south-side, blue-collar 6th district.

The 1972 Johns Hopkins graduate was appointed to the Council in March of 1982, and quickly gained a solid reputation for himself as being a hard-working, diligent and creative lawmaker while chairing the important Budget and Finance Committee.

"I am most proud of the work I did in the last session on passing the pension supplement Bills Nos. 1478 and 1479, that aided the retirees and widows and widowers of our municipal, fire and police systems," said Councilman Murphy.

An attorney, Murphy has been carefully nutured along the clubhouse political route by the savvy boss of the city's 19th Ward, the plucky ex-Councilman, John J. Hines.

Councilman Murphy, a southwest Baltimore resident, was an alternate delegate to the 1984 Democratic Convention in San Francisco, and from 1978-1982, he served with distinction as the Chairman of the Baltimore City Democratic Central Committee.

In 1986, the speculation is that Congresswoman Barbara A. Mikulski (3rd D.) will seek a seat in the U.S. Senate. If that happens, Murphy would be in an excellent position to make a race for that coveted federal office.

With strong political, maritime and labor connections; on hands legislative experience; and impeccable educational and intellectual credentials;

Murphy could become the first congressman from South Baltimore in this century.

\*            \*            \*

\*Author's Note-Tim Murphy was a member of the Maryland House of Delegates from the 47th District. In the spring of 1993, he was the Chairman of the Budget and Finance Committee of the Baltimore City Council.

It was in that important role that Murphy championed the passage of the "MacBride Principles Bill" through the Council by a unanimous vote of that body. In May, 1993, the Bill was signed into law by his honor, Mayor Kurt Schmoke. It is beyond dispute that Murphy's strong support, along with Councilman Martin O'Malley's (now mayor of Baltimore), along with other key council members, was critical to the success of that legislation.

On Jan. 20, 1999, Murphy was appointed a judge on the District Court of Baltimore City, where he presently resides, by Governor Parris N. Glendening,

\*            \*            \*

# 51. Alan Murrell: A Giant of the Maryland Bar
## May, 1984

The son of a celebrated English sea captain, Alan Murrell was born in the sleepy Welch town of Barry, Wales.

His father, Frederick H. Murrell, won worldwide acclaim and honors in 1887, for leading the gallant rescue of all the passengers on a distressed Danish vessel off the Azores islands.

Since January, 1972, Murrell has served with great distinction as the appointed "Public Defender" for the State of Maryland. He is charged with the heavy responsibility of representing in criminal cases all indigent state defendants.

"It is the challenge," began Murrell, "that brought me to the criminal law practice. You are dealing with someone, a defendant, who needs help, and who is looking to his attorney to see to it that he gets a fair trial. You have to be professional."

In trying more than one hundred murder cases, Murrell has never had a defendant sentenced to death.

His two most memorable victories, prior to becoming Public Defender, involved the acquittal of a Anne Arundel County magistrate on bribery charges and of an Annapolis socialite on a 1st degree murder charge.

There can be no doubt that Murrell has created a state agency that has truly become a professional advocate for the indigent defendant.

Over the last hundred years, the Maryland Bar has produced some outstanding lawyers like a Roger Taney, Luther Martin, Harry Lord, Foster Fanseen, Steve Sachs, Patrick O'Doherty and Arnold Weiner.

Alan Murrell, at the peak of his legal career, is yet another example of such magnificent excellence.

*          *          *

## 52. Ed Hale: A CEO on the Rise
### May, 1984

"State-of-the-Art," is how Ed Hale describes the service performed by his container carrier firm, Port East Transfer, Inc. In just nine years, Hale's trucking company has mushroomed from transporting a mere 2,000 containers a year to over 50,000.

The success story of the 37 years-old Baltimore County native sounds like a page out of Horatio Alger primer.

"I just enjoy building a good, competitive service," added Hale. "In 1984, we will continue to expand," he prophesizes," and last year our sales totaled $10 million."

Presently, Port East, headquartered in Baltimore, employs 212 people, operates 13 terminals with a fleet of 150 trucks, and services shippers in every port east of the Mississippi and 34 states from Maine to Texas.

Hale is a definite throwback to the daring entrepreneur of over a century ago in this nation. He has fully computerized his operations, and his entire top management team possess business as well as trucking skills.

In 1975 when Hale embarked on his gutsy endeavor, the trucking industry was severely depressed. But, Hale saw a "need for an on-demand carrier to handle local drayage in and around Baltimore City."

The vision of the young man from Edgemere has become a reality, and today, Ed Hale owns a trucking company that is one of the fastest growing on the east coast of the United States.

*  *  *

Author's Note-In 1991, Hale, a Dundalk native, spread out into banking. He is now the chairman of the board of First Mariner Bankcorp, which has assets of close to $260 million and 16 branches located throughout Maryland.

*  *  *

## 53. Tom Hall & The Choral Arts Society
### May, 1984

At age twenty-eight, Tom Hall is the talented Music Director of the Baltimore Choral Arts Society which performs a wide repertoire of choral music.

Stuart Low, of *The Sun,* described his debut at a Goucher College concert in November, 1982, as "brilliant."

"Great art is nothing more than great ideas," began Hall, a New Jersey native who received his Bachelor of Music, *magna cum laude*, from Ithaca College and his Master of Music from Boston University.

Now, a Baltimore City resident, Hall strongly believes that classical music should be made more accessible to the general public, and that listening to live music can make a spiritual contribution to people's lives.

"Art is a fundamental pursuit, not ancillary to life, and it shouldn't be just a fringe thing for the people," he emphasized.

Hall helped prepare the chorus which participated in legendary conductor Leonard Bernstein's moving rendition of Mahler's "Resurrection" at the celebrated "Concert for Peace," held at the Washington Cathedral on January 8,1984.

"The human feeling was manifested at that concert. When the chorus sung *Augersteh'n*, 'Rise-Up', Hall concluded, it meant to me that there is, indeed, hope for mankind."

*       *       *

## 54. Ethel Ennis: Baltimore's Celebrated Vocalist
## May, 1984

"All these things that are happening to me now," says acclaimed vocalist Ethel Ennis, they are like the new birth."

Ennis is going through an exciting career renaissance that mirrors the changes taking place in her native Baltimore.

In June of this year, the self-described "progressive pop singer" will be opening her new restaurant and cabaret, "Ethel's Place," in the heart of the emerging cultural corridor of the city on the corners of Preston and Cathedral Streets.

In addition, a pictorial book on her life and times by local photographer, Sallie Kravetz, is due for release.

"I want 'Ethel's Place' to be kind of an embassy," continued Ennis," and, I am thrilled to have someone tell my life story the way I am and not the image they were trying to make me into. There are happier days ahead and everybody is going to feel it," concluded Ennis, a person of strong faith and vision.

From the fabled "Red Fox" bar on old Pennsylvania Avenue, to singing at the White House for two presidents; and after performing for ten years at the Maryland Inn in Annapolis; Ethel Ennis, a municipal treasure of musical quality, is coming home again.

\*           \*           \*

## 55. Mayor Thomas J. D'Alesandro, III: He Won the Day
### October, 1984

"I held at the goal line," began former Mayor Thomas J. D'Alesandro, III, in speaking of his tenure of office (1967-1971) during one of the most difficult crisises in the history of the municipality.

In April, 1968, urban America, including Baltimore City, exploded in a whirlpool of riotous civil strife that brought the city near total collapse.

Some of the over 250 cities nationally that suffered disorders, like Newark, have never fully recovered from the frightening ordeal.

"Baltimore bounced back with renewed vigor," continued D'alesandro with pride. The 55 year-old native of "Little Italy" gave special credit to his strong Cabinet that included men of exceptional courage and quality like: Robert Embry, Frances D. Murnaghan, Jr., (now a distinguished Judge of the 4th Circuit Federal Court of Appeals), W. Pierce Lineaweaver, George L. Russell, Jr., and the Police Commissioner Donald Pomerleau.

"I also had a very cooperative City Council," continued D'Alesandro, "and we were able to make the transition from the old to the new city, despite the tumultuous times that we were all living in."

For the past 14 years, D'Alesandro has been in the private practice of law with his long time associate, Jacob Milliman.

History will indeed record that not only did D'Alesandro make an heroic stand at the goal line for old

Baltimore, in April, 1968, but that he also, and even more importantly, won the day!

\*             \*             \*

## 56. Louie Goldstein: Comptroller *Par Excellence*
### January, 1985

My philosophy as to public service," says the eight term State Comptroller, Louis "Louie" L. Goldstein, "is to give a 100 percent effort and to offer a capital R.AS.- that is 'Recognition, Affection, and Security' to all the citizens and taxpayers of Maryland."

Goldstein, in a remarkable political career, has become part of the honored Free State's folklore. In fact, the General Assembly recently named the state's treasury building after him.

The Calvert County native lives on a rambling 600 acre estate, near Prince Frederick, called "Oakland Hall," with his wife, Hazel, and three children.

An innovative comptroller, Goldstein has insisted on competitive bidding on all state contracts, the placement of reserve state funds in interest-bearing accounts, and his was the first state agency to fully computerize its operations.

In 1938, Goldstein was elected as a delegate from Calvert County. He eventually moved over to the Senate, and even served a term as president of that prestigious body.

The World War II marine veteran has also been a delegate to the last nine national Democratic Conventions.

His only political defeat was suffered in the Democratic primary for the US. Senate in 1964 to young Joe Tydings.

Goldstein in 1972 won statewide office by over 342,000 votes and carried every county and Baltimore City.

The "God bless you all-real good" politico has made the "country boy" image almost unbeatable at the polling places.

"I am now serving as comptroller. But, the people are always asking me," Goldstein concluded, "to make the race for governor in '86, My goal is to continue to serve the people in whatever capacity they desire."

*       *       *

# 57. Mayor Theodore R. McKeldin: A Baltimore Original
## January, 1985

In the modern era, he was beyond dispute the State of Maryland's greatest political leader.

Theodore R. McKeldin (1900-1974) was twice mayor of the City of Baltimore (1943-1947)-(1963-1967), and twice distinguished governor of the State (1951-1958).

His earliest ambition was to study for the ministry. He claimed he was always "a frustrated evangelist."

Grandson of a Belfast, Ireland immigrant, who escaped from "the Great Famine of 1845," McKeldin grew up in South Baltimore at the corners of Ostend (then Stockholm) and Eutaw Streets. One of eleven children of a foot policeman. James A. McKeldin, he turned towards the law and also developed skills as a professional orator.

A Republican, he gained wide attention as the "Boy Orator of the GOP."

A courageous fighter for "Civil Rights," McKeldin was also a staunch defender of the young State of Israel. It was McKeldin who first launched the "Inner Harbor Redevelopment Program."

Friendship Airport, Liberty Dam and the Civic Center were other projects completed under his dynamic leadership, that always respected the democratic process and the right of dissent.

In 1952, at the Republican National Convention in Chicago. McKeldin was granted the high honor to nominate General Dwight D. Eisenhower for President.

For over forty years, McKeldin was closely associated with political kingmaker, the late M. William Adelson of Baltimore.

McKeldin could always be seen wearing a plastic, "Black-eyed Susan" in his coat lapel.

*   *   *

## 58. Judge John C. Byrnes: One of the Best
**August, 1984**

For over ten years, he served as a State Senator from Northeast Baltimore and earned for himself a reputation as a reform-styled politician.

Although some political insiders and muldoon clubhouse types considered John C. Byrnes a "politician dilettante," the weight of the evidence shows that he has had a praiseworthy career in both the law and in the Maryland legislature.

During the seventies, Byrnes served as the Chairman of the Ethics Committee of the Maryland Democratic Party.

In February of 1982, Byrnes was appointed as an Associate Judge of the Circuit Court of Baltimore City by Governor Harry Hughes.

In November, 1982, he won election, in a bitterly fought battle, to a full 15 year term on the Bench. Two other judicial incumbents, unfortunately, lost their seats in that brawl-like contest.

In recently addressing the problem of chronic juvenile crime, Judge Byrnes told the City's Grand Jury, "whole generations of young people are growing up in this country without any ethical sense of behavior."

The jurist has also expressed his deep concern about "the widespread availability of obscene and pornographic material in the city."

The Homeland resident is married to the former Helen Zimmerman McClausland and they have three children.

His father, the late Joseph R. Byrnes, was also a Circuit Judge in Baltimore, and a former President of the Maryland State Senate.

Respected by his colleagues on the Bench, and the Trial Bar, as a "hard-working, fair-minded trier of facts," Judge John C. Byrnes can be counted on by Baltimoreans to serve out his term of office in keeping with the highest traditions of the state's judiciary.

*       *       *

*Author's Note-On January 4, 2002, the State's Attorney for Baltimore City said she wouldn't appeal a decision made by Judge John Carroll Byrnes to free inmate Michael Austin. He had spent 27 years in prison on a faulty murder charge. Judge Byrnes had ruled in late December, 2001, after a full evidentiary hearing, and on the merits, that Austin's original criminal trial was "plagued by errors."

## 59. Helen Delich Bentley Fights for the Port
### April 14, 1999

What are the port's chances of winning a potentially huge shipping deal offered by Maersk Inc. and Sea-Land Services Inc.? Former Congresswomen Helen Delich Bentley says, "I can tell you that Baltimore is definitely in the running."

She is a consultant to the Maryland Port Administration, ex-chairperson of the Federal Maritime Commission, and also a long time advocate of local maritime interests.

At press time, the two shipping giants, Maersk and Sea-Land, presently located in Elizabeth, New Jersey, are considering whether to move south to Baltimore, head further north, or just stay put. They have announced that they want to build a new terminal somewhere in the Northeast shipping corridor. One cost estimate for such a project ran as high as $200 million. Maryland Governor Parris Glendening is on record supporting Baltimore's efforts to get the lucrative contract.

The good news for Baltimore is that politics and public funding are making the possibility of the two firms staying in the New York area a little sticky at the moment. New York's Governor George Pataki, a moderate Republican, and Christine Whitman, Governor of New Jersey, who is on the right fringe of her party, must both agree on an economic strategy to keep the shipping firms. The Port Authority is a bi-state operation of New York and New Jersey.

Its big revenue winners are its airports, like Kennedy, La Guardia and Newark, while its marine terminals usually run in the red ink. Recent figures indicate a deficit last year of $29.8 million for its terminal operations in Newark, Elizabeth, Brooklyn and on Staten Island.

In addition, a new port terminal in New York or New Jersey would mean additional and expensive dredging costs, along with the anticipated delays for obtaining federal permits and meeting the always difficult environmental guidelines.

A comparable Baltimore's operation, however, would probably need little dredging, but, if it were required, there is already an ongoing dredging project not too far from the Dundalk facility.

New York's Pataki wants to carefully consider all the pros and cons of the proposition, especially the bottom line. Whitman, on the other hand, models herself after the UK's Margaret Thatcher and is looking "to do a deal" and is ready to give the store away with incentives.

One insider speculated that she may attempt to use this situation "to upstage Pataki" as she did by appearing on April 12, at a union sponsored rally at the World Trade Center. Pataki, according to the *New York Post*, (April 13), has threatened to veto any deal unless a revised Port Authority gives him control "over cash-rich city airports."

Pataki has been mentioned as a possible vice-presidential candidate on the ticket of Texas Governor George W. Bush. Whitman is positioning herself to run for one of New Jersey's seats in the U.S. Senate. Her neoconservative politics finds her close to Steve Forbes, another announced Republican presidential candidate. In a volatile election year, politicos, tend to put their self interest before party unity.

Bentley believes the Dundalk Marine Terminal is the perfect spot for the shipping firms to relocate. The terminal, she underscored, in an April 12 interview, is a good one, but "it's over 40 years old now," and it is long overdue for some "serious refurbishing."

She sees any major improvements or additions to the Dundalk facility as simply part of keeping up with the competition. Bentley concedes that some of the railroad tracks in Baltimore are a problem, from either being too crowded or lacking height clearance, but that it's the kind of problem that can be taken care of quickly.

She praised the local private port interests and state officials for keeping Baltimore a first rate enterprise. Bentley says that overall the port is "doing very well," and that its cargo handling and gross tonnage numbers are up, and its movement of automobiles "leads the nation."

One New York maritime official told me that the Maersk/Sea Land combine presently brings in "over thirty percent" of that port's business. If that is an accurate assessment, then you can see why powerful New York waterfront interests would be very anxious to keep them home, and why Baltimore, or some other lucky port, would want to them to change locations.

There is obviously a lot at stake in successfully closing this important megadeal, especially for the future of the port of Baltimore.

Bentley concluded the decision could be made "at any time" and that she rates the Port's chances "as good."

*          *          *

*Author's Note-New York and New Jersey won out in the above port contract competition, but that didn't take anything away from the great efforts put out by Bentley on Baltimore's behalf. She served, with great distinction, in the House of Representatives for five term from Baltimore County. Bentley is a Republican and was also a former chairperson of the Federal Maritime Commission under President Richard Nixon. Earlier in her fabulous career, she was a maritime reporter for the *Baltimore Sun,* and produced a long running, and award-winning, television program entitled, "The Port that Built a City and State."

*          *          *

# 60. State Sen. George W. Della, Jr. : A Baltimore Legend
## August 19, 1982

In a ringing editorial, the *Baltimore Morning Sunpapers,* said of his City Council duties that, "He puts in more hard hours of work on citywide matters than any of his colleagues." His name has been synonymous with the politics of South Baltimore for over four decades.

For the last three years, he has served from the 6th Councilmanic District as chairman of the powerful Budget and Finance committee.

He is George W. Della, Jr. and he has been in the City Council for six years. He led the ticket in his 1979 in his bid for a full term.

At the age of 39, Della is ready to embark on a new career as a state senator from the 47th legislative district. He will replace his friend and mentor, the legendary Harry J. McGuirk, who is presently in a battle with Harry Hughes for the high office of governor.

"To tell you the truth," Della said. "I have been running for the state senate for over nine years. I expect to win this time and I will exercise my very best efforts to protect the interest of this city in Annapolis.

With veteran senators, like McGuirk, John Byrnes and Joe Curran leaving the senate, the city is going to need all the help it can get," he added.

"My father was president of the State Senate for 12 years," he continued," and served in that august body for 24 years. Someday, I would like to be president of the State Senate, too, just like my dad. But, in my first senate term, I would be satisfied with a good committee chairmanship, where I can look out for south Baltimore, the port, and the municipality."

Married to the former Beth Otter, Della is also proud of his work in city government. He emphasized, "In my three years as chairman of the Budget and Finance committee, there was an unprecedented reduction of the real estate tax rate for each fiscal year."

One of three children of ex-state senator, George W. Della, Sr., and the former Agnes H. Mattare, Della says, "My role models and political heroes, in addition to my father, were the likes of Franklin Delano Roosevelt, (a/k/a FDR), and Harry S. Truman, especially FDR. He was such a great action man. FDR knew how to cut the bureaucratic red tape and in his first 100 days in office, he got the country moving again."

Della concluded by saying that it was his unshakable conviction that, "Harry McGuirk is going to win. His candidacy Is being well-received in all areas of this state and he will make a great governor."

Della's opponent in the democratic primary is political unknown Robert B. Lewis.

The Della name has spelled power and success in local clubhouse politics. History has a tendency to repeat itself. The dream of the son can become the reality of the present.

Della, in the tradition of "Bib" Hodges, Dominic Leone, Mike McHale, Bill Hudnet, John Hines and Tom Fallon has been an outstanding city councilman for South Baltimore.

The state senate is Della's next forum. The people can be assured of strong, effective representation for the next four years. George W. Della, knows how to get the job done.

*      *      *

*Author's Note-George Della was victorious in 1982, in his race for the State Senate. He continues to this date to serve the people of South Baltimore, with skill and integrity, from the 47th Legislative District.

# Chapter Six

## Sports Icons & Stories, too

### 61. "The Greatest NFL Game," Colts Vs. New York Giants
**December, 1998**

In December,1958, I was working on the Baltimore docks as a long-shoreman for the Alcoa Steamship Co. I was living in Locust Point and was a Colts fan right from the start. Like many from the south side, I was excited about the upcoming championship game against the Giants. After a very good 1957 season, the Colts looked like the real thing in '58, with John Unitas, Lenny Moore, and Raymond Berry having banner years.

It may be difficult for pro sports fans of this era to realize with the megabucks Orioles' Camden Yards facility and Ravens' stadium, but back in the late 50s, Baltimore was considered a hick town.

In fact, it was boring, too.

There was no "Harborplace," National Aquarium, Meyerhoff Symphony Hall, Morris Mechanic Theatre, Center Stage, or $800 million subway system to be found. This was also long before the "Do-It-Now Mayor," the incomparable William Donald Schaefer, arrived on the municipal scene to do his unique version of urban renewal.

That other great attraction, "Fells Point," wasn't even on the tourist map. Then, it was just a run down neighborhood, featuring decaying warehouses and pot-hole-filled streets, drunks, and sleazy pubs, that even "Elvis" wouldn't be found dead in.

Although, the city has just gotten a new major league baseball franchise, (thanks to the herculean efforts of then-Mayor Thommy "The Elder" D'Alesandro), the no-names Orioles were a pathetic joke. In short, in 1958, Baltimore City was a "loser."

My unchecked enthusiasm, however, at age 21, led me to buy two tickets for the contest and to take my Highlandtown girlfriend with me. The tickets cost $4 each! Today, $4 might get you a large beer at a Ravens game, but not much more. The *Baltimore Sun*, ran a photo of some of us lucky fans lining up at Memorial Stadium on 33rd Street to buy the Colts/Giant ducats. I was thrilled to see my mug in it.

I was looking forward to driving to New York for the game, my first trip there, but decided at the last minute to take a train from Penn Station. We left early that morning, Sunday, Dec. 28, and were lucky to get a seat. It was very crowded.

After arriving in New York, we took the subway to the Bronx and to fabled "Yankee Stadium". I had a rush of adrenalin when I first sighted that legendary arena, a/k/a, "The House that Ruth Built."

When we got to our seats, the usher politely wiped them off and then stuck out his hand. I thought to myself, "He wants to welcome me to New

York by shaking my hand." I quickly found out by the look on his frowning face that he wanted a (gasp) tip! Under coercion, I gave him a quarter.

I was pleased to see other southsiders at the event, like John "Hopit" Haspert, Emmet Prenger, and Eli Burkum. Soon, after the game started, I got another jolt from the New Yorkers. When we would stand to cheer for the Colts,the locals would invariably yell at us in a loud mocking voice, "Sit down you farmers!" I had never thought of my self as being a farmer, although my late mother, Nora Thornton, was raised on a farm in the west of Ireland.

I'll leave the actual description of the rightly-labeled "Greatest Game" to the sport writers. My memories of it, however, will forever center around the dramatic final touchdown run by Alan "The Horse" Ameche, the pinpoint passing of quarterback Unitas, and the record breaking 12 receptions by the end Berry.

The train ride back to Baltimore was a special trip unto itself. The happy Baltimore fans were at a "Mach-3" level of unbridled celebration. Some of them were carrying parts of the goal post with them, others could barely walk to their seats from having one-beer-too many. It was a party train like no other. It lasted right through to our landing at Penn Station and spilled out into the joyful night on to Charles Street.

I felt then as I still feel today, that the victory by the Colts over the Giants, on that memorable day, by a score of 23-17, in the first NFL televised overtime championship game, placed the city in the pantheon of pro sports towns.

The Colts' victory also proved to me, and to many others of my generation, that Baltimore City was a winner, too!

∗       ∗       ∗

## 62. Remembering Sports Writer, John F. Steadman
## March, 2001

John F. Steadman was a popular sports writer in Baltimore for nearly fifty years. He died at the age of 73, on Jan. 1, 2001.

Steadman started his career as a journalist with the old *Baltimore News-Post* and ended it with the *Baltimore Sun*. I personally thought he was a very good writer in that *genre*, but not a great one.

He was too much of a "homer" to be a great writer.

Politically, Steadman came off as a reactionary to me. For example, I remember him marching in a union-sponsored parade, back in the '70s, in down town Baltimore, to support the Vietnam War and Richard Nixon's and Henry Kissinger's hawkish and blood-stained policies.

The sinister Kissinger, unfortunately, for our country is America's Iago. I was appalled to see Steadman in that pro-war demonstration.

Steadman also had an annoying habit of criticizing, in print, with little or no probative evidence to support it, the cause of Irish freedom. That kind of pro-Tory editorializing would quickly cause by temperature to rise about 100 degrees in 5 seconds flat.

Yet, at his funeral mass, a Celtic cross was proudly displaced on the front of the church funeral mass program, along with an Irish saying on its back. Go figure!

Steadman also hurt himself with me, and others, too, by his blind "hatred" for Bob Irsay (see, the *Boston Globe's* Will McDonough's comments on Steadman in the *Baltimore Sun*, 01/27/01). I think history has given the late Irsay, a former owner of the Baltimore Colts, who took the team to Indianapolis, a bum rap.

And, Steadman, more than anyone else in Baltimore, was responsible for driving him out of town and for demonizing the persona of that poor devil. I think Steadman, over time, had crossed the line as a journalist and he simply over identified with the Colts.

Here's a question for all of the Bob Irsay haters out there in Charm City: "What is the difference between what Irsay did to Baltimore and Art Modell did to Cleveland?" If there is a difference, I would like to know exactly what it is.

Saying all of that, however, Steadman still deserves sincere recognition for being a very good sports writer and a decent and honest fellow. He was a member, too, of the National Sportswriters and Sportscasters Hall of Fame, no small accomplishment. And, from all accounts, he was a "good" Catholic man.

His funeral mass was held at St. Jude's Shrine on Paca St. in Baltimore, on Jan. 5, 2001, and it was attended by many sports figures, local politicos, and loyal friends of the deceased.

Although, Gregory Kane of the *Sun* did point out in his column (01/28/01), by way of comparison, that the late Augie Waibel's funeral, (He was a popular coach for many years at Poly H.S.), who died on Jan. 6, 2001, had a much bigger turnout, then did attend Steadman's.

The beloved sports scribe was buried at New Cathedral Cemetery, out on Frederick Road, where tradition says, many of the good Baltimore Irish are finally laid to rest.

May his soul rest in eternal peace. Steadman's many virtues, I'm confident, far outweighed his few, but minor, faults.

*          *          *

# 63. Babe Ruth: A Baseball Immortal
## January, 1985

"The greatest figure the world of sports has ever known has passed from the field. Game called on account of darkness. Babe Ruth is dead."

So wrote the dean of American sports writers, Grantland Rice, on August 17, 1948, on the death of the mighty Ruth.

George Herman "Babe" Ruth was a Baltimore original and her greatest son in the domain of sports. He was born in 1894, at 600 West Pratt Street, one of eight children.

His parents were both of sturdy German stock. His father owned a saloon at 426 W Camden Street, and Ruth's earliest years were spent living above that emporium.

Discovered by the legendary Jack Dunn, owner of the Orioles in 1914, Ruth was soon on his way to baseball immortality; first with the Boston Red Sox as a great pitcher, and then in a sensational 22- year career as a slugging outfielder with the New York Yankees, where he amassed a total of 76 records, many of which stand to this very day.

He was the "Battering Bambino" and the "King of Swat." Lifetime he hit 708 homers, and once knocked-out 60 home runs in one season. He also struck out 1,330 times.

Hollywood made a movie of his life in 1948 called "The Babe Ruth Story," starring the late actor, William Bendix.

In February, 1983, a stamp was issued in his honor.

Thanks to the vision and courage of the late civic leader Howard Owens, and former Mayor Thomas J. D'Alesandro, Ill, a memorial and museum for Ruth was begun at 216 Emory Street, one half-block south of his original birthplace, in 1968.

Today, Babe Ruth's Birthplace is a major tourist attraction for visitors to Baltimore.

          *                   *                  *

## 64. Bob Williams: All American Quarterback
### May, 1984

"Football has meant a lot to me. Notre Dame is a magic word. It opened a lot of doors for me," began Bob Williams, former All-American quarterback on Frank Leahy's outstanding 1949 national championship team, and now a very successful business executive in the greater Baltimore community.

Williams, a Towson resident, was so highly regarded for his football prowess for the "Fighting Irish," that he was nominated for the celebrated Heisman Memorial Trophy; finishing in 5th place in 1949, and in the 6th position in 1950.

During the early fifties, Williams played quarterback for three years in the National Football League for the Chicago Bears, under the tuleage of another fabled pigskin character, the late George Halas.

"Mr. Halas was very tough coach, recalled Williams fondly, "and loyal to old friends, almost to a fault."

Educated by the Jesuits at Loyola High School, Williams has gracefully made the transition from the transient glory of the sports world, to the more enduring field of high finance, as President of one of Maryland's most respected and growing institutions—Harbor Federal Savings and Loan Association.

"Harbor Federal, with five branches in the metropolitan area, has been in the top ten percent of profit-makers in the industry," concluded the hard-working Williams, and I feel very fortunate to be where I am."

*　　　　*　　　　*

# 65. Bob Irsay: Live and Let Die
## February 5, 1997

Bob Irsay, a self-made millionaire, devout Catholic, loving father and devoted husband, and former owner of the Baltimore/Indianapolis Colts, died recently at the age of 73.

His last years were spent gallantly fighting off a very serious illness. Published reports indicated Irsay had suffer a stroke that made his final days both difficult and painful.

None of this seemed to matter to his half-baked critics, most of them unable or unworthy to hold this fine man's jockstrap. Irsay had accomplished more in his lifetime as an entrepreneur than most of them could in several lifetimes. Ignoring the admonition of the great Romans to speak only good of the dead, these mealy-mouth wise guys, mostly from the media class, gleefully stomped on his dead corpse.

Shame on them.

After moving the Colts to Indianapolis in 1984, Irsay became one the most maligned people in sports history. Leading the charge against him, before and after he left town, was that pompous ass, John Steadman.

In spite-filled columns, he regularly hacked away at Irsay's persona from the sport pages of the *Baltimore Evening Sun,* and later, *The Baltimore Sun.* As far as Steadman was concerned, Irsay couldn't do anything right as the owner of the Colts. No cheap shot was beyond this blow-hard.

Steadman made life miserable for both Irsay and his family. And, who knows? Steadman's endless *ad hominem* tirades might have also contributed to Irsay's development of a problem with alcohol. I can only speculate on this subject. What I do know is that Steadman never showed any mercy or compassion towards Irsay. To this day he can't admit that Irsay had the justice of economics on his side in 1984.

Look, I was a long time Colt season-ticket holder. My devotion to the team that gave the NFL the likes of John Unitas, Raymond Berry, Lenny Moore, and Artie Donovan went back to the glory years of the late 1950s.

I even made the trip to New York's hallowed Yankee Stadium December 28,1958, to witness the Colts win the NFL championship against the Giants in the first sudden-death overtime game. And unlike windbag Steadman, I paid to get in to see that historic contest!

But the fact of the matter, forgotten in the vicious verbal assaults on Irsay's hard-earned reputation, is that the fans in Baltimore failed to support the team in a fashion consistent with maintaining an NFL franchise. They were spoiled rotten by the successes of the Unitas and Bert Jones-eras. They thought Baltimore was always suppose to have a winning team. This is pure nonsense.

I remember that last dismal season before the Colts left town. I took my brother-in-law to one of the games. He is from State College, Pennsylvania, home of Penn State, an institution with a long history of football heroics under the legendary coach Joe Paterno. Memorial Stadium was half-empty that day, and many of the fans who did show up wore brown paper bags over their heads.

My brother-in-law was shocked by how the fans treated the players. He felt, as I did, that it was depressing to even go to a game under such negative circumstances. The 1984 Colt team could have sued the fans for non-support and won.

The simple truth is that Irsay, from a business perspective, was fully justified in moving his team to another major market, where he could expect a proper return on his investment.

He gave Baltimore plenty of chances to give him a better day, but the then-Mayor, William Donald Schaefer wasn't up to the situation. Schaefer lost the Colts by sheer incompetence, ego-tripping, and gross stupidity.

Another character assassin in this saga, who must be mentioned is Michael Olesker, also of the *Baltimore Sun.*

Usually, he bores his readers to tears scribbling about the "Block," or Boogie Weinglass, or his old Park Heights neighborhood. But after Irsay's death, Olesker charged that Irsay had committed the most infamous act in Baltimore sports history. He totally forgot the late weasel Abe Watner, who sold the earlier Colt All-American Conference franchise back to the NFL in the 50s for a song, and the NFL folded the team.

Look, it's time for all of us to sing from the same hymnbook. Irsay is dead, the Ravens are here now, and, the Irsay bashers, like Steadman and Olesker, should get a life.

*       *       *

## 66. Sports Lobby Shafting the Taxpayers
## March, 1996

Ken Griffey, Jr. signed a contract recently with the Seattle Mariners. He will be paid $8.5 million a year to run around the bases, hit that little white ball out of the park, and mug for the TV cameras.

When Griffey penned his $34 million, four-year deal, he declined to wear a Mariner uniform. Instead, he decked himself out in his finest digs for the photo opportunity, displaying over every inch of his body the corporate images of the products he personally endorses for even more millions a year. Yuk!

Meanwhile, on the franchise owners' front, Art Modell hijacked the Cleveland Browns to Baltimore to play in a $200 million stadium to be built with public funds.

These two garish examples epitomize the sea of change that has washed over major league sports in the last decade or so. The idea that a player, or club, has any loyalty whatsoever to the city it represents is only wishful thinking nowadays.

Fond memories of great performances, team memories of golden moments, are abandoned for individual greed. Anything for the almighty dollar. Anything.

In the past, it was usually the player that was exploited buy the owner. But those days are gone forever. Now it's the taxpayers who are getting the shaft and the shafter is this power special interest that I call the "Sports Lobby."

The "Sports Lobby" is loosely made up of the professional franchise owners; the overpaid players and their slick agents; sports writers and their newspapers; the businesses that sell sporting goods and their advertising agencies; TV sports networks, like ESPN; and those ubiquitous quasi-public stadium and arena authorities.

Taxpayers are regularly asked to pay for new stadiums and arenas that benefit the Sports Lobby and fat cat sky box owners, but titles to such expensive facilities are immediately placed in the hands of a quasi-public authority, like the Maryland Stadium Authority. Shades of William Donald Schaefer's notorious "Shadow Government."

Art Modell's "free lunch," courtesy of Governor Parris Glendening, includes the following: a 30-year, rent-free, property-tax-free lease for a 70,000-seat stadium, with 100 percent of revenues derived from parking, concessions. advertising, 108 luxury boxes, and 7,500 high-priced club seats. In addition, Modell will receive up to $75 million in "relocation expenses" to be raised from the sale of personal seat licenses (PSL), which entitle the purchasers to buy season tickets. He'll also get a 10 percent "management fee" and 50 percent of the profits for all non-NFL events staged in the stadium, including college games and rock concerts.

Experts are predicting the price tag for the new football stadium in Baltimore could go as high as $300 million, while the proposed lottery revenues will probably be inadequate. In addition, it is expected that Orioles owner Peter "Me Too" Angelos will invoke his "parity clause" to get the same kind of sweetheart lease deal as Modell.

Tickets for the planned ten NFL home games, after forking out the exorbitant PSL fee, will be far outside the economic means of the typical middle class family. For instance, how many people do you know who will be able to shell out $1,100 in order to line up to buy one of Modell's NFL season ducats?

One of the leading cheerleaders for the Glendening giveaway is the *Baltimore Sun*. Its out-of-touch editorial staff has acted like a propaganda wing of Art Modell's PR Machine during this media circus. *The Sun* claims the new stadium will stamp the city as "first class," increase the "quality of life," and be a "huge boost for the local economy."

Numerous studies insist that tossing public money into stadiums and arenas for privately owned professional sports teams produce only marginal benefits at best. (Well, what do you expect from the oracles at the *Sun?*)

This is the same British-First organ that mindlessly championed the mass destruction of Baltimore's world-class streetcar system after WWII and our charming Belgian granite-laid streets, all in the name of "progress"-i..e., (read the grasping Automobile and Highways Lobbies.)

Down the road in Prince George's County, millionaire owner Jack Kent Cooke is planning to spend his own money to build a stadium to house his NFL Redskins team. Cooke, however, is trying to shake down the taxpayers for $78 million to construct new roads into his emporium. The public should tell him to get lost, too.

At the moment, the resources of the state are seriously strained. Education, rebuilding our infrastructures, job-training programs, genuine economic development and police and fire protection should be our priorities. Corporate welfare is a no-win proposition for Marylanders, as is the anti-working class attitude of Newt Gingerich and his Jacobin band in the Congress. The Modell stadium deal should be axed.

At press time, both Modell and Cooke have offered some concessions to stem the rising tide of protest throughout the state to their proposed deals. The General Assembly will have to decide this matter during this session.

If the members of the Senate and House of Delegates know what's good for their careers, they will put the "public interest" before the interests of the "Sports Lobby."

*　　　　*　　　　*

# 67. John Unitas: The Golden Arm
## January, 1985

He was called "The man with the golden arm," and he wore number 19 on his jersey. His name was John Unitas, and for 18 glorious years he quarterbacked the Baltimore Colts into the hearts of thousands of its partisan fans.

His records on the gridiron are legendary; 290 touchdown passes completed, and over 40,000 yards gained.

At 51, Unitas is a successful business man, surrounded by a happy family life, with his wife Sandy and their three children. Unitas also has five children from his first marriage.

His "Golden Arm" restaurant on York Road in Baltimore is a popular eatery, noted for its long, chic bar, over which hangs a large portrait of the near-mythical No. 19 in action on the football field.

The Pittsburgh native joined the Colts in 1956, straight from the sandlots of that city after graduating from the U. of Louisville in 1955.

Cameron C. Snyder of *The Sun* said, "Unitas will be remembered as a giant among pro football players, although he never weighed more than 197 pounds. He looked frailer than that, but he withstood years of physically demanding NFL wars."

In July, 1979, Unitas was inducted into Pro Football Hall of Fame. Fifteen bus loads of Colt Corral members, the largest invasion in the 17 years of the Hall of Fame ceremonies, made the trip to Canton, Ohio.

Tex Maude, writing in *Pro Magazine,* summed-up Unitas well with this comment: "He quit after the 1973 season. He went out of the game with the same dignity and class he showed as a player. It will be a long time before we see the likes of Johnny Unitas again."

*      *      *

## 68. Charley Eckman: A Sportsman for All Seasons
## January, 1985

One of Maryland's most beloved sports figures is Charley Eckman. For over forty years Eckman has done it all- trainer, player, coach, referee, scout and sportscaster.

For almost two decades Eckman has also been the voice of sports for WFBR-AM radio in Baltimore.

"Sports has been a way for me to make a living, and also my whole life," says Eckman, now a young sixty-four and longtime Glen Burnie resident.

At sixteen, Eckman, who was raised in West Baltimore, began refereeing basketball games around town at places like the Cross St. Market and 14 Holy Martyrs.

After service in WWII, Eckman moved up to the National Basketball Assn. as a referee, and later as a coach for the Western Division champs, the Fort Wayne Pistons (1955-1957). Eckman even found time to become chief judge of the Orphans' Court of Anne Arundel County.

Eckman labeled Tom Gola of LaSalle as the best all- around college basketball player, and Jim Lacy, former Loyola immortal, as the best pure shooter.

On the pro side, Eckman picked Jim Pollard in the all around talent category, and the legendary "Jumping Joe" Fultz of the Philadelphia Warriors as a pure shooting wizard.

The "tell-it-like-it- is" sportscaster says he does what comes naturally. "I talk from experience-I relate to the guy on the street. And, when I retire from announcing," Eckman says, "I'm going back into politics!"

\*       \*       \*

Letter Published in the *Baltimore Sunday Sun*, January 9, 2000.
Sports Section

January 2, 2000
Dear *Sun* Sports Editor:
Re: Charley Eckman

One of our city and Maryland's finest sports' sons was the late, great Charley Eckman. He was born in West Baltimore and made a solid reputation for himself as a basketball player, coach, referee, scout and as a colorful sportscaster. For the longest time, he was "Mr. Basketball."

After service in WWII, he became a profession referee in the National Basketball Association. He then went on to coach the Fort Wayne Pistons to the championship of the Western Division the 1955-57 seasons. He even found time later in his fabulous career to serve as the Chief Judge of the Orphans' Court in Anne Arundel County.

John Steadman's list of ten Baltimore-born sports legends was good, but I found it incomplete. The incomparable Charley Eckman deserved a place in that illustrious group.

Sincerely,
Bill Hughes

# 69. Art Donovan: Pro Football Hall of Fame
## August, 1984

"My greatest moment in a Baltimore Colt's uniform was when we came from behind to beat the San Francisco Forty-Niners in December of 1958 to win the conference title for the first time," recalled Art Donovan.

Now 60 years of age, and the father of five children, the genial Donovan can look back, with pride, on a professional football career that spanned from 1950 to 1962 with the Baltimore Colts as a defensive tackle.

A bona fide Hall of Famer, enshrined at Canton Ohio, after his playing days were over, Donovan rates one of his former coaches, Weeb Eubank, as "maybe the greatest coach ever."

"Eubank took two of the worst teams in football, the Baltimore Colts and the New York Jets, and made them into World Champions," said Donovan.

Donovan credits the former legendary coach of the Cleveland Browns, Paul Brown, as being "the father of modern football," and Don Shula, now coach of the Miami Dolphins, as "definitely the heir-apparent to both Eubank and Brown."

Donovan picked former opponents Stan Jones (former U. of Maryland footballer), Bruno Banducchi, Jim Ringo of the fabled Packers, and Bill Walsh of the 49ers, as just some of the offensive linemen he admired the most.

For running backs, he ran off the names of Ollie Matson, "Hugging Hugh" McLhinney, and Rick Zares, as being among the best he ever faced, although "there were so many to remember," he added.

The WW II Marine Corp veteran is very busy these days managing, with his wife Dorothy, the Valley Country Club in Riderwood, Baltimore County. The fashionable tennis and swimming club, a family-owned business, also caters to parties and weddings.

Few people realize that Donovan's father was the late ring referee, Arthur B. Donovan, Sr., considered by many sport's experts to be the finest boxing official in all of pugilist history.

It is, indeed, appropriate, that the son, Arthur B. "Art" Donovan, Jr., has been able to carve out for himself, such a unique and special identity on the football field.

That effort has also brought much joy to him, his family, and to his legion of loyal fans in the Maryland area.

\*             \*             \*

## 70. Jim Mutscheller: The Classic NFL Tight End
## May, 1984

"I didn't know that we played sudden-death. I thought that if we ended up in a tie, then that was it," fondly recalled former Baltimore Colts end Jim Mutscheller.

In the historic overtime win over the New York Giants on December 28, 1958 in Yankee stadium, it was the reliable "No. 84," Jim Mutscheller who came within one yard of scoring the winning touchdown on a gutsy pass from quarterback John Unitas on the Giant's ten yard line.

I always had a lot of confidence in Unitas's passing ability," added the Beaver Falls, Pa. native, who caught five passes in that classic of all pro football contests.

At Notre Dame, Mutscheller played in 1949, on a national championship team under the legendary gridiron coach Frank Leahy. Bob Williams, a Baltimore native, quarterbacked that fabled team and won for himself "All-American" honors in the process.

After hanging up his cleats in 1961, Mutscheller has been a highly successful insurance agent with the National Life Insurance Co. of Vermont.

The Guilford resident still considers the '57 Colts team, because of its "run attitude," a better overall team than the celebrated '58 champs.

As a place to live and work, Mutscheller has found the Baltimore area to be "the best in the whole country."

---

# Chapter Seven

---

## Ode to the Memories

### 71. Bygone Locust Point: Halcyon Days in Baltimore
**March 7, 1990**

The Locust Point of my early youth bustled with maritime commerce and social activities during the years of World War II. It was commonplace to find hardy dockworkers, twenty-four taverns, gung-ho sailors and soldiers, drunken brawls, merchant seamen, floating dice games, some loose women, a fast buck and festive block parties.

It was a time also of air raid drills, black-outs, ration stamps, crowded church services, unfounded fears of foreign spies, buying coal by the bundle, church-sponsored "May" processions, "National Boh" beer on draft, shoe shine boys, patriotic parades, newspaper hawkers, a cop walking his beat and electric street cars.

I grew up in Locust Point over fifty-one years ago. As a child, it was a magical kind of moment that I didn't think was ever going to end. It was a very exciting period, too, like watching a big budget movie being made and it seemed like everyone was growing old but me.

The peninsula, formerly entitled "Whetstone Point," juts out into Baltimore harbor, with historic Fort McHenry at its easterly point, and with Fort Avenue literally splitting it down the middle.

Its landed boundary on the west is Lawrence Street, and within its confines could be found around 3,000 residents, mostly of Polish, German, Irish and English extractions.

The area contained three precincts of the 24th Ward. It had Roman Catholic, German Lutheran, and Episcopalian church parishes; one funeral parlor; a gas service station; assorted industries, including a cinder-block company and even a blacksmith; Our Lady of Good Counsel parochial school and P.S. 76, and spacious Latrobe Park, with its baseball, softball, and soccer fields.

On its north side were situated the sprawling dock terminals, first opened by the B&O Railroad in 1849. The B&O, then one of the largest and finest private employers in the state also owned and operated the massive grain elevator at Andre and Beason Streets.

On its southern end were the Port Covington docks, owned by the competing Western Maryland Railroad, which also included a grain elevator and ore and coal piers.

Just outside of the Point on the Key Highway, the Bethlehem Steel Corporation maintained the then

largest drydock and shipyard facility in the country. That 35-acre site, plus a 14-acre facility adjacent to Fort McHenry, worked around the clock, seven days a week, on cost-plus government contracts during WWII.

It built and repaired hundreds of "Victory," LST's and "Liberty" ships in the massive war effort. It employed tens of thousands during this hectic period, including many women in jobs formerly held by men. The long black limousines used by the company executives could be seen parked outside the its facility, with their well-groomed chauffeurs standing by at the ready.

The "Soap House" (as it was called by the locals), the Proctor & Gamble plant, world famous for its "Ivory" soap, was at the foot of Haubert Street. It was also producing at its capacity during this era. The "Sugar House," its next-door neighbor, owned by the American Sugar Refinery, with the huge neon sign on top of it, was just as busy, making the famed "Domino" sugars.

At night, the banging noise of steel pipes being loaded onto ships by the longshoremen could regularly be heard. The longshoremen were hired to work the ships, and were commonly referred to as "stevedores." After loading or discharging its cargo, a ship, accompanied by a tugboat, would make its way carefully out into the main shipping channel of the harbor.

This would be preceded by a concerto of short blasts from each vessel's whistle, as the larger ship was towed safely away from the dock. Even to this day, the burst from a ship's whistle is a haunting melody to me, recalling fond memories of yesteryear.

During the early morning hours, the business agent for International Longshoremen's Local 829 on Hull Street could be heard barking out, over his loud speaker, the daily order for labor for longshoremen gangs. The gang carrier would then hire on the spot, what men he would need for that day's work. This "shaping-up" process was later immortalized in the movie "On the Waterfront," which starred the great actor Marlon Brando.

There were five separate I.L.A. hiring halls located on the Point. The largest, for the stevedores, was divided into two separate locals: one for the blacks and one for whites. The other union halls were for the grain workers, who worked on bulk grain ships; the talleykeepers, shiprunners and checkers, (Checker's Union); and one for the receiving and delivery clerks, (Front Door Local).

My father, the late Richard Patrick Hughes, Sr., worked on the waterfront for over 40 years as a shiprunner out of I.L.A. Local 953 (Checker's Union). His job was to supervise the loading and discharging of cargo onto the vessels. This was long before containerization transformed the industry.

In those days, the lot of the longshoremen was a hard one indeed. Most of the cargo had to be moved by hand. The work was very difficult, took special skills, and was extremely dangerous, with long and erratic work hours. Fatal accidents were not uncommon.

Cargo with live ammunition was loaded at the Hawkins Point Terminal, located further out in the harbor, on the southern shore of the Patapsco River. A general cargo ship would be loaded with military goods, equipment, and troops, to capacity, if the freight was available. Some of the vessels never made it to their final destination, falling victim to German "U-boats" in the treacherous waters of the North Atlantic. The stowage for these vessels had to be exact for safety reasons.

Longshoremen, with their ubiquitous hooks in the back of their pants, worked tirelessly to maintain the ship's tight schedule. Many of them also drank, fought, and played hard at the same level of intensity. A good slugfest outside of one of the neighborhood bars on Friday evening between the longshoremen wasn't out of the ordinary. In fact, the during the "dog days of summer," (and before the invention of television), it was actually expected.

Usually the "Marquess of Queensberry" rules automatically applied, and no one was taken unfair advantage of by the combatants, or their unofficial seconds. The last man standing was normally declared the winner, and if the fight was going too bad for one of the participants, some wiser head normally intervened and declared the match over. After the battle, everyone, including the two principal fighters, would return arm-in-arm to the bar for yet another round of drinks.

There was a terrible war going on in Europe and in the Pacific. But to me as a youngster, those places might well have been on the planet Mars. That reality, for the most part, only came through when I went to the "Deluxe" movie house on Fort Avenue (at Lowman St.) on Saturday afternoon. Just before the feature, and the eagerly-awaited "Serial," the Deluxe ran a news-of-the-world segment. It was only then that I heard about celebrated incidents, like the Normandy invasion, the "Battle of the Bulge," and the fall of Berlin; and about our military heroes: Patton, MacArthur, and Eisenhower.

I remember seeing German prisoners-of-war laboring down at the "Lumber Yard" opposite Latrobe Park (at Decatur St.) This was just before the war ended. Some of my neighbors gave them water to drink, which they gratefully accepted. In retrospect, they appeared relieved to be alive and out of the fighting.

In front of the B&O's;Riverside "Round House," (on Fort Ave., near Lawrence St.), there were stored thousands of huge life rafts-stocked twenty high. They said it was surplus war goods.

There is, however, one other memory of the war still sketched in my psyche. I recall vividly seeing a photograph, or a drawing, in our Sunday morning newspaper. It was on the cover of the magazine section. It showed a beleaguered soldier, either U.S. or one of our allies, kneeling, with his hands tied behind his back, and his head lowered onto a block. An angry-looking Japanese soldier towered menacingly above him with his sword raised high preparing to do the foul deed on his helpless victim. For war propaganda and morale purposes, the picture worked, charging up feelings of intense hatred towards the Japanese. It definitely belonged in the classic category.

We lived then at 1237 Haubert Street. Several times a week, only a half block away, the B&O Railroad would bring a train, loaded with raw materials, through Marriott Street and into the Proctor & Gamble warehouse, and then it would carry out finished products from an earlier shipment. My twin brother and I would sit on the curb and watch the train go into the plant, and wait patiently for it to come out. The engineer always rewarded us with a blast or two of his whistle as he went by our sidewalk position. It also helped that there was a tavern directly across the street, that just happened to be one of the train crew's favorite watering hole.

From our front stoop, the faces and sounds of merchant seamen from all over the world could be seen and heard. The seamen from India and the Orient had the habit of walking down the street in single file, usually with their hands folded behind their backs. The Europeans preferred to travel in packs of three or more, and normally walked abreast of one another.

The typical icons in most of the small row houses on the Point consisted of portraits of President Franklin D. Roosevelt and/or Pope Pius XII. Some of the taverns also carried a picture of the great labor leader, John L. Lewis.

Lewis, the indefatigable boss of the National Miners' Union, actually called a strike during World War II. Needless to say, the Point was a bastion of strength for trade unionism, whose residents took deep pride in their work and in their union membership.

The 1100 block of Haubert Street was known as "Fairy Alley," since so many Irish had lived there. *(Author's Note-The other theory, probably more accurate, is that is was called "Ferry Alley," because the harbor ferry left from the foot of Haubert St. to travel twice a day to Broadway over in Fell's Point, See, *Locust Point Wards, Vol. 1, Plate L, G. M. Hopkins,* Librarian of the Congress, at Washington, D.C., entered according to the Acts of Congress, 1876.)

The Toolan family was raised there, and one of their sons became the Roman Catholic Bishop of Mobile, Alabama.

Woodall and Stevenson Street area was called "Leadtown," since it had been the site of the "Maryland White Lead Works". Reynolds Street was referred to as "Garrett Park." It had formerly been part of an estate owned by the distinguished Howard family of Baltimore and environs.

Sam Meisel owned a very successful ship chandler's business at Fort Ave. and Towson St, which had been started by his father. He lived on the

Point and died there at a late age. When asked why he hadn't moved out to the suburbs, he answered,"Why should I? I know you, knew your father and his father before him. And when I walk down the street in Locust Point, I am always addressed as 'Mr. Meisel'. In Pikesville, I would be just another old man."

Everybody who worked on the docks in those days appeared to have a nickname of some sort. Colorful monikers, like "Horse Collar," "Half-Dead," "Iggy," "Gassy," "Snake-Eyes," "The Ox," "Hackey," "Stumper" and "The Senator" were bantered about.

In the summer months, an elderly man, who fixed umbrellas, while you waited would make his rounds walking around the neighborhood. He was very proud of his craft and took great pleasure in watching the wonderment of us "street kids" at his magic-like achievements. The "A-rabs," vendors who sold vegetables and fruits from the back of a horse-drawn wagon, could also be seen, and especially heard, hawking their wares in the back alleys and streets into the early evening hours.

The political boss of the Point was the late, beloved Ed "Judge" Daugherty. He lived in the 1100 block of Hull St. and was a checker on the waterfront. He had also served as a "Sitting Magistrate".

Judge Daugherty was associated with the still-dominant Stonewall Democratic Club, which has longed played a key role, mostly positive, in the life of the community. He was highly respected as an honest and good man, who had helped many constituents with their problems.

There was also a nurse from the City's Health Department who made periodic visits to the neighborhood, especially to homes with expectant mothers. Our family physician, Dr. Arron Sollod, made house calls as a matter of course.

During WWII, one of the military parades I particularly remember had Mayor Theodore R. McKeldin in it. There were the usual marching bands, soldier units, and flags in it, too.

But I especially recall seeing the mayor seated on the back of a jeep as the parade went down Fort Avenue (at the intersection of Hull St.)

towards Fort McHenry. He was waving to the crowd and enjoying himself immensely. Somebody was complaining bitterly that, "He's a Republican," but I remember my father saying to the man that it didn't matter, because McKeldin was an "alright guy."

President Roosevelt, deeply loved by the people, died on April 12, 1945. The Point mourned his loss, as did the nation. Germany and Japan both surrendered later that year.

The great war was finally over. The halcyon days of the Point as a place of mass employment had also come to an end. Its people and industries had met the difficult war challenges. The changing global economy and "modern times," however, have regretfully taken their toll on my old neighborhood.

The legendary Bethlehem Steel shipyard on Key Highway is gone forever, ready to be converted into an apartment/condominium complex. I.L.A. Local 829 is now part of the folklore of labor history. Its predecessor union has moved to East Baltimore. The B&O Railroad and Port Covington docks have been taken over by the Maryland Port Administration, and soon, the *Baltimore Sun's* modernized printing plant will be added to the Port Covington area.

The Point will probably never be the same place again, and maybe some will say, "That's a blessing."

But, my memory of those grand and glorious WWII days, and Locust Point's part in it, will remain with me forever.

*            *            *

## 72. The Final Exile of Nora Thornton of County Mayo
### December 28, 1988

My mother died recently at the age of 87. She was simply worn out by the vicissitudes of life. In many ways, especially considering her last years of illness, she welcomed death.

"Oft in the stilly night, ere slumber's chain has bound me. Fond memory brings the light of other days around me," wrote the great Irish poet, Thomas Moore (1779-1852), in "The Light of Other Days."

Born Nora Thornton in the village of Tavanaghmore in the County of Mayo, she was one of six children-two boys and four girls. One of her brothers, Patrick, died in his youth with the flu. The other, Mickey, a lovable rebel from the days of the Irish Civil War, died earlier this year in Ireland at the age of 88. Mom was destined to be the last of her clan.

The remains of her ancestral home, rocky and weather-battered, still sit on top of a hill, near the Pontoon bridge, overlooking pristine Lough Conn. It's a truly lovely place with a magnificent view of the surrounding countryside and of the usually snow-capped Mount Nephin. The town of Foxford, world famous for its wool, is only a couple of miles down the road.

And, the Irish bard continued, "the smiles, the tears of childhood years, the words of love then spoken."

But the stunning beauty of the wild landscape, (like for many of today's Irish), wasn't enough to sustain life for her. Her father's decision, unfair as it was, was made for dire economic reasons: The girls had to go! The farm couldn't sustain a living for all of them, and only Mickey's help was needed to make the farm viable.

And go they did-one by one. Mary married and moved to the next village of Stonepark-Brogan. The other two girls, Katherine and Anne, left for Scotland, preparing the way for my mother to follow.

It must have been a painful time for my mother, as it was for her sisters. Through no fault of her own, except the accident of birth in a country for centuries dominated by an alien power, she was required to turn her back on everything she had come to cherish. Even to her last days, she could hardly speak of it without filling-up with emotion.

"Sad memory brings the light of other days around me," said the poet.

There she was-a farmer's daughter, with a basic education received in a one-room school house being torn away from the bond with family, friends, and native land. Her parents took her on that fateful day by donkey and wagon to the local railroad station. She was then put on a train for Dublin, and from there on to a ferry to Scotland to meet her sisters. From that sad day of departure and farewell in 1915, she was never again to see her loving and brokenhearted parents.

In 1918, she made her way to America, working, as many of the "green horns" did in that era, as a live-in domestic in a fashionable neighborhood of Baltimore. Later on, she would meet my late father, Richard Patrick Hughes, a longshoreman. They would marry and raise a family of nine children. As the fates would have it, my father's parents were also from the village of Tavanaghmore.

Despite a mostly comfortable and good life in America, and two joyful visits to Ireland in her later years, my mother never quite got over her abrupt loss of the world of her youth. That became clearer to me as the years flew by. The forced leaving had cut a deep wound-a spiritual sort of death.

"The eyes that shone now dimmed and gone. The cheerful heart now broken," concluded Moore.

So that when the Grim Reaper finally did call on her on October 8, 1988, my old Irish mother was waiting and ready for him.

The final exile held no fear at all for Nora Thornton, a tired, bone-weary, but gallant daughter of Erin.

\*       \*       \*

# 73. Only The Memories Last: The Death of JFK, Jr.
## March 15, 2000

The report a few weeks ago that John F. Kennedy Jr.'s plane was missing off Martha's Vineyard brought back a flood of memories.

On the day his father was assassinated, Nov. 22, 1963, I was working in the court house as a clerk.

I remember an obese cop trudging into our office saying he'd had heard on the radio that President Kennedy had just been shot in Dallas. Then, he started telling us in great detail about a recent hernia operation he'd had. I looked over at my fellow clerks, Morris Cohen, Hector D'Alesandro, and Irv Katz, and I believe that we all wanted to throw up in unison. Our president had been gunned down and this vulgarian was showing us the scars from his surgery.

That night back in my old neighborhood, Locust Point, I was looking for some place to grieve over the loss. I was hoping my church, Our Lady of Good Counsel, would do something special. Instead, it decided to hold its regular Friday night bingo session, like nothing terrible had happened in Dallas that morning. To say I was disappointed in their reaction would be an understatement.

Two days later, on a Sunday, I was watching television. My daughter, Lisa, was just learning to walk. She kept parading in front of the TV set as the Dallas police brought out the prime suspect in the Kennedy assassination, Harvey Lee Oswald. Out of the crowd, a man later identified as Jack Ruby, fired a gun, striking Oswald. I had just witnessed the first televised murder.

It was a double whammy! First, the president was slain, and then, his supposed assassin, Oswald, was killed in front of a national TV audience. The country was traumatized and looking for something to hold onto.

At his father's funeral, JFK Jr, or as he was then known, "John John," gave it to us. Standing outside of St. Matthew's Cathedral in Washington, D.C., he saluted his father's coffin as it passed by. It was also John-John's third birthday. That symbol has endured because it struck a deep chord in our collective psyches. I think it also helps to explain the spontaneous outpouring of mourning over his tragic death.

Like JFK Jr., I have a private pilot license to fly a single engine aircraft. Much of my training back in 1981, was done over the usually haze-covered Eastern Shore and the waters of the Chesapeake Bay. My flight school was located at BWI airport. I can certainly identify with JFK Jr, knowing that flying over water at night with poor visibility can be very challenging for a beginner pilot.

My only glimpse of JFK Jr happened in February, 1994. I was attending a news conference, on behalf of WBAI's Radio Free Eireann program, held at the Waldorf Astoria hotel in New York City. At the time, I was a commentator on the weekly NYC show. The occasion was the first visit to the U.S. of Sinn Fein leader-Gerry Adams.

I had just finished interviewing former Boston Mayor Kevin Flynn, in the lobby of the hotel about the event, when I noticed a very young looking JFK Jr. walking by. I made eye contact with him and he gave me a friendly nod back, along with that trademark smile of his. I've regretted ever since not getting a comment from him about the Adams visit.

Historically, the Kennedy tribe originated in the south of Ireland, in County Cork. Their progenitor, Patrick Kennedy, came to Boston, in 1848, to escape the great famine in Ireland. Two to four million people died in that man-made holocaust, although there was more than enough food in Ireland to feed the starving peasants. But, the British landowners insisted it all be shipped back to England. Patrick Kennedy was one of the lucky ones. He had survived to give birth to a fable American dynasty.

Now, the fates have again struck a Kennedy down. Unlike most of America, however, their family saga is played out on a public stage. It leaves the rest of us only with our memories, like that special one of a three-year old lad saluting his father's coffin so many winters ago.

*       *       *

## 74. Life with Harry J. 'Soft Shoes' McGuirk
**April 24, 1992**

It was one of those awful humid summer nights in Baltimore, nearly 37 years ago. We were all sitting around the Locust Point Democratic Club, dressed down to the basic essentials to escape the beastly elements, playing a little poker, drinking some warm draft beer, cursing the fates and puffing on our cigarettes.

The club was so close to the harbor you could hear the longshoremen loading the steel pipes on the Alcoa ship at Pier 9. I was 18 years old and working on the waterfront as a stevedore/checker out of ILA Locals 829 and 1429.

Suddenly, the front door opened wide and in strutted one of the 6th District's popular city councilmen, Tom Fallon, with his usual entourage of coat-holders, spear-carriers and drinking buddies.

Bringing up the rear was a stranger, a character right out of Central Casting, a double for the late comedian Ernie Kovacs, attired in a silk shirt and tie and colorful sport coat, with a full crop of wavy black hair resting atop a massive head.

"Hi," he said, warmly, "I'm Harry McGuirk." I asked him if he wanted a beer. He answered politely, "No thanks, I don't drink beer, but I'll have a Coke if you don't mind."

This was my introduction to the man who would dominate southside politics for most of the next three decades. Harry McGuirk, who died Monday, was to make a solid reputation for himself as a distinguished lawmaker in both the House of Delegates and State Senate. While he served in Annapolis, he was always a friend to the Baltimore city mayor and to his constituents in South Baltimore.

His legislative legerdemain became legendary. It was during McGuirk's long tenure as chairman of the Senate's Economic Affairs Committee that he demonstrated his ability to shepherd legislation through the maze of the General Assembly. Critics, and he had many, labeled him the "gray fox," a "political whore" and much worse. To his many faithful friends and staunch allies, however, he was the consummate lawmaker, the ultimate fixer.

He was, of course, always more than just an office holder to many of the citizens of predominantly working-class South Baltimore.

McGuirk was the boss of the powerful Stonewall Club, one of the city's last bastions of rough-and-tumble clubhouse politics. And despite the slurs of some liberals, the Stonewall, under his tutelage, was more open to candidates for public office than many organizations praised for their "democratic" procedures. What other political club gave the floor to political hopefuls from the Communist Party, to socialists, LaRouchies, and even to gadfly perennial candidate Melvin Perkins?

I got to know McGuirk on a more intimate basis during the 1970s, while I was the 24th Ward captain and lawyer for the club. As a master dispenser of municipal and state political patronage, McGuirk touched many lives, including mine.

In 1976, I ran as a Jerry Brown delegate to the Democratic National Convention on the Stonewall ticket in the 3rd Congressional District. I was confident of, victory, but reform politics spelled doom for me. I was wallowing in self-pity when I got a telephone, call from McGuirk late one night. Somehow, he had worked a deal to have me attend the convention as an "alternate" pledged to Sen. Henry "Scoop" Jackson.

I had little idea who Senator Jackson was and no idea of his record, but I did have an idea why the newspapers had taken to calling McGuirk, "Soft Shoes." He knew how to broker a political deal without a sound being heard by outsiders. This was his true genius. It was why his name is synonymous with old-time Maryland politics.

Jimmy Carter won the nomination in 1976. The Democratic convention was held, as this year's will be, In New York City's Madison Square Garden. McGulrk believed Carter, who had the delegate count sewed-up early, could beat the shaky President Gerald Ford in the general election. I remember him telling me while we were heading north on the New Jersey

Turnpike that he thought Carter would win, but not because the Georgian was the better of the two candidates. Rather, McGuirk said fallout from the Watergate scandal would continue to doom the Republicans. He was right as usual.

The Stonewall is the oldest Democratic club in continuous existence in Maryland. It was named after the great Confederate general, Stonewall Jackson.

Political giants like Joe Wyatt, Willie Meyers, Johnny Hines, Bill Hudnut, Tom Fallon, Leroy Fredericks, George Della, Sr., and Judge Ed Daugherty were all associated with it during its halcyon days.

But, the figure making the most lasting impression in the Stonewall gallery will be the incomparable Harry J. "Soft Shoes" McGuirk.

*        *        *

## 75. "And, That's a Wrap," for "Billyclub" at WBAI's *Radio Free Eireann*
### December 13, 1997

On September 23rd, I celebrated my 60th birthday, and to use a sport's metaphor, it reminded me that the clock is on the field. I've been blasting away weekly at *Radio Free Eireann* (RFE) **for over three years.**

**And, I must say that I have enjoyed every minute of it, as I did my four year spin as a pundit for the *Irish People* newspaper, when Martin Galvin headed INA. "Johnny Bob" McDonagh, one of RFE's producers, gave me my boost up in both endeavors. I thank him, Brian Mor, Liza Butler, and, my man, Mick Dewan, who I hope is listening in today, for all their wonderful support.**

**On this radio beat, I've met some truly great people, like the "Boston 3's" Martin Quigley, Richard Clark Johnson and Peter Eamon McGuire.**

I've also crossed swords with "Big Ian" Paisley and the Orange Order's czar, David Trimble. Many assignments took me to Capitol Hill, the seat of power.

And, I recall some memorable broadcasts from places, like Penn State College's football stadium, historic Harper Ferry, a hospital bed after heart bypass surgery, and on a jet 30,000 feet over Middle America, seated next to that splendid activist, Father Sean McManus.

Everyone knows the IRA called a cease fire on July 20 and that a Sinn Fein delegation had an afternoon tea, on Thursday, with Tony Blair, at 10 Downing Street. And, that is my problem summed up in a nutshell. My kind of attack journalism needs villains, and now the bad guys are getting written out of the script.

I've been an advocate for the cause of Irish freedom for over 25 years, and, it's time now for me to step down as the regular commentator for RFE. My fondest hope is that the "All Party Talks" will succeed in ending partition and will lead to a united Ireland.

On the Irish freedom front, clemency for Richard Clark Johnson, asylum for the H-Block 3, and freedom for Roisin McAliskey will remain at the top of my personal agenda. I will also carry on with my *pro bono* legal efforts with Ed Lynch's Lawyers Alliance, hawking my book, *Creating a New Ireland*, and developing my professional acting career.

My "Act III" will focus on the work of restoring the American Republic and crushing the New World Order scum bags. To that end, I will look for an opportunity to do a radio commentary on national political and cultural issues. If anyone knows of an opening, please contact me.

From time to time, I plan to return to RFE with a "Special Report" on a breaking news story. Finally, I send my sincere thanks and best wishes to each one of you for your past support of myself, RFE, and WBAI.

And, that's a wrap for Bill Hughes and his "Billycub" commentary for *Radio Free Eireann.*

---

# Chapter Eight

---

## Fighting for Justice

### 76. Bringing Closure to the Black Panther Era
**March 29, 1999**

Although the original Black Panther Party is history, one of its members is still languishing in prison in Maryland. His name is Marshall "Eddie" Conway. A former leader of the local Panther group, he has been behind bars for nearly 30 years.

In a highly controversial trial in 1970, Conway was convicted of murdering a white Baltimore City police officer and trying to shoot two others. He was given a life sentence.

Now, for a black man to get a fair trial, two years after the 1968 Baltimore riots, was difficult at best. When you add to it the fact the defendant advocated extreme radical politics, it was like pushing the envelope to its outer edge.

First, some historical background: The Black Panther Party was the white establishment's worst nightmare come true. Frustrated by what many Black activists saw as the limited success of the Civil Rights Movement, and the horrific murders of leaders, like the fiery Malcom X, and the revered Martin Luther King, they organized to change the system by "any means necessary." This proved, in a democratic society, to be both a seriously flawed and self-defeating strategy.

The establishment countered with a J. Edgar Hoover-inspired covert process called, "Cointelpro." It was formed to infiltrate and disrupt Black Nationalist organizations, and in particular, the Black Panther Party.

The FBI won the battle and the Black Panther Party was totally crushed. Many of its leaders were either killed, forced underground, or sent to prison. Some were fairly convicted of their offenses; others, however, fell into a miscarriage of justice category.

One such case involved Elmer "Geronimo" Pratt, who just had his 1972 conviction for murder overturned out in Los Angeles. The court said the prosecution wrongly suppressed evidence that the main witness against him was a government informant, who was paid by the police and FBI to infiltrate the Black Panthers. Pratt was lucky. He was represented on appeal by the celebrated criminal defense attorney, Johnny Cochran.

The case against Conway, too, was built primarily on the most dubious kind of evidence, a jail house informer. The snitch insisted that Conway, who never wanted the guy as his cell mate, had confessed to him about killing the police officer.

It is hard to believe that someone as politically conscious as Conway would blab to a total stranger about his supposed involvement in such an outrageous event. Unfortunately for him, he didn't have a Johnny Cochran type by his side at the trial table to protect his rights.

Conway had fired both of his lawyers. The first, who was privately retained, in a dispute over trial strategy and the second, who had been appointed by the court to defend him, but who did little to prepared for the trial. Conway had refused to cooperate with him.

Back in 1970, impoverished black defendants, in serious felony cases, had to face the music, without having the kind of adequate legal representation that they were rightfully entitled to under the Constitution. There wasn't any "Public Defender" system at that time.

Most importantly, there was no physical evidence linking Conway to the terrible crime. While he was in custody, two of the police officers that were also involved in the incident identified his photo as being one of the assailants on the night in question. The problem with that gambit was that Conway's attorney wasn't present and the witnesses were given two stacks of photos to look through.

Conway's mug was placed in both of them, unfairly suggesting he was the culprit. In the first stack a 1963 photo of the defendant was used and neither officer could make a positive I.D. When his 1970 photo was inserted, however, they both identified the defendant. The usual police lineup of suspects wasn't held either.

A lot of things in this country have changed since the tumultuous "Burn Baby Burn!" 60s, especially inmate Conway himself. He has earned three college degrees while in prison, and organized a computer literacy program for his fellow inmates. His conduct, too, inside the prison system has been exemplary.

I believe that the state of Maryland, through the Parole Board or Governor Parris Glendening should do the right thing. It is time to write closure to the Black Panther era. It is also time to free Marshall "Eddie" Conway.

Healing and reconciliation in the community require it.

\*　　　　　　　\*　　　　　　　\*

# 77. Baltimore's Bishop Murphy & the Arms Race
## June 6, 1983

Unless everyone becomes informed and politically active to find alternatives to the arms race, then everything we do is a footnote," says the Auxiliary Bishop of Baltimore, P. Francis Murphy. "All the issues that we deal with everyday, that are important if we allow a new generation of nuclear weapons to be built. Within 10 years, we will have 35 nations that possess nuclear weapons, and it will be near impossible to control these weapons."

In November of 1980, Bishop Murphy formally suggested to an assembly of U.S. Bishops that a pastoral letter dealing with war and peace in the nuclear age should be written by that influential body. That prescient suggestion was agreed to by the bishops and set in motion a process of monumental importance.

On May 3, 1983, in Chicago, the National Conference of Bishops voted 238-9 in favor of a 44,000-word teaching document, entitled, "The Challenge of Peace, God's Promise and Our Response." The statement marks an historic watershed on the bishops' involvement in U.S. government policy.

"At the completion of the Bishops' conference, I felt more than ever in my life the presence of God's spirit. The fact that 250 bishops in two days could approve a statement of such complexity was almost miraculous. It demonstrated their deep commitment on the issue and their profound understanding and knowledge of it," continued the soft-spoken Bishop Murphy in his office on the seventh floor of the Catholic Information Center at Mulberry and Cathedral Sts.

There are approximately 52 million Roman Catholics in the country, who represent more than 22 percent of the population and more than 30 percent of the U.S. Army's personnel.

In the Baltimore archdiocese, which roughly embraces the city of Baltimore, its metropolitan area and western Maryland, there are an estimated 430,000 catholics. The immense power and prestige of the Church and its growing and vocal concern on the seminal issue has sent shock waves through the conservative Establishment, the red-baiting White House, and the entrenched and grasping military-industrial complex.

The unprecedented pastoral letter, a product of three drafts and two years of disputed testimony, has for one of its centerpieces a call for a "halt" in the production and deployment of nuclear weapons, and endorses the concept of a nuclear freeze.

The document also strongly condemns the "first use" of nuclear weapons even in the face of a military defeat by conventional weapons. The letter states, "We do not perceive any situation in which the deliberate initiation of nuclear warfare on however restricted a scale can be morally justified."

"The challenge the bishops faced was that we have created a power in the 20th century that can destroy the planet and totally eliminate human life. The bishops looked at the moral dimensions of that power, and they looked at it from a vision found in the Hebrew scriptures and the New Testament. That vision speaks about a peace in the world that is based upon reconciliation, forgiveness, justice for everyone, and non-violence. That peace is far different from the type of peace that President Ronald Reagan talks about when he says, 'The MX missile' is a peacekeeper.' Reagan's concept of peace is totally removed from God's message of peace that we are speaking of," Bishop Murphy continued.

The total firepower of World War II only equally three megatons. The weapons on just one Poseidon submarine adds up to nine megatons, or the firepower of three WWII's.

The U.S. National Security Council estimates that in a full-scale nuclear war between the U.S. and the U.S.S.R.,140 million Americans and 113 million Russians would die. The Institute for Defense and Disarmament Studies believes both sides presently possess 50,000 nuclear weapons and the Quackers' *Friends Journal* says, "The existing nuclear weapons represent 18,000 megatons-equal to 6000 WWIIs."

"The U.S. government in their dialogue with us acknowledged that indirectly they have 40,000 sites targeted in the Soviet Union for nuclear weapons. They admitted if the U.S. were attacked first, they would massively retaliate, which is totally against the Catholic Church's teaching on war-even the 'Just War' theory. I think the strength of the pastoral letter is that it is not a passive document. But what we are saying is that even under the 'Just War' tradition of proportionality and discrimination, there is no way we can justify these questions on nuclear war," Bishop Murphy emphasized.

The Reagan Administration plans to spend $1.6 trillion on the mindless arms race in the next five years. The emerging grass roots "Freeze Movement" was successful in getting the House of Representatives on May 4, 1983, to adopt a mutually verifiable nuclear freeze resolution by a 278-149 vote. It is estimated by SANE (a nationwide disarmament group) that a weapon freeze now would save $84.2 billion over the next five years alone. Congress, however, recently approved $625 million in start-up funds to allow for the basing of the MX Missile-a weapon system of dubious military value, which has an ultimate price tag of $24 billion.

Jeanne Kirkpatrick is the controversial U.S. Ambassador to the U.N. and a staunch supporter of right-wing totalitarian governments, like those of El Salvador and Argentina. She is also on leave of absence from the faculty of the Jesuit-controlled Georgetown University in Washington, D.C.

Asked to explain the contradiction in the Church that has made such heroic sacrifices on behalf of the common people of these embattled regions, and yet can give aid and comfort to a Jeanne Kirkpatrick, Bishop Murphy replied, "There is great plurality and diversity in the Church. There are times when the truth of the Gospels is very much in conflict with the living reality of Catholic people-including Catholic institutions."

Bishop Murphy praised anti-war activist and poet Father Daniel Berrigan, S.J., saying, "I think Dan Berrigan and people like him, who have a prophetic stance, are most important people for the Church's ministry and they have provided a great service."

The prelate, who is the Western Vicar of the Archdiocese and the chairman of the Justice and Peace Commission, also said he generally agreed with the essentials of the recent pastoral letter of the Canadian Bishops, that denounced, "the scourge of unemployment," and held that the rights of workers are more important than profits. Bishop Murphy predicted the American bishops will, within the next two years, be publishing a pastoral letter on the economic system in this country.

In February, 1981, Georgetown U., under its president, the Rev. Timothy Healy, S.J., decided to give the British Prime Minister Margaret Thatcher, an award for humanitarian service. There was a predictable storm of protest from the Irish-American community and the supporters of Irish freedom because of the ongoing British colonial policy in the police state of Northern Ireland. Healy ignored the heated objections and went ahead and gave the honorary degree to Thatcher. Immediately thereafter, in the spring of 1981, the prime minister allowed 10 Irish hunger strikers to die over the issue of political status in a Belfast jail.

Bishop Murphy responded to that distressful situation by saying, "I do not agree with Catholic institutions inviting people, especially to get honorary degrees, when their political positions are so much in opposition to what we would consider the gospel values. Therefore, I would have serious questions about the fact that they would invite someone like Margaret Thatcher. I also had serious problems about President Reagan being invited to the University of Notre Dame. We have to always be ready to raise the moral issue, that often gets us into conflict, other than endorsing people we should not."

Locally, the administration of Loyola College have, with arrogance and insensitivity, pushed ahead with a plan to purchase the Wynnewood Towers, an apartment house on Cold Spring Lane, and convert it into a dormitory for students. The conversion, besides taking valuable property off the tax rolls, will cruelly displace 186 elderly tenants.

One of the tenants is the former five-term member of the Baltimore City Council from the Fifth District and one of the most respected labor and civil rights lawyers in the nation, the Hon. Jacob J. Edelman. Bishop Murphy declined to comment directly on that bitter imbroglio, but he did add, "I am concerned about the perception this has had in the community and I am always concerned about the rights of senior citizens."

The 1980 U.S. Census showed Baltimore City, despite the hype of the municipality's propaganda machine, as being the eighth poorest urban center in the country. Queried whether the Archdiocese has seen substantial proof of that shameful fact, Bishop Murphy said, "We have evidence from our pastors and ministers in Baltimore, who say that the present stress on their parishes and families is much greater than it was a few years ago. We are now giving out more food and more money for rent, basic needs, and utilities. That is just another reason why I am so strongly supporting the campaign of 'Jobs With Peace,' under the leadership of its able director Sister Katherine Coor."

Bishop Murphy concluded the interview by remarking, "I consider the pastoral letter, as an institutional document, to be the most significant event in the total Church history. It has widespread support; it has direction; and it is moving."

In the early part of this century, there arose a legendary churchman in the Baltimore diocese, who became an unrepentant champion of the working class, the under privileged, and the poor. His name was James (Cardinal) Gibbons (1834-1921).

Bishop P. Francis Murphy, on the issues of the arms race and social justice, is fearlessly following the progressive path of that memorable "Prince of the Church."

          \*                \*                \*

# 78. Ethnic Cleansing in Ireland: A Millennium Perspective
## January February, 2000

"I will not ignore 'ethnic cleansing' in Kosovo."[1]-British Prime Minister, Tony Blair

The idea that Great Britain has any moral standing to intervene in another nation's civil war because of supposed "ethnic cleansing" is simply preposterous. As a ruthless imperial power, it wrote the book on subjugating other races.[2] Fortunately, in the case of its American colony, it was repelled.[3] But, only after it had suffered military losses at Baltimore's Fort McHenry and New Orleans in 1814.[4]

Other British-held territories in China, India, Africa, Australia, Asia, the Middle East, Central and South America, weren't as lucky.[5] In fact, the 200,000 indigenous peoples of Tasmania were literally wiped out by the British.[6] Slave trading, piracy and opium running, were also part of its notorious practice of empire building.[7]

With respect to Ireland, ethnic cleansing has been the essence of British rule dating from the Anglo-Norman invasion of 1169. One of its earliest racist laws, enacted in 1367, was the "Statute of Kilkenny." It prohibited intermarriage between the British and (Gaelic) Irish under penalty of death. To the British, the Irish were subhuman.

If one thinks of Irish history as a play, crafted in London's Whitehall by its bureaucrats, at the direction of powerful wirepullers, where the actors (read individuals, political parties, military, police, etc.) are given certain roles, but the end result is already known by the wirepullers, then the tragic drama of Ireland under British rule can be understood.

Since British outrages against the Irish are so many, space requirements permit me to cite only a few of the more egregious ones.[8]

The Great Terrors

In 1520, when Henry VIII broke with Rome, it added religion to the bias against the Catholic Irish. Under Henry's daughter, the murderous

Queen Elizabeth I (1533-1603), the killing fields of Ireland ran red with the blood of innocent victims. It is estimated 1.5 million Irish peasants were starved or "put to the sword" and much of their lands seized by English predators, while she reigned.[9]

By the time the zealot Oliver Cromwell arrived on the scene, the Irish were ripe for more carnage. "It has pleased God to bless our endeavors," he wrote of the mass slaughter in 1649, by his Puritan troops of 3,552 Irish inhabitants of the seaport town of Drogheda, just north of Dublin. He pompously continued, "I am persuaded that this is a righteous judgment of God upon these barbarous wretches."[10]

This Drogheda massacre is one of the leading examples of the insidious British policy of ethnic cleansing in Ireland. Another is Cromwell's sacking of Wexford and the killing of 2,000 of its citizens.

The infamous "Cromwellian Settlements" followed his conquest of Ireland. Millions of acres of land (41 percent of Antrim, 26 percent of Down, 34 percent of Armagh and 38 percent of Monaghan) were allocated to English Protestant settlers. The landowners of Irish birth were either killed, banished or forced out to Connaught in the west of Ireland, where it was hoped "they would starve to death."[11]

A Cromwell biographer labeled this massive confiscation of Irish lands, "by far the most wholesale effort to impose on Ireland the Protestant faith and English ascendancy."[12] The British policy of colonizing Ireland with Protestants still has repercussions which are felt today on the streets of Belfast.

From 1649 to 1652, one-third of the population of Ireland was destroyed. Petty, an English historian says, "660,000 Irish people were killed."[13] Twenty thousand Irish boys and girls also were sold into slavery to the West Indies. The Irish peasant farmers that survived were forced to pay rent to their usurpers. Once prosperous home grown industries were also destroyed because they "competed with British factories."[14]

The memory of the holocausts under Elizabeth I and Cromwell have been forever seared into the psyche of the Irish race. Cromwell's evil idea that Irish Catholics were "barbarous wretches" has, too, unfortunately, passed into the British mindset.[15] Parliament reacted to Cromwell's crime against humanity in Ireland by passing an infamous Resolution that legitimized ethnic cleansing. It stated, "The House doth approve the execution done at Drogheda, as an act both of justice to them and mercy to others who may be warned by it."[16]

After the shaky British monarchy was restored in 1660, under Charles II, the vicious propaganda against Irish Catholics continued unabated. Many of the "vilest pamphlets" hyping the threat of a supposed "Popish Plot" against the Crown were printed in Holland.[17]

When James II, Charles' brother, succeeded him as King of England and Ireland in 1685, the hopes of Irish Catholics rose. His defeat, however, by the forces of William of Orange, at the Battle of the Boyne in 1690, on July 12, brought renewed disaster.

More confiscations of Irish lands followed and the adoption into law of the notorious "Penal Laws" in the late 1690s. Their net effect was to hold that, "The law does not presume any such person to exist as an Irish Roman Catholic."[18]

As time passed, there were periodic, but failed, rebellions in Ireland. In 1845, with nationalist aspirations at their lowest ebb, the moans of the starving were heard. The potato crop was blighted and famine stalked the land.

## The Irish Genocide

Author Thomas Gallagher sets the scene for this unspeakable tragedy in his moving testament to the Irish dead, *Paddy's Lament:* "A famine unprecedented in the history of the world, a chapter in human misery to harrow the human heart was about to start, and even little children could see its quick, sure approach in the nakedly fearful eyes and faces of their parents."[19]

By the mid-19th century, Ireland was a country of eight million, mostly peasants. As a result of years of exploitation, they survived as tenant farmers and were never far from economic disaster. They were forced to exist on a single crop: the potato. A disease turned the potato into a foul slime. When the Irish masses turned to the British government for relief, they received the back of London's hand.

Meanwhile, "Food, from 30 to 50 shiploads per day, was removed at gunpoint (from Ireland) by 12,000 British constables, reinforced by 200,000 British soldiers, warships, excise vessels, and coast guards... Britain seized from Ireland's producers tens of millions of head of livestock, tens of millions of tons of flour, grains, meat, poultry and dairy products-enough to sustain 18-million persons."[20]

Gallagher estimates two million died from the famine. Writer Chris Fogarty, however, places the numbers "murdered at approximately 5.16 million... making it the Irish holocaust."[21] Distinguished legal scholars, like Professors Charles Rice of Notre Dame U. and Francis A. Boyle, U. of Illinois, believe that under International Law, that the British pursued a barbarous policy of mass starvation in Ireland from 1845-50, and that such conduct constituted "genocide."[22]

## The Wrong of Partition

An armed uprising occurred in Ireland, on Easter Monday, 1916. It was quickly crushed and its leaders executed by firing squads on the orders of General John "Mad Dog" Maxwell.[23]

In the next general election, in 1918, Sinn Fein, the Republican Party, won 75 percent of the seats allocated to Ireland in the London Parliament. In defiance of Great Britain, its representatives set up an independent parliament known as *Dail Eireann* (Assembly of Ireland). London replied with massive violence, spearheaded by the "Black and Tans," fascist storm troopers.

Two years of war ensued with the Irish Republican Army, (IRA) fighting the British to a stalemate.[24] In 1921, a truce was declared. During negotiations for an Anglo-Irish Treaty, British Prime Minister, David Lloyd George, issued an ultimatum to the Irish delegation: Sign a draft treaty or face immediate and "terrible war."[25] The signing led to a bitter civil war and the partition of Ireland, with the six northeastern counties becoming the bogus state of "Northern Ireland."

After the civil war ended, Eamon De Valera became Prime Minister of the "Irish Free State," which consisted of the twenty-six counties in the South. On July 1, 1937, a Constitution was adopted by his government rejecting partition and any oath of allegiance to the British Crown.

## Six County Police State

Since the late 60s, British rule in the North of Ireland has been marked by events, like "Bloody Sunday,"[26] the "Dublin-Monaghan Bombings,"[27] and the death of the "Ten Hunger Strikers."[28] It has employed political assassinations, a shoot-to-kill policy, raiding of private homes, plastic bullets, the repressive Diplock Court system, tear gas, surveillance, torture and deportation in order to suppress the Irish.[29]

As resistance by the IRA to the occupation intensified, so did renewed oppression.[30] Actions, like the torching of Catholic churches, and the murders of attorneys Patrick Finucane and Rosemary Nelson, have underscored its policy of terror.[31] Although British officials regularly deny any responsibility for Loyalist (read Protestant, Unionist or Orange Order) terrorism, strong evidence suggest the contrary.[32]

Thanks to American activists, Ex-British Army Captain, Fred Holroyd (MI 6) revealed to a C-Span audience details of Britain's "dirty tricks" in the Six Counties. British tactics included murders, bombings, framing of innocent victims, black propaganda and kidnappings.[33]

Holroyd said the Special Air Service (SAS), undercover military personnel that are licensed to kill, are controlled directly by the office of the

Prime Minister and the Cabinet, and that the SAS, often referred to as "Margaret Thatcher's Praetorian Guard," ran spies into the 26 Counties.[34]

British wrongdoing didn't stop at the Irish shores. It also unsuccessfully opposed the MacBride Principles, U.S. sourced anti-discrimination legislation, which promoted equal employment opportunities for Catholics in the sectarian dominated Six Counties.[35]

## Conclusion

A "Peace Process" in Ireland, was boldly initiated, in 1993, by Sinn Fein's Gerry Adams and the Social Democratic Labor Party's John Hume. It eventually evolved into the 1998 "Good Friday Agreement."

Unionist prevarications, however, and the reluctance of Blair's Labor government to trump the Orange Card, despite having a 179-vote majority in the Parliament, have brought it to the brink of failure. Keep in mind that on December 19,1993, the London Sunday Times reported a secret Anglo-Irish deal to "smash the IRA, if a peace deal is rejected."[36]

Some now wonder, if the "Peace Process" is yet another example of Perfidious Albion's dirty tricks. They ask, "Will British ethnic cleansing return once again to Ireland and with a fury that would shame even Cromwell?" Only the wirepullers at Whitehall know for sure the answer to that troubling question.

If the past 831 years is prologue, we would do well to heed it.

## ENDNOTES

[1]. Tony Blair, "Kosovo: Our Responsibilities Do Not End at the Channel," *London Sunday Independent*, Feb. 14, 1999.

[2]. John Michael, *The Way of the Aggressor*, (Flanders Hall, 1941). During the Boer War, (1899-1902), the British created the first concentration camps, in which "26,663 women and children died," p. 69. And, in India

between 1860 and 1900, it is estimated "thirty million" starved to death under British rule, p. 64.

[3]. A. J. Langguth, *Patriots: The Men Who Started the American Revolution,* (Touchstone, 1988).

[4]. Anthony S. Pitch, *The Burning of Washington: The Invasion of 1814,* (Naval Institute Press, 1998).

[5]. J. M., *The Way of the Aggressor.* In New Zealand, of the Maoris natives only "50,000 survived" British extermination, p. 65.

*[6]. Ibid,* p. 64.

[7]. Hugh Thomas, *The Slave Trade,* (Simon &;Schuster, 1997). When John Hawkins, a notorious pirate and slave trader, was knighted by Elizabeth I, he chose as his crest "a manacled negro." And, slave trading was to remain one of "England's foremost sources of income until well into the nineteenth century,"J. M., *The Way of the Aggressor,* pp. 66-67.

[8]. Seamus MacManus, *The Story of the Irish Race,* (Devin-Adair Co., 1921).

[9]. J. M., *The Way of the Aggressor,* p. 20.

[10]. Frederick Harrison, *Oliver Cromwell,* (Omni Publications, 1888), p. 139.

[11]. J. M., *The Way of the Aggressor,* p. 20.

[12].F.H., *Cromwell,* p. 147.

[13]. J. M., *The Way of the Aggressor,* p. 21.

[14]. F. H., *Cromwell,* p. 149.

[15]. William Cobbett, *A History of the Protestant Reformation in England and Ireland,* (Tan Books, 1896).

[16]. F. H., *Cromwell*, p. 149.

[17]. Captain A. H. M. Ramsay, *The Nameless War*, (1952, Ramsay).

[18]. Robert Kee, *The Green Flag, Volume 1: The Most Distressful Country*, (Penguin Book, 1972).

[19]. Thomas Gallagher, *Paddy's Lament: Ireland 1846-1847*, Prelude to Hatred, (Harcourt Brace Jovanovich, 1982), p. 8.

[20]. Chris Fogarty, "The Mass Graves of Ireland: 1845-1850," Oct. 26 and Nov. 2, 1996, *The Irish People*, NYC.

[21]. *Ibid*, Oct. 26, 1996, p. 9.

[22]. Advert, Irish Famine/Genocide Committee, "The Famine Was Genocide," *The Irish People*, NYC, March 1, 1997, p. 14.

Early in 1992, Gallagher told me, "The Famine isn't taught in the Irish schools. And, I could find nothing on it either at New York Irish Historical Society."

An excellent educational tool on the Famine is, "The Great Irish Famine Curriculum," authored by the Irish Famine Curriculum Committee, and chaired by James V. Mullin, (January, 1996).

[23]. Peter De Rosa, *Rebels: The Irish Rising of 1916*, (Doubleday, 1991).

[24]. Tim Pat Coogan, *The IRA: A History*, (Roberts Rinehart Publishers, 1993).

[25]. Robert Kee, *The Green Flag, Volume 3: Ourselves Alone*, (Quartet Books, 1976), p. 155.

[26]. On Jan. 30, 1972, 14 civilians were shot dead by British paratroopers, in occupied Derry, during a peaceful civil rights march.

[27]. On May 14, 1974, 33 people were blown to death in explosions in Dublin and Monaghan. Evidence pointed to collusion between the Royal Ulster Constabulary (RUC), the British Army, and Loyalist paramilitary groups in the terrorist attacks.

Jim Smith, "Hub Recalls Victims of '74 Bombings," *Irish Echo,* May 18-24, 1994.

[28]. In the spring of 1981, British Prime Minister Margaret Thatcher permitted ten jailed IRA men to die on hunger strikers over the issue of their status as political prisoners.

[29]. Rona M. Fields, *Northern Ireland: Society Under Siege,* (Transaction, 1980).

[30]. T. M. C., *The IRA*, pp. 259-423; and, *Joe Doherty, Standing Proud: Writings from Prison and the Story of His Struggle for Freedom,* (National Committee for Joe Doherty,1991).

Joe Doherty was incarcerated from 1983 to 1992, in the Metropolitan Correction Center, in NYC. I had the chance to visit and exchange correspondence with him. Doherty, a resourceful and talented individual, was the first and only IRA man, jailed in the U.S., to write an op ed article for a major U.S. newspaper, the *Baltimore Evening Sun*, March 17, 1989. He was deported to the UK, in 1992, and finally released from prison on Nov. 6, 1998, under the terms of the "Peace Process" (See Christy Ward's excellent account of the Doherty's saga in *The Irish People*, Nov. 14, 1998).

Martin Quigley and Peter Eamon McGuire were two other IRA members imprisoned in the U.S. for a period of time during the 90s. I also visited with them; Quigley at FCI Allenwood, PA., and McGuire at FCI Cumberland, MD. I found them to be sincere, genuine, highly intelligent individuals, and driven by the finest of patriotic impulses. They were both returned to the Republic of Ireland to finish their prison sentences and have since been released from custody.

Richard Clark Johnson is an American citizen and a highly-respected radar engineer. He was jailed for ten years, in 1989, on dubious evidence, for supposed weapons running charges connected to the IRA. No weapons were ever found. Like many, I believe Johnson was railroaded by our government to please Margaret Thatcher (See Robert P. Connolly, "Free Speech Failed Last IRA Prisoner in U.S.," *Boston Herald*, Sept. 5, 1999). I visited with Johnson, too, at FCI Allenwood. He was released from federal custody on Oct. 17, 1999.

[31]. Patrick Finucane, a 38 year-old Belfast solicitor, was shot to death in his home, on Feb. 12, 1989. The Ulster Freedom Fighters claimed responsibility. Rosemary Nelson, a prominent civil rights lawyer, age 40, was murdered on May 15, 1999, in Lurgan, in the Six Counties, by a car bomb. She had previously received death threats allegedly from the Royal Ulster Constabulary (RUC).

On June 15, 1999, I attended a meeting at the British Embassy in Washington, D.C. One of the purposes of the session was to demand an inquiry totally independent of the RUC into the murder of Nelson. Some of the other activists present were: Professor Gerry Coleman, Kathleen Kelly, Gavan Kennedy, Professor Jack Worrell, Richard Harvey, Esq. and James Fitzpatrick, Esq.

I pointed out to the Embassy officials that New Jersey attorney Edmund E. Lynch had written numerous letters, in 1997 and 1998, to Northern Ireland Office (NIO) officers about the repeated death threats to Nelson. On Feb. 12, 1999, Lynch even met personally with RUC head, Ronnie Flanagan, for over two hours, and again raised the issue of death threats against Nelson. The Embassy officials vigorously defended the conduct of the RUC, but promised to look into "our concerns."

[32]. John Stalker, *The Stalker Affair: The Shocking True Story of Six Deaths and A Notorious Cover-Up*, (Viking, 1988); Sean McPhilemy, *The Committee: Political Assassination in Northern Ireland*, (Robert Rinehart,

1998); Ed., "To Serve Without Favor: Policing, Human Rights, and Accountability in Northern Ireland," (Human Rights Watch, 1997); and, David Leigh, *The Wilson Plot: How the Spycatchers and Their American Allies Tried to Overthrow the British Government,* (Pantheon Books, 1988).

[33]. Liz Curtis, *Ireland: The Propaganda War*, (Pluto Press, 1984).

[34]. A C-Span program, originating from the National Press Club, in Washington, D.C., on Oct. 18, 1993, carried Holroyd's press conference. I participated in it as a reporter representing WBAI's Radio Free Eireann in NYC.

[35]. Father Sean McManus, *The MacBride Principles: Genesis and History and The Story to Date*, (Irish National Caucus,1993). The MacBride Principles became a federal law in 1998.

[36]. Andrew Grice and Michael Prescott, "Secret Anglo-Irish Pact to Smash IRA," *London Sunday Times*, Dec. 19, 1993.

*       *       *

# 79. Philip Berrigan & the Anti-Nuke Movement
## January 12, 1983

"I was an imperial citizen, the citizen of an imperial empire, every bit as decadent and twisted and sick as the British Empire and the Roman empire. It was obscene, the monumental injustice of it all," says James Cunningham, a 41 year-old former attorney from Laguna Beach, California.

Cunningham is a resident of Jonah House, described by one of its founding members, Philip Berrigan, as a "non-violent resistance community dedicated to working against nuclear weapons and nuclear omnicide."

Berrigan, a former Josephite priest, now a graying 59 year-old, and his wife, Liz McAlister, their three small children and a half-dozen other adults make up the activist, anti-war Reservoir-Hill-located group.

"I owned 26 suits, 40 pairs of shoes, three cars, land and all of that," Cunningham continued. "I had it all. I was a criminal lawyer and made a lot of money doing it. But it was terrible, especially when I considered 40,000 children starved to death each day, according to the United Nations, because of factors directly relating to malnutrition. After the Vietnam War, I simply went to sleep."

Congressman James Jones, a Democrat of Oklahoma, recently said on the House floor, "If we spent $1 million every day since the birth of Jesus, we would have spent half of what the administration wants to spend on the U.S. military in the next five years, or $1.5 trillion."

"The people do not have the voice of representation in Washington, D.C.," says Berrigan of the 1968 *Catonsville Nine* and more recently as one of the *Plowshare Eight* defendants. Along with his brother, the Jesuit priest and well known poet, Daniel Berrigan, Philip and the *Plowshare Eight* were convicted of destroying a Mark 12A nuclear warhead with a sledge hammer at General Electric plant in King of Prussia, Pennsylvania on September 9, 1980. In January of 1981, Philip was sentenced to three-to-10 years in prison and 10 years probation for what he describes as "his crime of peacemaking." He is now appealing that verdict.

"The insanity of the legal system," Cunningham added, "is best epitomized in a short hand version by the movie,

*And Justice for All.* All of those things in that movie happened to me, but only in spades: the alcoholic judges, the sex-pervert prosecutors, the innocent people being f….. over, the guilty being thrown in these hell holes, the child-molester cops, the drunk cops, the drug-addict cops and the awful sickness of making people be stoolies and have them killed later. The amorality of it all, at one point, came to me. It came to me that what I was involved in here was a pagan religion that worshipped death."

The 43 year-old Liz McAlister, a former Sacred Heart nun and college history teacher, says she has seen, "tremendous changes" and positive results in the quality and quantity of non-violent resisters to the global war preparations. McAlister added,"The arms race isn't something out there. It is something that comes out of our own guts. It comes out of the way we live against other people, and, in putting walls around who will and will not be our community; namely, the nuclear family. It is well-named by the way."

Berrigan, who was arrested yet again over the Christmas holiday at a Pentagon demonstration, added, "The government is less and less representing the people. So that is why a movement has to be built in this country, if we are going to make it. The government has to be restored to the people and only the general public can do that." He said although the 'Freeze Movement' has its ambiguities because, "It fails to address the possession and stockpiling of nuclear weapons; nevertheless, it warranted praise as a 'first step' in an evolving process towards sanity."

Cunningham, who voluntarily resigned from both the California and Oregon Bars in 1980, recently completed a six month jail sentence for damaging a missile hatch on a Trident submarine, located at Electric Boat Company, in Groton, Connecticut. He belongs to a group of defendants, known as the *Trident Nine*.

"Trident submarines were just like the courts that I was practicing in," Cunningham emphasized. "Instead of a judge, they had a captain of a ship. Instead of lawyers, they had a lot of crew men, who were going around under the water, like in a monastery. They chanted with each other. They went through all the rituals; celibacy, obedience, just like the monastery; except that they were worshipping death and calling it deterrence and peacemaking, and all kinds of things. They were torturing the language to death. They don't go to mass underwater. It's too difficult for them."

Cunningham faces six more months in prison, if he fails to make restitution for the property damage done to the submarine. He is going to refuse to pay the damages and says, "The judge is a classic liberal, who is trying to play both sides and he is just really in a lot of psychic turmoil over our case. He is Jewish and very well read on the Jewish tradition. We kept hitting on that theme during the trial, that the Trident submarine is just an oven without walls. We spray-painted 'U.S.S. Auschwitz' on the side of the *USS Florida* 728."

"It brings me back to my profession, the end of the world will be legal. The entire civilization could go up in smoke and it would be eminently legal; perhaps the most legally supported, legally analyzed, legally talked about, legally sanctioned event in all of human history. What does that say about the law?"

Cunningham continued, "I saw poverty in the 'Third World' when I was in the Navy. I saw poverty in the streets, when I was a social worker, and poverty in the courts, when I was a lawyer. And up at the pinnacle, I saw this judge, who represented death. So, when I heard about a Trident submarine, I didn't hear it in some vacuum. When I heard about a submarine two football fields long, with 24 missiles, each having 17 warheads, and the range was 6,900 miles, and the accuracy within 90 feet, and they told me about what a 'first-strike' was, God damn-I was over the edge."

All of the Jonah House residents that I talked with were encouraged somewhat by the recent statement of the National Conference of Catholic Bishops attacking among other things, the morality of the first-strike use of nuclear weapons by any of their possessors.

Berrigan said, "For 37 years, there has been a grand silence from the church both Catholic and Protestant, on this important issue, and now, it has been broken. But, I don't think they have gone far enough."

             \*             \*             \*

# 80. Abolish the Death Penalty
## March 7, 2001

Re: HB 102-Abolish the Death Penalty
Testimony-House of Delegate's Judiciary Committee
Thomas Hunter Lowe Building
Annapolis, Maryland

Mr. Chairman and Members of the Committee:

My name is William Hughes. I am an attorney and an author from Baltimore City.

I don't believe the state of Maryland should be in the business of executing convicted criminals. This is a barbaric practice that has no place in a civilized society.

The death penalty doesn't deter criminals either. What it does do is teach the wrong lesson that it is alright to kill, if you have a supposedly righteous cause and the power to carry it out.

When a society stoops to executing defenseless individuals, it also erodes the more enduring values of our Republic. Revenge is not one of those values, nor is it a virtue. The state should not be used as a tool to balance some mythical scale of justice that has its roots in the biblical era.

HB 102 is also timely. It is clear from recent statistics that it is the poor and minorities who are disproportionately the victims of the death penalty hysteria. If you're wealthy, the chances are you will be able to retain the best kind of legal representation and even if you don't beat the case, such a defendant will more than likely escape receiving the ultimate penalty.

The recent murder case involving one of the DuPonts comes to my mind. He was able to plead the insanity defense in his situation.

In addition, statistics compiled by the "National Coalition Against the Death Penalty," show that since 1972, 69 people convicted of a capital offense in this country and awaiting the death sentence have since been found innocent and released from custody. Twelve states and the District of Columbia are without capital punishment laws.

Let Maryland join that group.

This Committee should be aware that death penalty cases for indigent defendants cost the taxpayers, too, through their funding of the state's "Public Defenders Office."

Equity and justice demand an end to the state's killing machine. HB 102 warrants the approval of this honorable Committee.

*           *           *

# 81. A Devil's Advocate for a Saintly Man
## January-February, 1999

As the "Iron Curtain" has disintegrated over Eastern Europe, the memory of one of dictator Josef Stalin's most heroic opponents-the late Eugenio Pacelli has come to mind. He was known to the world as Pope Pius XII.

His pontificate lasted from 1939 to his death in 1958. By force of strong character, a rich intellectual heritage, and genuine spirituality, Pius XII led the Church through one of its most turbulent periods-World War II (1939-1945).

As his pontificate unfolded, he faced perilous dangers to his own person, to the Church, and to the survival of Catholicism. Pius XII was a virtual hostage, *a la* Lebanese-style, in the Vatican during most of the WWII period. Italy was then under the absolute domination of the fascist, anti-clerical dictator, Benito Mussolini. Adolf Hitler's Germany, also rabidly anti-Catholic, was preparing to invade Poland, with Stalin's Bolshevik-infested regime, and Italy, as its Axis cronies.

Stalin, the quintessential cult-of-personality psychopath, despised the Church. His warped communist ideology, enforced by fanatical Bolshevik cadres and demonic Commissars, was dedicated to destroying everything associated with the peoples of the Christian West. Nevertheless, the Pope bravely blasted Hitler's pact with Stalin and railed against the rape of Poland by the Nazis hordes.

In the mega-carnage that followed, an estimated 50 million people lost their lives. Stalin would later join the Allies: the U.S., Britain and France, but only after Hitler's shocking invasion of the Soviet Union in 1941.

In the summer of 1943, after Mussolini was overthrown by partisans, the Nazis took over total control of the city of Rome. It is beyond dispute that Hitler, then paranoiac over heavy military losses sustained on the Eastern front against the Red Army, easily could have dissolved the entire Vatican establishment in one murderous raid.

Fortunately, Pius XII lived to see the Church survive. He never wavered in his abhorrence of Hitler or Stalin. After WWII, evidence of the "Jewish Holocaust" (the mass killing of European Jewry by the Nazis) became known. World opinion was outraged. There also was created the need for scapegoats and a cleverly crafted red herring when awkward questions arose for the surviving Jewish people.

"Why did the Jews, through their own leaders, cooperate with the Nazis in their own destruction?"; "Why did the Jews abandon their apparently successful economic boycott of pre-WWII Nazi Germany?"; and, "Why did millions of Jews go to their death like lambs to the slaughter?"

These were some of the major queries raised by intellectuals and historians, like Ben Hecht, and especially, Hannah Arendt. Arendt called the Zionist complicity in the tragedy one of the "darkest pages" in the history of their race. Many found the questions raised by Arendt and Hecht too painful to face directly.

Pius XII, now dead, became a convenient target for revenge and a distraction from the issue of Zionist complicity raised by the dissidents. Both Zionists, and non-Jews, began accusing Pius XII of responsibility for the death of the Jews by his so called "silence" regarding the mass exterminations. The Christian bashers regularly portrayed Pius XII in plays, articles, books, movies and television documentaries, as a crass tool of the capitalists, an uncaring bureaucrat, and a heartless cleric. Nothing could have been further from the truth, but these slanders continue until the present day. Although some have bravely spoken out on this matter, most have elected not to do so for fear of being labeled an "anti-Semite" by Zionist zealots. The truth, however, must be told and Pius XII, like other historical figures, is entitled to a defense.

First, some background on Pius XII. As a young priest, he was trained in diplomacy and Cannon Law. He came from an ancient Roman family that had long been in the service of the Vatican. He was known as a tireless worker, well-read, and experienced in global affairs.

In 1929, the young Pacelli was appointed secretary of state for the papacy. During his tenure, a compelling papal encyclical, *Mit Brennender Sorge*, was issued in German in 1937. No epithets were omitted in its condemnation of Nazism. Hitler was described as a "mad prophet of repulsive arrogance." It is beyond rebuttal that such a provocative encyclical could not have been issued without the consent of Pacelli.

After Hitler's success in the Czech Sudetenland, however, and his diplomatic coup in reaching the "Munich Agreement" with Britain and France, he secured the overwhelming support of the German populace. Despite all of that, Nicholas Cheetham said in his *Keeper of the Keys,* the gutsy German bishops, with the Vatican's approval, which included Pacelli, a key diplomat, "courageously denounced concentration camps, mass deportations, the organized euthanasia of the infirm, the confiscation of Church properties, and the corruption of the youth by semi-pagan teachings."

Respected historians now agree that the "Jewish Holocaust" didn't begin until after the Wannsee Conference, held on January 20, 1942. The meeting was chaired by SS Gestapo Chief, Reinhard Heydrich, Heinrich Himmler's deputy.

As late as Christmas Day, 1942, Pius XII still persisted in publicly denouncing the evils of totalitarianism, which invoked violent German protest. He was repeatedly threatened with physical retaliation. The

Vatican, under his stewardship, had saved over 400,000 Jews from certain death, more than all other institutions, churches and governments put together. Records at Israel's *Yad Vashem* memorial now indicate, according to the author of *Pius XII: Greatest Dishonored,* that the Pope's humanitarian efforts actually saved over 860,000 Jewish lives.

Margherita Marchinone underscores in her book, *Yours Is a Precious Witness,* that "while 67 percent of European Jews were killed, 85 percent of Italy's Jews were saved" and that the people who know best-"credit Pius XII for this moral victory." Thousands of Catholic priests and nuns also paid the supreme penalty for opposing Hitler.

Recent events have demonstrated that Pius XII's role during this period has also been subjected to a double standard by his vindictive Zionist critics. While he was expected to express opinions against the Nazis, despite being under the equivalent of house arrest, Zionists today regularly refuse to speak out against Israeli atrocities in the West Bank, Gaza and southern Lebanon. What flagrant hypocrisy!

A celebrity "Jewish Holocaust" survivor, Elie Wiesel, was requested to give his opinion on the *Intifada,* the gallant Palestinian uprising in the occupied West Bank and Gaza. He declined to condemn Israel's barbaric treatment of the Palestinian people, which has been documented by leading human rights groups, like Amnesty International and by the United Nations. Wiesel's excuse, despite living in the safety of the Christian West, was that his answer might aid Israel's enemies. The deafening silence of the vast majority of the American Zionists to Israel's abysmal human rights record must also be taken into account in this brouhaha.

Just imagine if the shoe were on the other foot in this controversy. Suppose Christian intellectuals had accused Judaism of being responsible for the crimes of Stalin, since many of the Bolshevik leaders were indeed Jewish (See, Stuart Kahan, *The Wolf of the Kremlin* and Malcom Muggeridge's *Winter in Moscow*). The outcry from the Zionists would have been monumental. In fact, Karl Marx, the founder of Communism, and Leon Trotsky, a Bolshevik leader, who became Stalin's top rival, were

Jewish, while the sinister Vladmir Lenin, whose Bolsheviks snuffed out an attempt at democracy by Russia's Mensheviks, was half-Jewish.

Question: Why did the Zionists at a world conference of members, according to the *London Daily Express,* (03/24/34), target Germany for destruction, and not also the Soviet Union, where Christians were being butchered left and right? And, what, if any, explanation is there for the Zionist silence about Stalin's genocide against the Christian masses? It is estimated that over 50 million died under the Communist "Evil Empire".

On the media front, one of Pius XII's severest critics has been the *New York Times* newspaper, long a vehicle for Zionist misinformation and as a shameless apologist for Israel's wrongdoing. In a book by S. J. Taylor, *Walter Duranty: Stalin's Apologist,* it was revealed that the *NYT's* reporter on the Soviet Union, the late, British-born Walter Duranty, was a shill for Stalin's propaganda machine.

The Ukraine genocide/famine of 1932-33 was one of the greatest man-made disasters in history. Stalin's henchman in this massive crime against humanity was the evil Lazar Kaganovich, a Jew, also was one of the signers of the genocide document, which condemned to death 25,000 Polish Catholic officers at the *Katyn Forest Massacre* in the spring of 1940. Millions of peasants perished in the forced collectivization in the Ukraine. The *NYT* not only missed the story, but also covered it up. The tragedy was called "mostly bunk".

Stalin's blood-stained purge trials of 1928, 1934, and 1936 also were reported as nothing more than "justice served."

Meanwhile, the *Washington Times* revealed in a shocking article (07/17/90), that only one million Jews had died at Auschwitz, a Nazi death camp, and not the four million as originally claimed by the Zionists. Three hundred thousand non-Jews also perished there. Researchers at Israel's *Yad Vashem* memorial admitted the new Polish figures were correct. This new evidence would cut in half the Zionist's original claim that six million Jews had died under the Nazi regime. It would also raise the question, "Why did the Zionists grossly exaggerated the original numbers of Jewish victims?

Finally, it must be stated that Pius XII's conduct can be judged only within the context of the unique circumstances of WWII in Europe. When that is done, the vile canard against his reputation by the Christian bashers must be dismissed as being factually unsupported and a damnable lie.

He will then be seen as a compassionate friend of humanity and a humble servant of his God.

*       *       *

# References

Hannah Arendt's *A Report on the Banality of Evil: Eichmann in Jerusalem*, Penguin Books (1963); *The Jew as Pariah*, Hannah Arendt, Grove Press (1978); Ben Hecht's *Perfidy*, Messner (1961); *Zionism in the Age of Dictators*, Lennie Brenner, Crown Heim, London and H. Hill, Westport, Conn. (1983); *Pius XII and the Holocaust*, a Reader, Catholic League Publication (1988); *Keepers of the Keys*, Nicholas Cheetham, Charles Scribner's Sons (1983); *Pius XII: Greatness Dishonored*, Michael O'Carroll, C.S.Sp., Latare Press, Blackrock, Co. Dublin; "In Memory of the Katyn Massacre," *Washington Times*, 03/27/95; *The Other Holocaust-The Terror Famine in Ukraine*, Peter J. Lorder, *Barnes Review*, 07/96; "Stalinist Boss Dies; Oversaw Reign of Terror," David Remnick, *Washington Post*, 07/27/91; L. M. Kaganovich, 'Stalwart of Stalin', Dies at 97, *New York Times*, Francis X. Clines, 07/27/91; *Jewish History, Jewish Religion*, Israel Shahak, Pluto Press, (1994); "A Pop Quiz on the Middle East," Charlie Reese, *Orlando Sentinel*, 02/08/98; and "What Price Holocaustomania?," Dr. Alfred M. Lilienthal, *Washington Report on Middle East Affairs magazine*, April, 1998.

*       *       *

Author's Note-In the notorious *Dachau* concentration camp, located in German, 1,213 priests, of 17 nationalities, were liberated by the U.S.

Army, on April 29, 1945. There were 30,000 inmates in the dreaded facility at that time. During all of WWII, 2,670 members of the clegy were detained at *Dachau*. Dying at the camp were 621 members of the clergy, of which 598 were of the Roman Catholic faith. Hauled away from the camp to their deaths in the "transport of the invalids," were 332 clergy members, of whom 325 were Roman Catholic priests. (Source, *And Who Will Kill You*, Bedrich Hoffmann, Pallottinun, Poznan, Poland, 1994.)

# 82. Agony of Lebanon
## July, 1996

"Even the dead can't rest in Lebanon," Habib D. Ghanim emphasized before an activist group in Washington, DC, on Friday evening, April 26, 1996, at a meeting entitled, "Israel Out of Lebanon-Stop the Bombing."

Ghanim is an Arab-American of Lebanese ancestry. He said the Israelis' recent shelling of Lebanon "destroyed in 16 days, what it took the people almost 16 years to rebuild. They even bombed cemeteries in their blatant attacks on the civilian populations. Every day that the bombing goes on means another year of rebuilding for the suffering people of Lebanon."

Casualty figures indicate over 150 people were killed in Lebanon, of whom 13 were Hezbollah fighters. The rest were civilians. Many more were injured, and over 500,000 Lebanese were driven out of their homes.

A cease-fire was announced earlier in the day that Ghanim spoke. Media speculation suggested that Israel had launched its offensive, entitled, "Grapes of Wrath," to boost Labor's standings in the polls, prior the May 29 election. Tel Aviv claimed otherwise. It said the invasion was in retaliation for Hezbollah's shelling of northern Israel and the suicide bombings by Hamas guerrilla that took 59 lives.

Ghanim said the accord wouldn't work. "It fails to address the root cause of the violence in Lebanon," he claimed, "which is the Israeli occupation of 440 square miles of that country and their desire to seize the waters of the Litani River."

Candace Wagner, a union activist at the protest meeting, demanded that all US aid to Israel be ended. The audience gasped when she reported, "$78 billion has gone to Israel since 1948, with $6.3 billion going in 1996 alone-about $17 million a day" (*Washington Report on the Middle East,* 04/96).

I wondered what the people in Baltimore City, living with budget cuts in library, education and fire protection services, would say if they knew Israel was getting all those freebies.

According to Ghanim, the damage to the economy of Lebanon from the Israeli invasion "could reach a half billion dollars." He charged that the Israelis deliberately destroyed power stations, reservoirs and roads in order to "make the people suffer and for them to turn on each other."

Ghanim maintained that the Israelis were "using innocent people as a political tool, but their strategy backfired. The people are now more united than ever. The Hezbollah resistance is now seen as a matter of national pride."

Wagner said there were nightly pickets, all throughout the bombings in front of both the White House and Israeli Embassy in Washington, although the media pretended otherwise. One White House protest, led by Arab Americans, was attended by 4,000 activists.

Another participant at the meeting, who asked not to be identified for this story, told me, "I believe the Israelis have every right to defend themselves against suicide bombers and to go after the wrongdoers, but I do think they went too far."

Nevertheless, the Likud Party, led by a right wing extremist, Benyamin Netanyahu, did win the election. His victory doesn't bode well for Mideast peace, a settlement of the Jerusalem question, or Lebanon's future.

Some American Christian leaders believe the situation was bad enough when Labor was in power. On March 6, 1995, Baltimore's Cardinal William Keeler, Kara Newell of the American Friends Service Committee, and six other officials, in an open letter to President Bill Clinton, called the Israelis' action into question. They blasted Tel Aviv for seizing the lands of the Palestinians, planning a "Greater Jerusalem", and for violating the rights of Muslims and Christians.

Meanwhile, the *Baltimore Sun*, (06/05/96), which editorially condoned Israel's rampage in Lebanon, trumpeted, "American support for Israel is permanent." Daniel Berger, one of its columnists, (06/08/96), praised Netanyahu as a "super Israeli nationalist." (This same Daniel Berger has made a career out of demonizing Irish nationalists as "terrorists.")

The *Nation* magazine, (05/06/96), however, sharply criticized the Israeli invasion of Lebanon for "violating the rules of international humanitarian law, as codified in the Geneva Convention." Since 1978, Israel has occupied southern Lebanon in violation of UN Resolution 425.

Ghanim concluded his remarks by saying, there were at least two American citizens killed by the Israelis in their shelling of the UN post at Qana (Cana), on April 18. "They were school-age children from Dearborn, Michigan, who were visiting relatives.

The Bible says Jesus performed one of his first miracles at Qana, when he turned water into wine. Now, the Israelis with their vicious attack on the UN post, have literally turned water into blood," he sadly observed.

*       *       *

## 83. Remember the USS *Liberty*
## June 8, 1996

This morning, I attended a very moving memorial service at the Arlington National Cemetery, located on the south side of the Potomac River. It honored the memory of the 34 Americans, who died on board the USS *Liberty*, on June 8, 1967. Another 171 were seriously injured. The memorial service was held at the "Mass Grave" site, and was sponsored by the "No Greater Love Committee."

A Navy chaplain said a prayer at the ceremony. There was also a wreath-laying ceremony and the playing of taps.

A good percentage of the impacted *Liberty* crew, like their skipper, Captain William McGonagle, were of Irish stock. The *Liberty* was a U.S. Navy intelligence ship.

While in international waters, in the Mediterranean Sea, it was deliberately attacked, with bombs, rockets and napalm by the Israelis. They knew it was an American ship, but lied about it.

One new theory is the Israelis may have been trying to cover up their ethnic cleansing of over 1,000 Arab POWs, during the 1967 War (Source, *Washington Report on Middle East Affairs* magazine, June, 1996.)

James Ennes, a lieutenant on the *Liberty*, and a native of Newark, N.J. believes the Israel attack itself was a "war crime." His book, *Assault on the Liberty* (Random House, 1980), gives a riveting account of that fateful day.

Many Americans know the name of Leon Klinghoffer, who was killed by PLO guerrillas a few years back. But, the names of the unsung *Liberty* seamen, who died in that Israeli sponsored terrorist attack, are now lost to history because of congressional fear of retaliation from the powerful Israeli Lobby.

I demand that Congress do it duty: investigate the *Liberty* affair, call Captain William McGonagle, and the other survivors to testify at a public hearing.

And, let justice, finally, be done for our fallen heroes.

*       *       *

*Author's Note-Captain William McGonagle died on March 3, 1999, at age 73. He was awarded the Medal of Honor in 1986 (see, Richard Pearson, "William McGonagle Dies: Captain of USS *Liberty*," *Washington Post*, March 9, 1999).

# 84. America Returning to its Populist Roots
## December, 1991

Americans are mad as hell, and they aren't going to take it anymore!

They feel alienated from the brokers of power in Washington, D.C. The 39 percent protest for David Duke in Louisiana reflects that reality, as did Sen. Harris Wofford's stunning senatorial upset victory in Pennsylvania over Richard "Tricky Dick" Thornburgh.

When organized labor held their recent rally in the nation's capital, over 250,000 participated. You could feel the dissent rising in the air.

The collective outrage is beyond the usual spectrum of right and left politics. Race isn't a significant factor in it either, despite the attempts of hysterical editorial writers to make it so.

The failure of many S & Ls and banks; the shaky state of some pension systems; Wall Street rats running amok in the merger mania and junk bond scandals; rampant street crime and drug use; the scourge of AIDS; a depressed economy; the BCCI debacle; and congressional skullduggery have all contributed to the growing disenchantment.

Bill Moyers, a respected commentator, blames our present mess on a "mercenary culture," in which myopic politicians view posterity as being "the next election." (*Washington Post,* 09/09/01).

A populist vein has been struck that is almost spiritual in nature. Naturally, it is disparaged by the elite snobs that run the country. Some of the vilification of Duke, as with Alabama's George C. Wallace's presidential candidacy in 1968, is aimed at discouraging other politicos from picking up his "throw-the-bums-out" banner.

I reject all racist opinions that may fairly be attributed to Duke. But, he was subjected to a flagrant double standard by the media. His message on crime, the welfare cycle, and quotas deserved a serious discussion. Duke was consistently referred to by TV newsreaders as "an ex-KKK leader and Adolf Hitler admirer." These same Persian Gulf cheerleaders don't dare describe Israel's prime minister Yitshak Shamir as an "ex-terrorist and former member of the Stern Gang."

The origins of populism can be traced to our brave rebels at Valley Forge and the gallant defenders of Fort McHenry in the War of 1812-14. Its intellectual beginnings can be found in our Declaration of Independence, our Bill of Rights, the Constitution, and in President George Washington's "Farewell Address" in May, 1796. In it, Washington warned against "the mischiefs of foreign intrigues" and the evils of factionalism.

The movement to set term limits for elected officials is also generated by populist instinct, as is the ongoing taxpayers' revolt now germination in our cities, states, and halls of congress.

In a sentence, populism can be defined as taking care of America's interest first, and advocating freedom, self-determination, and equal opportunity for all.

George Wallace said there wasn't "a dime's worth of difference between the two parties." He was right. Since World War II, this nation has gone from colossus status to pitiful has-been. Both political parties have played a part in that debacle.

Any idea that New York's Mario Cuomo will ride to our rescue is pure wishful thinking. Cuomo is just a northern version of Jimmy Carter. Cuomo also lacks the courage to say "no" to the lobbyists for special interests, the New York Times, and the Council on Foreign Relations.

Unlike partisans for the Eastern Establishment, I don't believe our decline as a world power has been accidental. Even an inept Congress has acknowledged that conspiracies exist in the economic field. This is why they have enacted anti-price fixing laws.

Why not a conspiracy also in the political arena? If grasping individuals can get together to fix prices on the sale of retail goods, why can't others, greedy for political and economic power, jointly plan to reduce America to a vassal state?

You think this is a preposterous idea? Then explain how Britain, Germany and Japan are vigilant in protecting their own industries, resources, and labor from foreign exploitation, but we aren't? I believe that our self-censoring media have consciously chosen to keep this truth from the American people.

Remember also, that if a giant conglomerate can be taken over by outsiders to bleed it dry, then so can a country. It's the same rip-off at work.

As a conspiratorial example, take the JFK assassination. You know that Lee Harvey Oswald didn't act alone when he murdered the president on November 22, 1963. The Warren Commission report that Oswald was a lone desperado is pure bunk to most Americans. JFK may have been the first U.S. president killed to make the world safe for the "New World Order."

He wanted to disengage from Vietnam, work out a deal with Red Cuba's Fidel Castro, and crush the anglophile-infested CIA into a thousand pieces. JFK was a threat to the agenda of the shadowy globalist mob. His murder has been covered up for over 23 years.

I assert that America itself, as a national entity, is also on a hit list. It stands today vulnerable to the caprices of these alien predators.

At press time, activists were arrested protesting state budge cuts at Governor Schaefer's Baltimore office. You can expect more demonstrations in the future, with the focus shifting to Washington, D.C.

With the dissolution of the Russians' "Evil Empire," the Establishment has been caught short, substituting a "sinister force" to justify a $300 billion-plus defense/security budget. But fear of terrorism isn't going to do it. Most people can't afford vacations anyway, and are more afraid of the local thugs that prowl their own streets than they are of some obscure enemy-from-without.

President George Washington also warned about alienating "any portion of our country from the rest." The insidious anti-populist elements want to divide North against South, black against white, women against men and conservative from liberals.

The notion that America's interests should come first is an anathema to the Establishment and their apologists. This is why columnist Fred Barnes could denounce a Patrick Buchanan presidential candidacy as a naked appeal to "nativist, protectionist, and isolationist interests."

Is not Duke-Buchanan that they really fear, but the end to the fraud, waste and corruption that they so viscerally represent.

This growing cause is as natural as apple pie, and as American as our 4th of July. If it doesn't come to power soon, there won't be any America left for patriots to celebrate.

*　　　　　*　　　　　*

Author's Note-The highest value in the land is the Republic (*Res Publica*). In a Republic, all power is derived from the people (*Imperium Populus*). No individual, group, special interest, clique, or combination of any kind whatsoever has the right to put its grasping interests above the Republic (*Pro Bono Publico*). If such a party does attempt to do so, it becomes *ipso facto*, an enemy of the people (*Sic Semper Tyrannis*). And, it should be treated as an enemy and a cancer (*Imperium Legum*) on the body politics (*Res Publica Est Res Populi*).

# 85. The People Control Act of 1993
## May, 1993

Is there something deep inside you that thinks the United States government may have overreacted slightly at Waco, Texas? Have you ever considered the idea that you, like the late David Koresh, and his hapless followers, could possibly be the target of zealous agents of the federal establishment because of your political activism?

Maybe, it was the sight of all those armed FBI and Treasury Department detectives storming the compound of the religious cult back on February 28 that jolted our psyches a little? Or, could it have been that TV image of a huge M-60 tank battering holes and shooting tear gas into the fortress on April 19?

You thought the cops in LA were bad?

The final tally shows 86 Branch Davidians now dead, which include 24 innocent children. One of the dubious justifications for the Vietnam-like attack on the cultists was to save the children from abuse. The government spread the false rumor, despite the fact there wasn't any evidence to support it. The White House apologist said that "Protecting the kids was the ultimate rationale for going in."

General William Westmoreland, the ex-Vietnam War Hawk, couldn't have said it better.

Now, ask yourself this question, "Do U..S. Police agencies need more power from the Congress to abuse its citizens?"

Well, irrespective of what you think, my friend, I've got some distressing news for you. A lot of powerful people on Capitol Hill believe that the FBI, especially its growing anti-terrorists sleuths, do need more ammunition. This is why the "Crime Control Act of 1993," (SB 8) has already been assigned to the Judiciary Committee, chaired by Sen. Joseph R. Biden, Jr. (D-Del).

This Bill, which should be labeled, "The People Control Act of 1993," is endorsed by political dinosaurs, like Senators Strom Thurmond (R-SC); Alan Simpson (R-WY); and Bob Dole (R-KA).

There are 43 Republicans in the senate, and many of their colleagues think just like they do on crime-related issues. SB 8 incorporates provisions dealing with Sen. Biden's SB 266, "Comprehensive Counter Terrorism of 1991," and SB 265, titled, "Terrorism Death Penalty Act of 1991." Both of those Bills contained language which can charge law-abiding citizens of being agents of offering support to terrorist organizations.

Politically active organization and labor unions are clearly vulnerable to prosecution under the deliberately vague provisions of SB8. A fist fight at a demonstration or picket line would qualify as a "terrorist act." An individual or organization who had or should have had knowledge that an associate (probably an agent provocateur) might commit a terrorist act can have that associate's property seized by the government.

Written like the notorious RICO laws, citizens who allowed their home or real property to be used for such an assembly would start out presumptively guilty before a Star Chamber-like tribunal.

Those who drafted SB 8 probably felt no need to tighten the definition of the words and phrases. Like Humpty Dumpty in Lewis Carroll's *Alice Through the Looking Class,* they say, in effect, "Please don't trouble yourselves trying to find out what our words mean; they mean what we say they mean, no more and no less."

Or to put it differently, SB 8 can be made to work selectively by the Establishment where its words will mean what the U.S. Attorneys say what they mean, no more and no less; and where the federal courts will become no more than a public place where punishments can be seen to be imposed.

The ghosts of Joseph Stalin's dreaded Commissars have to be pleased by the draconian provisions in this monster Bill. If it passes as written, the Congress might as well shred the U.S. Constitution. Our revered Bill of Rights will be its first victim. Citizen of this Republic will live in terror of federal bureaucrats. Opposition to government policy, both domestic and foreign, will become a memory of the past.

If your rights are trampled on by agents trying to prevent so-called "terrorist acts," Section 2337 of the Bill will prohibit you from filing a civil suit for damages against either the "United States or Foreign Government." Gee, I wonder what "foreign government" the Bill is trying to protect from litigation? Couldn't be the "New World Order" gang, could it?

The mere thought of a dark conspiracy at work is enough to get the "G-Men" to legally move against any activist or his group. Under provisions of SB 8, property forfeiture, arrest, huge fines and long prison sentences can result from "activities which appear to be intended toward violence."

Any picket line which is alleged to have blocked public access could qualify to "intimidate or coerce a civilian population" or "to influence the policy of a government by intimidation or coercion."

In the prosecution of any cases under SB 8, discovery of witnesses and evidence against the accused will be sharply limited. The Bill will also allow illegally obtained evidence to be used at a trial, if the arresting officer thought the search was in "conformity with the Fourth Amendment."

At press time, no Democratic version of a Crime Bill had been introduced in either the Senate or the House. President Bill Clinton stated, at his April 23 press conference, "I think we need to go forward on the crime bill." I pray he didn't mean SB 8!

The fact that Sen. Biden has previously championed many of the God-awful provisions now contained in SB 8 should give all progressives and libertarians pause for concern. As chairman of the Judiciary Committee, he can call for a vote on SB 8, without conducting any public hearings.

Biden has a nasty habit of not consulting interested parties on controversial Bills before sending them to the floor for a final vote.

If anybody is looking to the House of Representatives to save them from SB 8 becoming law, don't bother calling House Speaker, Tom "Bad Check" Foley. He has built a career caving into special interests. Common Cause, one of the most respected advocates of campaign election reforms, recently reported that Foley has received nearly $2 million in PAC moneys over the last 10 years. A member of the David Rockefeller's front group, the Council on Foreign Relations, the House

Speaker has long lost any affinity for the needs of citizens to be protected from the excesses of their own government. Foley could care less!

The Bush-Quayle "Omnibus Crime Bill," was blocked on October 2, 1992, by sheer dumb luck, simply because it would have also limited gun sales in this country. The Senate failed to invoke closure to cut off a Republican filibuster, so the Bill was allowed to die. It contained many of the onerous provisions, now enshrined in SB 8; like increased penalties for certain offenses; and, weakened the ability of death row prisoners to challenge their sentences.

Concerned citizens should immediately contact their Representatives in the House, and their two U.S. Senators, and express their reservations about SB 8. Any group that might possibly be impacted by this Crime Bill should also insist on their congressperson sending them a copy of it.

Express your opinions on SB 8 to your elected officials, with a copy of your letter going to: Hon. Joseph R. Biden, Jr., Chairman of the Judiciary Committee, U.S. Senate, Washington, D.C., 20510.

As the politicos to state their positions on SB 8, in their return correspondence to you or your organization.

*          *          *

Author's Note-Over time, some of the more egregious provisions mentioned above have in fact become law. Check out, "The Anti-Terrorism Act," pushed a few years back by Arlen Specter (R-Pa) and Charles Schumer (D-NY), then a member of the House. He is now the senior senator from New York. It calls for "secret trials, based on secret evidence" for non-citizens suspected of wrongdoing.

Specter, earlier in his dismal career, was the legal adviser to the Warren Commission. He came up with that ridiculous "Magic Bullet" theory, that helped to derail an effective investigation into the murder of JFK. Schumer is a rabid gun control addict and the chief advocate in the congress of the legally dubious "Hate Crime" schemes.

Another draconian law, enacted in 2001, entitled, "The U.S.A Patriot Act," drives a wooden stake deep into the heart of some of our most precious civil liberties. It was sponsored by the Bush-Cheney Administration. Liberals in the congress, however, like Sen. Barbara Mikulski (D-MD) and right wing conservatives, such as Rep. Peter King (R-NY), joined together to shred our Bill of Rights by voting for this baleful measure. How can these people sleep at night? Didn't they take a solemn oath of office to uphold the Constitution?

# Notes

**Sources of Articles and/or Letters**
**Chapter One: Heroes, Heroines & Mavericks**

1. Baltimore's *City Paper.*
2. Letter to Rep. Mario Biaggi (D-NY) from the author.
3. *Maryland Life Magazine.*
4. *Baltimore Chronicle.*
5. *Baltimore Enterprise.*
6. *Ibid.*
7. The Baltimore Press.
8. *Ibid.*
9. *Ibid.*
10. *Ibid.*
11. Baltimore's *City Paper.*
12. *Maryland Life Magazine.*
13. Baltimore's *City Paper.*

**Chapter Two: The Reality-Challenged**

14. *The Baltimore Press.*
15. Posted on Amazon.com.
16. Letter to Father Healy from the author.
17. *Baltimore Sentinel.*
18. *Maryland Life Magazine.*
19. *The Christian News*, New Haven, MO.
20. *The Baltimore Press.*
21. *Maryland Life Magazine.*
22. *The Jeffersonian*, Towson, Maryland.

## Chapter Three: Taking on the Establishment

23. *The Jeffersonian, supra.*
24. *The Baltimore Press.*
25 *Journal of the Social Justice Review*, St. Louis, MO.
26. *The Baltimore Press*
27. *Ibid.*
28. *Ibid.*
29. *Ibid.*
30. *Ibid.*
31. *Ibid.*
32. *Maryland Life Magazine.*
33. *Social Justice Review, supra.*
34. *Baltimore Sentinel.*
35. *Baltimore Enterprise* and also published in the *Congressional Record,* Vol. 127, No. 185, on Dec. 11, 1981.
36. *Baltimore Sentinel.*

## Chapter Four: Clubhouse Politics

37. *Baltimore Sun.*
38. *Maryland Life Magazine.*
39. Baltimore's *City Paper.*
40. *The Baltimore Press.*
41. *Ibid.*
42. Posted on the Internet.
43. *The Baltimore Press.*

## Chapter Five: From the Land of Pleasant Living

44. *The Jeffersonian, supra.*
45. *Maryland Life Magazine.*
46. *Baltimore Chronicle.*

47. Baltimore's *City Paper.*
48. *Maryland Life Magazine.*
49. *Baltimore Chronicle.*
50. *Maryland Life Magazine.*
51. *Ibid.*
52. *Ibid.*
53. *Ibid.*
54. *Ibid.*
55. *Ibid.*
56. *Ibid.*
57. *Ibid.*
58. *Ibid.*
59. *The Baltimore Press.*
60. *Baltimore Enterprise.*

## Chapter Six: Sports Icons & Stories, Too

61. *Baltimore Chronicle.*
62. *Ibid.*
63. *Maryland Life Magazine.*
64. *Ibid.*
65. *Baltimore's City Paper.*
66. *Baltimore Sentinel.*
67. *Maryland Life Magazine.*
68. *Ibid.*
69. *Ibid.*
70. *Ibid.*

## Chapter Seven: Ode to the Memories

71. *Baltimore Chronicle.*
72. *The Western People,* Ballina, County Mayo, Ireland.
73. Internet.

74. *Baltimore Evening Sun.*

75. NYC's WBAI, *Radio Free Eireann* program.

## Chapter Eight: Fighting for Justice

76. *The Baltimore Press*

77. *Baltimore Sentinel.*

78. *Social Justice Review, supra.*

79. Baltimore's *City Paper.*

80. Testimony before Md.'s House Judiciary Committee.

81. *Social Justice Review, supra.*

82. *Baltimore Sentinel.*

83. NYC's WBAI, *Radio Free Eireann* program.

84. *Baltimore Sentinel.*

85. *Ibid.*

# About the Author

William Hughes was born in Baltimore, Maryland, on September 23, 1937. He spent his boyhood playing on the streets of Locust Point, which included historic Fort McHenry, the inspiration for our National Anthem.

In the late 1950s, he earned an Associate in Arts degree during the day at the University of Baltimore, while working as a longshoreman, in the evenings, on the docks.

Hughes was a deputy clerk in the local state court house in the early 1960s, and attended the U. of Baltimore Law School at night. He received his Juris Doctor Degree, in 1964.

Since 1964, Hughes has been an attorney in general practice in Baltimore. He is a member of the Maryland and District of Columbia Bars.

In 1966, he was appointed as a Special Assistant State's Attorney for the Municipal Court of Baltimore.

From 1969 to 1981, he worked in the City Solicitor's Office in Baltimore and was chief of its Litigation Division from 1977 to 1981. He served under Mayor Thomas J. D'Alesandro, Jr. and Mayor William Donald Schaefer.

Hughes has written political articles for Baltimore's *City Paper*, *Maryland Life Magazine*, the *Baltimore Enterprise*, *The Baltimore Press*, the *Baltimore Sentinel*, *Baltimore Chronicle*, and NYC's *Irish People* newspaper. His byline has also appeared in many other publications, e.g. *Newsday*, the Camden *Courier-Post*, New York's *Irish Echo*, Philadelphia's *Irish Edition*, and *Irish America* magazine.

He was a commentator for WBAI's popular, weekly *Radio Free Eireann* program in New York City, from 1994 to 1997.

His first book, *Creating a New Ireland: A Tribute to the Irish Lobby,* is a collection of his essays on the issue of Irish Freedom. It highlighted the work that had been done in this country by activists to launch the Irish Peace Process. It was published in 1995 and is available online from Amazon.com.

*Andrew Jackson vs. New World Order* is Hughes' second book. It is historical fiction set in the 18th century, having strong satirical overtones and a compelling message for all of today's patriots. It was published by Authors Choice Press, in August, 2001. It, too, is available online, from iuniverse.com, Barnesandnoble.com, and Amazon.com

Hughes has traveled widely over the years, making many trips to Ireland, Canada, and the United Kingdom. He has also been to the Soviet Union, Iceland, France, Germany, Sweden, Switzerland, Austria, Finland, Spain and Israel, as well as many countries in Central and South America.

Presently, he is on the adjunct faculty of the Dundalk Community College and the U. of Baltimore Law School.

A professional actor, Hughes, who performs under the stage name of "Liam Hughes," is also a member of AFTRA, SAG and the AEA. He had a supporting role In John Waters' comedy classic, *Pecker,* and in Steve Yeager's film, *On the Block.* Television audiences have seen Hughes in *Homicide: Life on the Streets* and *America's Most Wanted.*

He lives with his wife, Ann, in Baltimore.

Hughes' web site can be found at:

http://liamhughes.home.mindspring.com.

0-595-21551-3